THE MODERN POETS

M. L. ROSENTHAL

The Modern Poets

A CRITICAL INTRODUCTION

OXFORD UNIVERSITY PRESS

LONDON   OXFORD   NEW YORK

Acknowledgments to:

Random House, Inc., and Faber & Faber, Ltd., for permission to quote from W. H. Auden's *Collected Poetry*, copyright 1945 by W. H. Auden, and from his poem, 'It's no use raising a shout' from *Poems*, copyright 1934 by Modern Library, Inc.

John Murray for permission to quote from John Betjeman's *Collected Poems*.

Houghton Mifflin Co. and Chatto & Windus, Ltd., for permission to quote from Elizabeth Bishop's *Poems*.

Paul Blackburn for permission to quote lines from 'The Assistance,' reprinted from *The Dissolving Fabric*; and from 'The Term.'

Liveright, Publishers, N.Y. for permission to quote from Hart Crane's *Collected Poems*, copyright © 1933 (R 1961), by Liveright Publishing Corp.

Harcourt, Brace & World, Inc., for permission to quote lines from: 'i like my body when it is with your,' copyright 1925 by E. E. Cummings, 'i sing of Olaf glad and big,' copyright © 1931, 1958 by E. E. Cummings, 'Buffalo Bill's,' 'my love,' 'ladies and gentlemen this little girl,' and 'good-by Betty, don't remember me,' copyright 1923, 1950 by E. E. Cummings, 'r-p-o-p-h-e-s-s-a-g-r,' copyright 1935 by E. E. Cummings, 'who's most afraid of death? thou,' copyright 1925, 1953 by E. E. Cummings, '(ponder, darling, these busted statues,' copyright 1926 by Horace Liveright, renewed 1953 by E. E. Cummings, all reprinted from E. E. Cummings's *Poems 1923-1954*; and for permission to quote 'silence,' © 1958 by E. E. Cummings, reprinted from E. E. Cummings's *95 Poems*.

Harold Matson Co. and Jonathan Cape, Ltd., for permission to quote from C. Day Lewis's *Collected Poems 1929-1933* and *A Hope for Poetry*.

Norman Holmes Pearson, owner of the copyright, for permission to quote from Hilda Doolittle's poems.

Oxford University Press, Inc., and Chatto & Windus, Ltd., for permission to quote from Richard Eberhart's *Selected Poems*.

Harcourt, Brace & World, Inc., and Faber & Faber, Ltd., for permission to quote from T. S. Eliot's *Collected Poems 1909-1962*, copyright 1936 by Harcourt, Brace & World, Inc., © 1963, 1964 by T. S. Eliot; from *The Cocktail Party*, copyright 1950 by T. S. Eliot; from *The Family Reunion*, copyright 1939 by T. S. Eliot; from 'Burnt Norton,' 'East Coker,' 'The Dry Salvages,' and 'Little Gidding' reprinted from *Four Quartets*, copyright 1943 by T. S. Eliot; and from his *Selected Essays 1917-1932*, copyright 1932 by Harcourt, Brace & World, Inc., © 1960 by T. S. Eliot.

Indiana University Press for permission to quote from Kenneth Fearing's *New and Selected Poems*, © 1956 by Kenneth Fearing.

Holt, Rinehart and Winston, Inc., and Jonathan Cape, Ltd., for permission to quote from *The Complete Poems of Robert Frost*, copyright 1923, 1928, 1930, 1939 by Holt, Rinehart and Winston, Inc.; copyright 1936 by Robert Frost; copyright renewed 1951, © 1956, 1958 by Robert Frost; copyright renewed © 1964 by Lesley Frost Ballantine.

City Lights Books for permission to quote from Allen Ginsberg's *Howl and Other Poems*.

Holt, Rinehart and Winston, Inc., for permission to quote lines from Horace Gregory's 'Interior: The Suburbs' from his *Collected Poems*, copyright 1941 by Horace Gregory.

The Trustees of the Hardy Estate, Macmillan and Co., Ltd., and The Macmillan Company,

New York, for permission to quote from Thomas Hardy's *Collected Poems*.

Oxford University Press, Inc., for permission to quote from Gerard Manley Hopkins's *Poems*.

Randall Jarrell and Faber & Faber, Ltd., for permission to quote from Randall Jarrell's *Selected Poems*; and to Harcourt, Brace & World, Inc., and Faber & Faber, Ltd., for permission to quote from his *The Seven-League Crutches*, copyright 1951 by Randall Jarrell.

Random House, Inc., and Hogarth Press, Ltd., for permission to quote from Robinson Jeffers's *Tamar*, copyright 1924 by Peter G. Boyle, copyright 1925 by Boni & Liveright, copyright 1935 by Modern Library; from *Roan Stallion*, copyright 1925 by Boni & Liveright, copyright 1935 by Random House, Inc.; from *Such Counsels You Gave to Me*, copyright 1937 by Robinson Jeffers; and from *Be Angry at the Sun*, copyright 1941 by Robinson Jeffers.

Little, Brown & Co. for permission to quote from Stanley Kunitz's *Selected Poems 1928-1958*, © 1957, 1958 by Stanley Kunitz.

Marvell Press, Hessle, Yorkshire, for permission to quote from Philip Larkin's *The Less Deceived*.

The Viking Press, Laurence Pollinger, Ltd., the Estate of the late Mrs. Frieda Lawrence, and William Heinemann, Ltd., for permission to quote from D. H. Lawrence's *Sea and Sardinia*; and from *The Collected Poems of D. H. Lawrence*.

Denise Levertov for permission to quote from her *Here and Now*.

Harcourt, Brace & World, Inc., and Faber & Faber, Ltd., for permission to quote from Robert Lowell's *Lord Weary's Castle*, copyright 1944, 1946 by Robert Lowell; and to Farrar, Straus & Giroux, Inc., and Faber & Faber, Ltd., for permission to quote from his *Life Studies*, © 1956, 1959 by Robert Lowell; and from his *Poems 1938-1949*.

The Macmillan Company for permission to quote from Hugh MacDiarmid's *Collected Poems*.

Faber & Faber, Ltd., for permission to quote from Louis MacNeice's *Collected Poems*, copyright 1937, 1939, 1940 by Louis MacNeice.

Ellen C. Masters for permission to quote lines from 'Daisy Fraser' and 'The Hill' reprinted from Edgar Lee Masters's *Spoon River Anthology* (Macmillan 1914, 1942).

Oxford University Press, Inc., for permission to quote from F. O. Matthiessen's *The Achievement of T. S. Eliot*.

Alfred A. Knopf, Inc., and Rupert Hart-Davis for permission to quote from W. S. Merwin's *Green with Beasts*, published 1956 by Alfred A. Knopf, Inc.

The Macmillan Company for permission to quote from Marianne Moore's *Collected Poems*.

Grove Press, Inc., and Faber & Faber, Ltd., for permission to quote from Edwin Muir's *Collected Poems*.

Howard Nemerov for permission to quote from his poetry.

Grove Press for permission to quote lines from 'The Kingfishers,' reprinted from Charles Olson's *The Distances*, copyright © 1950, 1951, 1953, 1960 by Charles Olson; to Charles Olson and Corinth Books, Inc., for permission to quote from his *In Cold Hell, in Thicket* and from *The Maximus Poems 1/10*.

New Directions and Arthur V. Moore for permission to quote from Ezra Pound's *The Cantos*, copyright 1934, 1937, 1940, 1948 by Ezra Pound; from *Personae: The Collected Poems*, copyright 1926 by Ezra Pound; and from *The Literary Essays*, all rights reserved.

New Directions for permission to quote from Herbert Read's *Collected Poems*, all rights reserved.

New Directions for permission to quote from Kenneth Rexroth's *In Defense of the Earth*, © 1956 by New Directions.

The Macmillan Company for permission to quote from E. A. Robinson's *Collected Poems*.

Doubleday & Company, Inc., and Beatrice Roethke, administratrix of the estate of Theodore Roethke, for permission to quote lines from Theodore Roethke's 'Give Way, Ye Gates,' 'The Shape of Fire,' copyright 1947 by Theodore Roethke, reprinted from his *Praise to the End*; and for permission to quote lines from his 'The Lost Son,' copyright 1947 by Theodore Roethke, reprinted from his *The Lost Son and Other Poems*.

Harcourt, Brace & World, Inc., for permission to quote from Carl Sandburg's *Smoke and Steel*, copyright 1920 by Harcourt, Brace & World, Inc., renewed 1948 by Carl Sandburg; and from *The People, Yes*, copyright 1936 by Harcourt, Brace & World, Inc.; and to Holt, Rinehart and Winston, Inc., for permission to quote from his *Chicago Poems*, copyright 1916 by Holt, Rinehart and Winston, Inc., renewed 1944 by Carl Sandburg.

New Directions for permission to quote from Delmore Schwartz's *In Dreams Begin Responsibilities*, copyright 1938 by Delmore Schwartz, and from *Vaudeville for a Princess*, copyright 1950 by New Directions.

Random House, Inc., for permission to quote from Karl Shapiro's *Poems of a Jew*, copyright © 1940, 1941, 1942, 1943, 1944, 1946, 1947, 1948, 1951, 1953, 1956, 1957, 1958 by Karl Shapiro.

Random House, Inc., and Faber & Faber, Ltd., for permission to quote from Stephen Spender's *Collected Poems*.

Alfred A. Knopf, Inc., and Faber & Faber, Ltd., for permission to quote from Wallace Stevens's *The Necessary Angel*, copyright 1947, 1951; and from *The Collected Poems*, copyright 1923, 1931, 1937, 1954 by Wallace Stevens.

New Directions, The Trustees of the Dylan Thomas Estate, and J. M. Dent & Sons, Ltd., for permission to quote from Dylan Thomas's *The Collected Poems*, copyright 1939, 1942, 1946 by New Directions, copyright 1952, 1953 by Dylan Thomas; and from his *Letters to Vernon Watkins*.

Ivan Obolensky, Inc., for permission to quote from Charles Tomlinson's *Seeing Is Believing*.

Harcourt, Brace & World, Inc., and Faber & Faber, Ltd., for permission to quote from Richard Wilbur's *Things of This World*, © 1956 by Richard Wilbur; from *The Beautiful Changes and Other Poems*, copyright 1947 by Richard Wilbur; and from his *Poems 1943-1956*.

New Directions for permission to quote from William Carlos Williams's *The Collected Earlier Poems*, copyright 1938, 1951 by William Carlos Williams; from *The Collected Later Poems*, copyright 1944, 1948, 1950 by William Carlos Williams; and to Random House, Inc., for permission to quote from *The Desert Music and Other Poems*, copyright 1949, 1951, 1952, 1953, 1954 by William Carlos Williams.

Mrs. W. B. Yeats, The Macmillan Company, A. P. Watt & Sons, Ltd., and Macmillan & Co., Ltd., for permission to quote from W. B. Yeats's *Collected Poems*; from *The Variorum Edition of the Poems of W. B. Yeats*; from *The Autobiography of William Butler Yeats*; from *Essays*; from *A Vision*; and to Rupert Hart-Davis, Ltd., for permission to quote from *The Letters of W. B. Yeats* (Wade, ed.).

Portions of this book appeared in their original form in The Nation, The Yale Review, Poetry (Chicago), The New Republic, *and* College English, *and in* Symbols and Values: an Initial Study, *copyright 1954 by the Conference on Science, Philosophy and Religion in Their Relation to the Democratic Way of Life; distributed by Harper & Brothers, all rights reserved.*

Permission to use these materials is gratefully acknowledged.

For my mother

Foreword

Not only poets but critics, teachers, editors, and many others have long been concerned about the formidable but quite unnecessary barriers between poetry and the general reader. One of my aims is to provide a catalyst to help break down those barriers. Without offering an exhaustive survey of *all* the modern poets and poetic currents, I have tried to plot a view that will suggest the range of our poetic landscape and its relation to that crisis of personality the modern mind has had to face for more than a century.

The book therefore begins with some comment on the resistance to rapport between poet and reader, on the character of the poetic sensibility revealed to us by the moderns, and on the many and varied continuities between poetry of the past and that of our own time. It then turns to the great germinative figures of Yeats, Pound, and Eliot—all of them extremely sensitive to the rôle of tradition—and to other important figures among the older moderns. It concludes with chapters on the prophetic, visionary, and rhetorical writing of Lawrence, Crane, and the 'thirties and on the poetry that has risen to the fore in the past two decades, from Dylan Thomas on. Needless to say, I have had to make painful omissions in order to keep to my main purpose. If the Muse takes notice, I pray her pardon.

There are genuine poets everywhere—sparkling, energetic spirits of every variety—and very few of them receive anything like public recognition. As poetry editor of a national magazine I have met and corresponded with hundreds of these 'unknown' figures who have, often, written beautiful, interesting work. They create a subjective expression of contemporary life in its individual meanings, a vital flow constantly reshaping the realities of the world into human, aesthetic dimensions. Some of them, such excellent poets as Ramon Guthrie, the late Dilys Laing, Theodore Weiss, and Ben Belitt, are familiar to the smaller community of their fellow-poets and other people aware of the current state of the art, if not to the largest audience. (We have unfortunately but a few groups like the one at Dartmouth in which poets can read and show their work to each other and receive criticism of the most practical kind, and in which the encouragement of beginners by masters and the candor of peers can be expected.) Most poets, though, are known to a few people only—an established poet who has encouraged them, an editor or two, a teacher, a few other writers in similar circumstances. And many lack even this limited kind of relationship. Yet without these 'unknowns' we could have no great poetry; they are the living matrix within which that poetry is actually written.

M. L. ROSENTHAL

Suffern, N. Y.
July 1960

Contents

THE MODERN POETS

ONE

Poetry Past and Present

1. THE WIDENING OF SENSIBILITY

Quite different from the comfortable assurances drifting down from public rostrums and from publicity offices are the exacting demands of our poets. What are we to do with Hamlet's elegiac mockery as he fingers Yorick's skull, or with the brutality of William Carlos Williams in his poem 'Death'?

> he's dead
> the old bastard—
> He's a bastard because
>
> there's nothing
> legitimate in him any
> more
>   he's dead . . .

Even professional critics and poets know the dismay that unfamiliar poetry can arouse at first hearing: another call to the abyss, another reordering of life, of the intelligence. An unexpected widening of sympathies and of sensibility threatens to release our dark, subversive, inward self; we fear engulfment by all that we protect ourselves from feeling too intensely. Yet a nagging desire to experience just such a widening persists; we long to face the mysterious depths of self for which the poet speaks with the evasive frankness of our own deepest thoughts. The poet, by bringing the problems of life into his aesthetic orbit, transforms them and reveals far more about our whole contemporary meaning than we ever thought possible.

Of course whatever is perceived with freshness and immediacy, with all the senses alert, seems disturbing, 'unorthodox,' although prevailing manners and systems are inevitably but approximations

3

of situations already obsolete. The liveliest minds will always dance among discrepancies, ironies, possibilities, truths and pretensions, life and death. Probably a gap is unavoidable at any given time between what the poets are saying and doing and what the common reader imagines they say and do. Too, the reader's refusal to allow a poem to come close enough may account for his casual rejection of it. The 'obscurity' we hear so much about is generally not obscurity at all, is not anything in the poem itself. What makes a poem seem difficult is usually a matter of perspective. Some quite comprehensible but unexpected shift of manner or thought, like those life confronts us with daily, may be the key.

Curiously the most marked stylistic break between past and present in poetry is not, as is commonly assumed, a break from forthrightness to riddle-making. It is from relative formality to simplicity and directness; an unpretentious intimacy, an awareness of everyday life, has been brought into poetry more emphatically than before. In fact Jules Laforgue commented on this development as early as 1885.* In his notes on Charles Baudelaire, he observed that his fellow countryman and poet was 'the first to write about himself in a moderate confessional manner and to leave off the inspired manner.' 'The first to speak of Paris from the point of view of her daily damned (the lighted gas jets flickering with the wind of prostitution, the restaurants and their air vents . . .)' and to 'accuse himself rather than appear triumphant,' Baudelaire 'shows his wounds, his laziness, his bored uselessness at the heart of this dedicated, workaday century.' He brings to literature 'the boredom implicit in sensuality,' the consciousness of 'neurosis,' the feeling of 'damnation on this earth.'
Although Laforgue's comments apply almost as well to Catullus and other poets who can hardly be called 'modern' he points out something particularly contemporary in Baudelaire's attitude: the suddenly morbid awareness of an individual life out of tune with the proclaimed ideals of its age, and paradoxically, the sense of being but one of the doomed many interned in megalopolis. The

* *Selected Writings of Jules Laforgue*, ed. and trans. William Jay Smith, Grove Press, New York, 1956, p. 211.

law of life becomes that of a living mass death; understandably, one of the crucial symbols of modern poetry, in English at least, becomes Dante's pictured prisoners in the antechamber of Hell, 'wretches never born and never dead,' worthy of neither blame nor praise. These are the citizens of T. S. Eliot's Waste Land, who, lacking all moral perspective, mechanical in their motions, are trapped by their bodily selves and are incapable of meaningful commitment either to good or to evil. The modern city is their habitat:

> Unreal city,
> Under the brown fog of a winter dawn,
> A crowd flowed over London Bridge, so many,
> I had not thought death had undone so many . . .

Thus writes Eliot, echoing both Dante's *Inferno*, III, and Baudelaire's 'Les Sept Vieillards': '*Fourmillante cité, cité pleine de rêves,/ Où le spectre en plein jour raccroche le passant.*' (Swarming city, city filled with dreams, where spectres in full daylight confront the passerby.) The changes in poetic attitude so apparent in these lines have affected virtually all our poetry. That the general reader has so little realized this, that his resistance to 'modern' poetry continues, is no doubt a measure of the continuing vitality and shock-value of the Baudelairean vision. The work that this book considers is not in fact modern innovation, but grows out of a modern tradition.

The most powerful impulses in our poetry still derive from the later William Butler Yeats, from Ezra Pound, and from Eliot. This is grounded in part on their relation to tradition and on their aesthetic achievements, in part on the character of their cultural criticism. Knowing them, we understand D. H. Lawrence better, and Hart Crane, and the revolutionary voyages of the 'thirties. We find more comprehensible the continuing absorption with translation and with certain mystical, Classical, Provençal, and Symbolistic motifs. This continuity is apparent in values, in craftsmanship, in symbolic statement, in psychological insight. Nor is that gaiety lost which informs the older poets—Williams dancing

naked before his mirror celebrating the knowledge of his own isolation, Wallace Stevens making jokes about death, Eliot perceiving the crudely comic—or the absolute, unblinking honesty behind it.

The cultivation of a special kind of subjectivity too has been
continuous. Thresholds of candor, even of morbidity are crossed
so that the multiple meanings of experience may be explored. The
Romantics and Whitman, and then Yeats and Lawrence, prepared us for the sexual immediacies of Dylan Thomas and Robert
Lowell. Life's 'normal' associations are distorted, dissolved in
nightmarish terror in Howard Nemerov's brilliant sequence 'The
Scales of the Eyes' as in Eliot's 'Rhapsody on a Windy Night.'
The 'Rhapsody' is a perfect embodiment of the new-old tradition. As the protagonist here moves through the city streets
everything is twisted and distorted, 'held in a lunar synthesis.'
The moon herself, queen of this night realm, is not the chaste
goddess Artemis but a witless old whore who 'winks a feeble eye.'

> The moon has lost her memory.
> A washed-out smallpox cracks her face,
> Her hand twists a paper rose,
> That smells of dust and eau de cologne. . . .
> The reminiscence comes
> Of sunless dry geraniums
> And dust in crevices,
> Smells of chestnuts in the streets,
> And female smells in shuttered rooms,
> And cigarettes in corridors
> And cocktail smells in bars.

It is she who whispers the incantations that dissolve 'the floors
of memory' and 'of all its clear relations,' its 'divisions and preci-
sions.' Under her crazed spell, in her light and that of the street
lamps, the world is seen as foul, death-ridden. A witch—in the
figure of a filth-bedraggled prostitute—leers from a doorway, which
opens on her obscenely, 'like a grin.' The motif of sexuality reduced to horror and sterility is carried through the poem, some-

times only by suggestion, sometimes openly and powerfully. It is somehow associated with the pictures of rusty springs in factory yards and dead branches cast up on the shore, and with a series of terrible, silent, greedily snatching movements that emphasize the automatic depravity, as it were, of animal nature: a cat devouring a bit of rancid butter in the street, a child's hand grabbing and pocketing a toy, a crab gripping the end of a stick.

We may, if we wish, call this a sick vision of life. But we cannot ignore the possibility, and it is this possibility the poem explores, that the nighttime world may be the real world. It is the world of day that, in this experiment of the imagination, is illusory—the world in which things make sense, in which one can make plans, strike heroic and moral attitudes, speak in 'the inspired manner,' in which the memory can teach and guide. Night blots out illusion and selects for intenser focus the images of the vilest reality only. Hence the bitter irony of the poem's conclusion:

> The lamp said,
> 'Four o'clock,
> Here is the number on the door.
> Memory!
> You have the key,
> The little lamp spreads a ring on the stair.
> Mount.
> The bed is open; the tooth-brush hangs on the wall,
> Put your shoes at the door, sleep, prepare for life.'

> The last twist of the knife.

'Rhapsody on a Windy Night' speaks for only one strain in Eliot's work as in modern poetry generally. But it is an important strain and has led to the occasional complaint that our poetry is merely negative, alienated, and 'pessimistic.' Poetry can be affirmative even when it cuts painfully into the bone so as to affirm the marrow. Moreover, poetic affirmation, even at its simplest, as in most of Longfellow, may have *some* of the sadness and mystery of the more difficult moderns: 'I heard the trailing garments of the Night/ Sweep through her marble halls!'

According to René Char, the poet is a person of 'unilateral stability'; * that is, he makes something unique by transmuting general ideas and commonplace reality into aspects of himself. In the process his artistic sensibility moves into the foreground and becomes the determining element; it is this creative alchemy, I think, which makes poetic speech normative—something that at once reveals the terrible silent poverty of most lives and the vast richness which is ours for the asking, and thus suggests an ideal. Who would not wish to be able to communicate love and its heightenings of sense-alertness as Richard Wilbur does in 'The Beautiful Changes'?

> One wading a Fall meadow finds on all sides
> The Queen Anne's Lace lying like lilies
> On water; it glides
> So from the walker, it turns
> Dry grass to a lake, as the slightest shade of you
> Valleys my mind in fabulous blue Lucernes.

As we have seen with 'Rhapsody on a Windy Night,' there is a darker function of the poet's awareness in the absolutely candid recognition of things as they are. Thus Williams's lines on death, quoted a little earlier, or these of Eberhart's:

> I saw on the slant hill a putrid lamb,
> Propped with daisies. The sleep looked deep,
> The face nudged in the green pillow
> But the guts were out for the crows to eat.
>
> ('For a Lamb')

Again, such candor is not new in poetry of this age. What is new is its insistence on the 'morbid' themes, not in scattered pieces only but in great quantity, by many writers. 'I always thought of ——,' a poet wrote to me, 'as our rosy-cheeked boy, the lover of life, who could make allowances for all human troubles and really mean it. But I've been reading his latest book and can see,

* René Char, *Hypnos Waking*, ed. Jackson Matthews, Random House, New York, 1956, p. 59.

in poem after poem, the maggot behind that cherubic smile. Death on every page!'

Death on every page, though often it is the death (and rebirth) of our civilization that is the real obsession. In modern poetry, we are more and more presented with the need to counteract the apparent suicide, or at least the self-betrayal, of a culture. 'The pure products of America,' writes Dr. Williams, 'go crazy.'

> No one
> to witness
> and adjust, no one to drive the car
>
> ('To Elsie')

The prevailing modern poetic assumption is that, in submitting to organization, institutionalization, and mechanization for their own sake we are in danger of losing touch with the springs of joy and vitality: delight of the senses, tradition and ritual, self-realization within a truly human context. Randall Jarrell's 'A Girl in a Library' shows a typical 'Home Ec.' or 'Phys. Ed.' major asleep in a college reading room. His satire is tempered by compassion for her as an innocent victim of her times who might at least, in another age, have been one of the anonymous 'braided maidens singing as they spin.' The poem concludes with an affirmation of the girl's 'real' or archetypal meaning, as opposed to what the civilization would make of her:

> . . . and I have seen
> Firm, fixed forever in your closing eyes,
> The Corn King beckoning to his Spring Queen.

Our poetry since the 'twenties might almost be described as a concerted effort to re-establish vital continuities with whatever in the past is myth-making, wonder-contemplating, and strength-giving, and to discover widened, fresher meanings. From *The Waste Land* to Muriel Rukeyser's *Elegies*, from Pound's 'The Return' to Crane's self-analyses, the spectacular psychological struggle for such continuity and cultural breakthrough made for a richly varied yet unified literature. At his best the modern poet, whether he descants on apeneck Sweeney or on the revolutionists stopping for a glass of orangeade or on 'the immovable critic twitching his skin like a horse that feels a flea,' has with Democritus and Shakespeare the gifts of laughter and of faith in human possibility.

2. SOME WORKINGS OF TRADITION

Just as our first acquaintance with poetry goes back to the buried impressions of infancy and to the songs and games of childhood, so the art itself summons up its whole history in every poem. It brings the two kinds of memory, historical and private, into single focus. Past and present illuminate each other—one might almost say they shape each other—as if a single Author outside Time were at work. The history of poetry is alive in any poet's work as much as are the echoing rhythms and melodies from his own early years.

The presence of the personal past may be easier to see. It is no trick, for example, to recognize Yeats's deliberate reversion, at the end of 'A Dialogue of Self and Soul,' to a childlike diction and rhyme—almost doggerel—to express the innocent ecstasy into which the poem flames:

> When such as I cast out remorse
> So great a sweetness flows into the breast
> We must laugh and we must sing,
> We are blest by everything,
> Everything we look upon is blest.

It is more difficult to observe the way in which the imagination of Yeats's forerunners has entered the lifeblood of this poem. In the climactic stanza preceding this one, the poet has affirmed the preciousness of life in the teeth of the worst it has to offer:

> I am content to live it all again
> And yet again, if it be life to pitch
> Into the frog-spawn of a blind man's ditch,
> A blind man battering blind men;

Or into that most fecund ditch of all,
The folly that man does
Or must suffer, if he woos
A proud woman not kindred of his soul.

To a reader also familiar with Matthew Arnold, the stanza recalls the ending of 'Dover Beach,' published in 1867, sixty-two
years before the 'Dialogue.'

Ah, love, let us be true
To one another! for the world, which seems
To lie before us like a land of dreams,
So various, so beautiful, so new,
Hath really neither joy, nor love, nor light,
Nor certitude, nor peace, nor help for pain;
And we are here as on a darkling plain
Swept with confused alarms of struggle and flight,
Where ignorant armies clash by night.

Each poem is, in its way, concerned with the question of
religious faith. Yeats's ditch in which a blind man is seen 'battering
blind men' has its obvious resemblances to Arnold's 'darkling
plain' where 'ignorant armies clash by night.' Both figures of speech
aptly project the human predicament in a world bereft of its certainties of faith. The very physical shape and rhythm of the two
stanzas, and the way they move into language of dark despondency,
are similar, cast in the same mold almost. When we find one of
Yeats's great poems reading in part like a deliberate revision of
Arnold's most famous single work, we may well remind ourselves
of the pervasive, active presence of poetic tradition. It is a chain
of flame. Its continuity, when it seems to be broken, is but smoul-
dering. Its forms and themes are constantly modified but never
entirely changed or lost, and the poets who take fire from it seem
in many ways re-embodiments of one another. Not only the
uniqueness of a poet's work, but also his ability to make use of
his heritage, is the mark of his originality. We shall find, writes
Eliot in a famous essay on the subject, 'that not only the best,

but the most individual parts of his work may be those in which the dead poets, his ancestors, assert their immortality most vigorously.' *

What, then, is the difference between such originality and imitation? Look again at the passages by Arnold and Yeats; the two are similar confessions of personal helplessness. But the curious fact is that 'A Dialogue' is both darker *and* happier than 'Dover Beach.' Arnold's *simile* 'as on a darkling plain. . ./ Where ignorant armies clash by night' does not strike as deep as Yeats's sharper *metaphor*, 'the frog-spawn of a blind man's ditch,/ A blind man battering blind men.' And Arnold's 'Ah, love, let us be true/ To one another!' is almost complacent next to

> . . . that most fecund ditch of all,
> The folly that man does
> Or must suffer, if he woos
> A proud woman not kindred of his soul.

Further, the end-of-century bitterness Yeats gives these symbols of lost meaning and of desire prepares us for a leap Arnold could never have contemplated. It is the leap *out of the nineteenth century*, truly, into a uniquely modern kind of redemption through self-acceptance. In his closing stanza, Yeats makes the speaking Self his crucial symbol after having thrown out a deliberately false lead in allowing the Soul to dominate the first part of the poem. Enmeshed in its suffering, pride, and sexual need, the Self projects out of the bleak limitations of its existence all that the Soul had threatened would be lost. It thereby appropriates to the living present the uncommunicable values of the Soul, which lie outside of life and are therefore inaccessible to human consciousness, to the living present—and then 'everything we look upon is blest.'

Literature is full of striking examples of the original use of tradition. Given resemblance of approach, theme, and mood, these convergences are inevitable:

* T. S. Eliot, *Selected Essays*, Harcourt, Brace, New York, 1950, p. 4.

> All day thy wings have fanned
> At that far height, the cold, thin atmosphere . . .
> > WILLIAM CULLEN BRYANT (1815)

> All afternoon the cloud-flown derricks turn . . .
> Thy cables breathe the North Atlantic still.
> > HART CRANE (1926)

The pitch and melody of these two pairs of lines, and their effect of wonder at the immensities of time and space brought into focus by bird and bridge, are almost identical. 'To a Waterfowl' and 'To Brooklyn Bridge' are varieties of the ode; Crane's poem absorbs the conventions represented by Bryant's work into a structure more daring and brilliant by far, and extremely 'modern' in its dramatic shifting of images. We might instance many other formal echoings of this sort, echoings that yet provide some new turn. Witness the old *ubi sunt* motif, in which the poet laments the irrecoverable past. Villon's fifteenth century 'Ballade of Dead Women,' in the Rossetti translation, is our best-known model:

> Tell me now in what hidden way is
> Lady Flora the lovely Roman?
> Where is Hipparchia, and where is Thaïs,
> Neither of them the fairer woman?

And the modern variations—just a few:

> Where are Elmer, Herman, Bert, Tom and Charley,
> The weak of will, the strong of arm, the clown, the
> > boozer, the fighter?
> > EDGAR LEE MASTERS ('The Hill')

> All that is piteous, all that's fair,
> All that is fat and scant of breath,
> Is Death's collateral . . .
> And General Grant and General Lee,
> Patti and Florence Nightingale,
> Like Tyro and Antiope
> Drift among ghosts in Hell . . .
> > BASIL BUNTING ('Villon')

> What happened to Robinson,
> Who used to stagger down Eighth Street,
> Dizzy with solitary gin?
> Where is Masters, who crouched in
> His law office for ruinous decades?
> Where is Leonard who thought he was
> A locomotive? And Lindsay,
> Wise as a dove, innocent
> As a serpent, where is he?
> > Timor mortis conturbat me.
> > > KENNETH REXROTH ('Thou Shalt Not Kill')

> Of Van Wettering I speak, and Averill,
> Names on a list, whose faces I do not recall
> But they are gone to early death, who late in school
> Distinguished the belt feed lever from the belt holding pawl.
> > RICHARD EBERHART ('The Fury of Aerial Bombardment')

The thought of our century is often called 'pluralistic,' because of our unprecedented awareness of all the choices and attitudes which are man's heritage as well as his possibility. Pluralism can be employed to evade responsibility; where we have so many alternatives we may be tempted to exploit the situation without committing ourselves. On the other hand, we are free to employ it as the infinitely rich resource it is, so that we can project our feelings into sympathetic rapport with other peoples and times and allow freer play to mind, will, and sensibility. The turn of a phrase, the handling of a line, may be a shorthand evocation of a whole way of thought associated with the poets of some past period. By the same token, the very choice of these poets rather than others as 'ancestors' is a sign that their way of speaking has special relevance for us—a 'modernity' that reveals something of ourselves. Donne's 'The Ecstasy' has appealed to twentieth-century writers in this way. It is a serious consideration of the spiritual meaning of sexual love, yet there is a colloquial spontaneity and punning fancifulness in it, too, that will not be bullied into silence by the near-sacred theme:

> Where, like a pillow on a bed,
> A pregnant bed swelled up, to rest
> The violet's reclining head,
> Sat we two, one another's best.

Again, Donne is quite modern in his trick of capturing a rhythm of prose exposition and using it in the more emotion-rousing context of poetry:

> We see by this, it was not sex;
> We see, we saw not what did move . . .

In a larger sense, there is *no* past poetry of value that is irrelevant. Blake's 'Ah! Sun-Flower,' for instance, is not intellectually sophisticated, or tough-minded, or colloquial. Yet it is a perfect embodiment of the Romantic awareness of the vast gulf between desire and possibility, and between both of these and actual fulfillment. It gives symbol within symbol of unrealized yearning. The 'sweet golden clime' toward which the sunflower turns is the region beyond death; those who are in it, the youth and maiden thwarted in *their* need, are still—there—in a region of dim aspiration only. The symbols of this poem, the sunflower particularly, are in themselves the theme and the *point* of the poem. As in Yeats's 'Who Goes with Fergus' or Kathleen Raine's 'Lyric,' no further moral is read into these reverberatingly melancholy symbols.

Eliot's *The Waste Land*, still considered by many people the prime example of a distinctively modern poem, is a symphonic composition using many traditional elements. The Waste Land itself is the landscape of barrenness and death which appears in medieval legendry around the quest for the Holy Grail. Also, it is like that dim region, neither here nor there, which holds the sunflower, the youth, and the maiden of Blake's poem—and, by no great leap of imagination, holds Dante's 'wretches never born and never dead.' And it is like the charnel hillside of Keats's 'La Belle Dame sans Merci'; or like the course over which the hero of Browning's 'Childe Roland to the Dark Tower Came' rides. *The Waste Land*, more complex, brings its concerns and symbolic methods sharply to bear on contemporary society as these other poems do not. But it is deeply imbued with their connotations, and is in fact a mine of 'influences' shrewdly calculated to bring out parallels and disparities between past and present which will heighten its major ideas. Its artful manipulation of these traditional elements illustrates the modern poet's increased consciousness of his sources. Eliot sometimes quotes these sources directly, as in the lines from Dante and others at the close of the poem which suggest his own (and our) spiritual state. Sometimes he parodies them, as in his echo of Goldsmith's lines on womanly chastity:

> When lovely woman stoops to folly and
> Paces about her room again, alone,
> She smoothes her hair with automatic hand,
> And puts a record on the gramophone.

The parody maliciously underlines the grotesque scene preceding it, which has shown modern sex as automatic and viciously impersonal.

Also, Eliot often reworks his sources. This happens with brilliant effect in Part II of *The Waste Land*, in a passage grounded on a famous description in *Antony and Cleopatra* (II, ii, 196ff.):

> The Barge she sat in, like a burnished Throne,
> Burnt on the Water . . .

Eliot follows Shakespeare's lines with exact parallelism at first, and retains throughout the passage enough of the latter's tone to keep the implied contrast between the passionate and heroic Cleopatra and the hysterically neurotic woman who is Eliot's subject clearly in view:

> The Chair she sat in, like a burnished throne,
> Glowed on the marble, where the glass
> Held up by standards wrought with fruited vines
> From which a golden Cupidon peeped out
> (Another hid his eyes behind his wing)
> Doubled the flames of seven branched candelabra

Reflecting light upon the table as
The glitter of her jewels rose to meet it,
From satin cases poured in rich profusion . . .

Where Cleopatra is revealed in open sunlight, her barge 'burning' on the water, the modern woman is seen in a dim, artificially 'glowing' interior, amid the mirrored reflection of candelabra and the winking glitter of jewels. The proximity of 'gold' and 'glitter' suggests the old proverb, and through it the lack of anything genuine in her life. Where Cleopatra is attended by 'gentlewomen' and pretty 'dimpled boys,' Eliot's lady has about her artifacts only, such as the golden Cupidons. One of the most telling differences is that between Shakespeare's

A strange invisible perfume hits the sense

and Eliot's

In vials of ivory and coloured glass
Unstoppered, lurked her strange synthetic perfumes,
Unguent, powdered, or liquid—troubled, confused
And drowned the sense in odours . . .

Eliot's 'revision' of Shakespeare stresses synthetic, not natural, fragrance, and with it a confusion and drowning of the senses rather than immediate impact and stimulation. Thus he underlines the degeneration of once-vital traditions, and announces that the exuberant secularism of the Renaissance has now reached dead end.

It is not, then, surprising to find that the most energetic inventors and experimenters are often the most sensitive to the voice of the past. When we see Odysseus re-established in various guises as the protagonist of Pound's major poems, or when we see William Carlos Williams preparing his reader for a vision of horror by using Dante's *terza rima* at the start of 'The Yachts,' we realize that to these poets the past is not a burden but a marvelous, inexhaustible source. For only the poet who feels himself somehow at the frontiers of his craft can use the past to make something new. Williams's essay on the painter Tchelitchew puts the issue more boldly, but he too is talking about the proper use of the past:

> Any who would know and profit by his knowledge of the great must lead a life of violent opposites. The deeper at moments of penetration is his mastery of their work, the more vigorously at other moments must he fling himself off from them to remain himself a man. But if he himself would do great works also only by this violence, this completeness of his wrenching free, will he be able to use that of which their greatness has consisted.*

His description of Whitman defines a traditional attitude of the innovator:

> Whitman . . . For God's sake! He broke through the deadness of copied forms which keep shouting above everything that wants to get said today drowning out one man with the accumulated weight of a thousand voices in the past—re-establishing the tyrannies of the past. . . . The structure of the old is active, it says no! to everything in propaganda and poetry that wants to say yes. Whitman broke through that.†

The most meaningful traditionalism and experimentalism meet in the drive for a sharply concrete, organically alive poetry that marks the first third of this century. It is interesting to look through the very influential anthology, *The New Poetry*, edited by Harriet Monroe and Alice Corbin Henderson in 1917, with revisions in 1923 and 1932, for its many evidences of this great new movement. 'Concrete and immediate realization of life,' the editors say, was its aim, and they quote Yeats to make their point clear.

> We wanted to get rid not only of rhetoric but of poetic diction. We tried to strip away everything that was artifi-

---

* Selected Essays of William Carlos Williams, Random House, New York, 1954, p. 250.
† Ibid. p. 218.

cial, to get a style like speech, as simple as the simplest
prose, like a cry of the heart. (p. xlii)

One source of the richness and diversity of this effort was its
international character. Foreign literatures and neglected work in
our own literature were ransacked for their manifold evocativeness
and for what could be learned from them about economy, musical
and organic form, tone, and the handling of imagery. Taking the
movement as a whole, you will find at one end of the spectrum
vigorous work that is structurally and technically loose but idio-
matically convincing, and at the other, work that is hard, precise,
and delicately modulated. A few instances from *The New Poetry*
will illustrate its varied scope:

> Did you ever hear of the Circuit Judge
> Helping anyone except the 'Q' railroad,
> Or the bankers . . . ?
>
> EDGAR LEE MASTERS ('Daisy Fraser')

> And the last sleeping-place of Nebuchadnezzar—
> When I arrive there I shall tell the wind:
> 'You ate grass; I have eaten crow—
> Who is better off now or next year?'
>
> CARL SANDBURG ('Losers')

> There is no rest for the mind
> In a small house. It moves, looking for God,
> with a mysterious eye fixed on the bed,
> into a cracked egg at breakfast. . . .
>
> HORACE GREGORY ('Interior: the Suburbs')

> The light is like a spider:
> It crawls over the water;
> It crawls over the edges of the snow;
> It crawls under your eyelids
> And spreads its webs there—
> Its two webs.
>
> WALLACE STEVENS ('Tattoo')

> You are clear,
> O rose, cut in rock;
> Hard as the descent of hail.
>
> H. D. ('The Garden')

> See, they return; ah, see the tentative
> Movements, and the slow feet,
> The trouble in the pace and the uncertain
> Wavering!
>
> EZRA POUND ('The Return')

3. HOPKINS, HARDY, AND THE 'RELIGION OF ART'

The most vital liberating force behind the extraordinary manipulations of traditional techniques and attitudes has been that most durable heritage of nineteenth-century post-Romanticism: the 'religion of art,' especially as allied with a belief in the 'life-force.' The faith that in some all-encompassing, germinative fashion art must discover and define for man his real perspectives has made it seem more and more important to test all its possibilities and resources. The last decades of the century saw philistinism in the ascendant. In Ezra Pound's words:

> Gladstone was still respected,
> When John Ruskin produced
> 'King's Treasuries'; Swinburne
> And Rossetti still abused.
>
> ('Hugh Selwyn Mauberley')

Against these circumstances the poets—their function and status increasingly discounted by the world around them—entrenched themselves by enshrining Beauty and ordaining themselves her priests. Rossetti expressed the central faith in 'Soul's Beauty':

> Under the arch of life, where love and death,
>   Terror and mystery, guard her shrine, I saw
>   Beauty enthroned; and though her gaze struck awe,
> I drew it in as simply as my breath.

Criticism, too, made the faith explicit. 'The principles of art,' wrote Arthur Symons, 'are eternal, while the principles of morality fluctuate with the spiritual ebb and flow of the ages.' * And Walter Pater argued that the poets desired mainly to bring to life 'a beauty born of unlikely elements, by a profound alchemy, by a difficult initiation, by the charm which wrings it even out of terrible things.' † Symons and Pater wished to place art and its motives beyond the reach of literal-minded morality. Yeats was conscious very early of the urgency of this fight for the very life of poetry and never wavered in his conviction that the artist's work preceded and transcended the moralist's.

The very nature of the fight, too, emphasized the dark side of art with its absorption in the secret and the forbidden as the way to self-discovery. In 1893, after he had received some recognition on his own, Yeats helped edit Blake's works. His prolonged rapport with their sexual frankness, mysticism, and deliberate reversals of familiar moral assumptions gave backbone to his own convictions and helped him see beyond current fashions in poetry. Two years later he was able to state incisively the fundamental artistic principle he had learned from the experience:

> . . . argument, theory, erudition, observation, are merely what Blake called 'little devils who fight for themselves,' illusions of our visible passing life, who must be made to serve the moods, or we have no part in eternity. Everything that can be seen, touched, measured, explained, understood, argued over, is to the imaginative artist nothing more than a means. . . .‡

The position is almost exactly the one taken by Symons in dealing with the accusation that one of his books was depraved: 'Whatever I find in humanity (passion, desire, the spirit or the senses, the hell or heaven of man's heart) is part of the eternal

* Arthur Symons, Preface to London Nights, 2nd edition, L. C. Smithers, London, 1897. See The Collected Works of Arthur Symons, Vol. I (London: Martin Secker, 1924), p. 166.

† Walter Pater, Appreciations, Macmillan, New York, 1903, p. 260.

‡ William Butler Yeats, Essays, Macmillan, London, 1924, p. 239.

substance which nature weaves in the rough for art to combine cunningly into beautiful patterns.' * It is the position implied in Eugene Lee-Hamilton's poem 'Baudelaire,' which shows how British poets, in the ferment of these issues and under the influence of French poets reacting to similar conditions, were forced to recognize the vile side of common existence and to incorporate that recognition—triumphantly—in their work:

> A Paris gutter of the good old times,
> Black and putrescent in its stagnant bed,
> Save where the shamble oozings fringe it red,
> Or scaffold trickles, or nocturnal crimes . . . †

The struggle for not merely sexual frankness but the right to use the facts of sexuality in all their aspects was important in the aestheticists' 'religion.' Although precedents abounded in Classical literature and in the writings of Chaucer and Shakespeare and in the seventeenth century, these writers found themselves opposed not only by Philistia but also by their own deep shock at their 'findings.' The influence of Whitman was long-delayed. They came to their sexual preoccupations and desire to startle in the lurid light of Poe's sense of depravity and morbid secrecy, deliberately cultivated and extended by his French followers, and of Blake's attempts in his day to shock and to convince by unanswerable paradoxes:

> And Priests in black gowns were walking their rounds,
> And binding with briars my joys & desires.
>
> ('The Garden of Love')

or

> Mutual forgiveness of each Vice,
> Such are the gates of Paradise . . .
>
> ('For the Sexes: The Gates of Paradise')

'The secret sensuous innocence' that Robert Bridges attributed to Eros can receive its true weight only after courage has been sum-

---

* Symons, op. cit. p. 166.

† Eugene Lee-Hamilton, *Sonnets of the Wingless Hours*, Stone & Kimball, Chicago and Cambridge, 1894, p. 103.

moned up to face sexuality at all. We can see the defiant note in
Henley's 'Hawthorn and Lavender':

> Love, which is lust, is the Main of Desire,
> Love, which is lust, is the Centric Fire.

And we can see it in very nearly the same language in the climactic
moment of Wilde's 'The Harlot's House.' The speaker and his
beloved find themselves one night under the windows of 'the
harlot's house,' watching the grotesque mechanical waltzing
shadows on the drawn blinds above the 'horrible marionettes' that
appear on the steps from time to time:

> Then, turning to my love, I said,
> 'The dead are dancing with the dead,
> The dust is whirling with the dust.'

> But she—she heard the violin,
> And left my side, and entered in:
> Love passed into the house of lust.

His description of the prisoners' degradation in 'The Ballad of
Reading Gaol' expresses a shock even greater than Blake's, no
doubt because of his own prison experience:

> . . . They starve the little frightened child
> Till it weeps both night and day:
> And they scourge the weak, and flog the fool
> And gibe the old and grey . . .

> Each narrow cell in which we dwell
> Is a foul and dark latrine,
> And the fetid breath of living Death
> Chokes up each grated screen,
> And all, but Lust, is turned to dust
> In Humanity's machine.

If Yeats shared the interests and outlook of his fellow poets in
the 'nineties, he was destined to outstrip all the others whose
names are linked with that decade. It is important to compare him

for a moment with two older contemporaries more powerful than Wilde or Symons, Dowson or Johnson. They were Gerard Manley Hopkins (1844-1889) and Thomas Hardy (1840-1928). A Jesuit priest and a modern skeptic, these two men represent extreme positions of the sort Yeats constantly balanced in developing his encompassing aestheticism. Since he was not deeply touched by the work of either poet, the relationships between their achievement and his are all the more indicative of the fact that the whole age had been tending toward Yeats's accomplishment.

Hopkins, in his youth, had shown promise in several arts. Once he was received into the Catholic Church and began his training for the priesthood, he disciplined himself for a long time by forswearing such 'worldly' pursuits. From his poetry it seems clear that a highly excitable, even irritable sensuousness often strove against his spiritual convictions and vocation. Hopkins does not in Yeats's manner seek to make himself independent of the quarrel of values by 'objectifying' it. He must remain within it, and take sides in the bargain. Few poetic moments are as poignant as the one in which the devout churchman, his defenses against the world's sights and sounds beaten down by the splendor of a kestrel hawk's triumph over buffeting winds against a brilliant morning sky, cries out his dismay in 'The Windhover':

> My heart in hiding
> Stirred for a bird,—the achieve of, the mastery of
> the thing!

Unquestioning faith is a necessary premise of Hopkins's poetry. His greatest poetic successes are those in which he converts his aliveness to the world of the senses into devotional inspiration. Even his metrics, the 'sprung rhythm' straining against the bounds of the conventional verse line, expresses his need to bring about such resolutions. By the close of 'The Windhover' we realize how subtly and passionately the bird's beauty and 'brute mastery' have been symbolically widened all along, from the dedication 'to Christ our Lord' through such images as 'kingdom of daylight's dauphin' and the series of figures showing the miraculous fires hidden in commonplace, perishing things, to the language of the closing line which so clearly suggests the Crucifixion. The buried implications of the chivalric and mystical phrasing come to light as soon as the poet tells himself how much more dazzling and dangerous than the bird's victory is the soul's effort in the communicant who dares imitate Christ and renounce the glory and excitement of the world. Hopkins is extraordinarily moving in his desire to go behind the personal conflict in which he is inwardly enmeshed and to force into view the divinity inherent in all things. As he says of God in 'The Wreck of the Deutschland':

> . . . tho' he is under the world's splendor and wonder,
> His mystery must be instressed, stressed . . .

It is less the faith itself than the *effort* that moves most of us so, and never more than in the 'terrible sonnets' in which, admitting he cannot quite wrestle the devil of his despair down, he yet *will* force the issue to the last. Thus, the ending of 'I wake and feel the fell of dark, not day':

> I am gall, I am heartburn. God's most deep decree
> Bitter would have me taste: my taste was me;
> Bones built in me, flesh filled, blood brimmed the curse.
> Selfyeast of spirit a dull dough sours. I see
> The lost are like this, and their scourge to be
> As I am mine, their sweating selves; but worse.

A predetermined result biases the curve of Hopkins's writing. Unless we share his particular beliefs we are more sympathetic with his conflicts—with the 'sweating self' and the 'heart in hiding' of a speaker whose sexual and psychic energies his images barely hold in check—than with his imposed resolutions. Hardy's emphasis is all the other way. He has the air of total immersion in the observable—the 'actual.' Characteristically, he is wry, ironically compassionate, anxious but unable to be detached. His genuine anguish derives from the essential stupidity of things: misdirected love, the unpredictability and the banalities of passion, the injustice of war, the supreme idiocy and betrayal that is death.

> Ah no; the years, the years;
> Down their carved names the rain-drop ploughs.
>
>   ('During Wind and Rain')

Hardy lacks the sustained and difficult fullness of self-projection of Hopkins at his best, but also stands clear of his tendentiousness. He is closer to what we may call folk-philosophy, and his grip on the reader has a correspondingly different source; the emotion comes straight and pure out of ordinary experience and folk-memory. A man sees a girl riding by with her fiancé, and is shocked and mystified to remember his own former intimacy with her; a lover, anxious to have a girl's father leave the two of them alone together, suddenly realizes that the older man actually has the greater claim on her. And beyond such transparent yet sharply felt themes and subjects, there are poems like 'The Souls of the Slain' and 'Channel Firing,' in which a pagan fatalism blends with disillusionment and with a feeling that, if there *are* any creeds of lasting value, they are those of the practical side of Christianity—simple love and concern. Hardy was quite able to allow contradictory premises to mingle in his work as they do in a people's thinking at any given time. He is nostalgic for the irrecoverable faith of the past (as in 'The Oxen') at the same time that his thinking is clearly in the spirit of the Enlightenment and its nineteenth-century heirs—Darwin, Spencer, Schopenhauer, and Arnold. The point is, he did not *like* the hard lessons of mechanistic science and of personal experience. Nor did he like many of the by-products of secularism, which he thought of as an 'ominous moving backward.' Among these were 'the barbarizing of taste in the younger minds by the dark madness of the late war,' the 'unabashed cultivation of selfishness in all classes,' and 'the plethoric growth of knowledge simultaneously with the stunting of wisdom.' In his 'Apology' (1922) he summed up these defects of a society without faith and called sentimentally and hopelessly for an intellectual program which Yeats (though Hardy had no knowledge of the fact) had for a long time been cultivating in his own fashion with ever more robust success:

It may indeed be a forlorn hope, a mere dream, that of
an alliance between religion, which must be retained unless the world is to perish, and complete rationality, which
must come, unless the world is to perish, by means of
the interfusing effect of poetry. . . .*

Hardy's longest poetic work, *The Dynasts*—'a drama of the
Napoleonic wars, in three parts, nineteen acts, & one hundred and
thirty scenes'—attempted to graft on to the dominant historical
and scientific determinism of the day this wan hope for the re-
emergence of faith through the mediation of poetry. Despite its
bulk it is an appealing reconstruction of history and interpretation of actual events in the light of the poet's view of man's
fate as arbitrary and perhaps pointless. But it forges no 'alliance'
between religion and rationality because Hardy lacks the necessary conviction and the necessary symbols as well. He does not
even approach the 'as if' position of Emerson, which to a certain
extent Yeats, also, held and which Hopkins simply carried to its
emotional limits: 'What difference does it make, whether Orion
is up there in heaven,' wrote Emerson, 'or some god paints the
image in the firmament of the soul? . . . Whether nature enjoy
a substantial existence without, or is only in the apocalypse of the
mind, it is ideal to me as long as I cannot try the accuracy of my
senses.' † But, as I have already suggested, it is *Yeats* who goes
beyond these as-if principles and makes the great reversal, liberating himself from the bonds of agnosticism and of dogma simultaneously by reducing both to subordinate status in an aesthetically
created universe of symbols. By this liberation he won through to
the passionate detachment, the concerned disinterestedness, toward
which the religion of art had long been carrying the modern spirit.

* Thomas Hardy, *Collected Poems*, Macmillan, New York, 1925, p. 531.
† Ralph Waldo Emerson, *Representative Selections*, ed. Frederick I. Car-
penter, American Book Company, New York, 1934, p. 33. (From Emerson's
1836 essay 'Nature.')

TWO

Yeats and the Modern Mind

I was unlike others of my generation in one thing only. I am very religious, and deprived by Huxley and Tyndall, whom I detested, of the simple-minded religion of my childhood, I had made a new religion, almost an infallible church of poetic tradition, of a fardel of stories, and of personages, and of emotions, inseparable from their first expression, passed on from generation to generation by poets and painters with some help from philosophers and theologians. . . . I had even created a dogma: 'Because those imaginary people are created out of the deepest instinct of man, to be his measure and his norm, wherever I can imagine those mouths speaking may be the nearest I can go to truth.' *

1. THE UNCONSENTING SPIRIT

Toward the end of his long career, William Butler Yeats wrote: 'I seek an image of the modern mind's discovery of itself.' † He never described his own work more truly or more succinctly. Yeats spoke to the modern mind in every way. The rise of nationalism and the political problems that were to create two world wars, the shattering and challenging effects of new science on old beliefs, the reopening of every question of truth and value—all these elements entered his imagination and were there absorbed and transmuted into the symbolic structure of his poetry.

This alchemy illuminates the development of his poetry. Yet, curiously, Yeats is the least 'experimental,' in any obvious sense of that word, of the great modern poets. He does not throw whole poems into free-verse forms, does not violate significantly the ordinary rules of syntax or grammar, never gives a poem over wholly to colloquial idiom and its rhythms. He endeavored rather to invigorate the tradition within which he wrote. 'All my life,'

---

* *The Autobiography of William Butler Yeats*, Macmillan, New York, 1938, pp. 101-2.

† William Butler Yeats, *The Words Upon the Window Pane*, Cuala Press, Dublin, 1934, p. 3.

28

he said, 'I have tried to get rid of modern subjectivity by insisting on construction and contemporary words and syntax.' * Similarly, his private life conformed to a traditional stereotype of 'The Poet.' In his hopeless passion for the actress Maud Gonne, his scorn for money grubbing and 'getting on in the world,' his excursions into faery lore and Celtic myth and the spirit world, in his ambition to bring about an Irish renaissance, he appears properly as a dreamer,† or as an Irish bard, or as a Keatsian Romantic. But it is as a spokesman for the modern human condition that Yeats reached his great stature. It is astounding to find a poet with his background and interests so deeply, even savagely, involved in critical contemporary issues. We may not like what he has to say in his couplet 'Parnell,' for instance, but how can we not feel its force?

> Parnell came down the road, he said to a cheering man:
> 'Ireland shall get her freedom and you still break stone.'

The poem speaks to our world of one of its great fears—the ultimate futility of political action. So does 'The Great Day':

> Hurrah for revolution and more cannon-shot!
> A beggar upon horseback lashes a beggar on foot.
> Hurrah for revolution and cannon come again!
> The beggars have changed places, but the lash goes on.

These examples may present an unfamiliar, embittered Yeats, but they show his sophisticated—and very contemporary—distrust of that callous demagoguery which battens on man's dearest hopes and ideals. His poem 'Church and State' also recalls the fearless cast of his mind and his extraordinary ability to give emotional weight and appreciation to mutually contradictory values. Like Blake's 'London,' this is a ferociously 'political' poem.

* *The Letters of William Butler Yeats,* ed. Allan Wade, Macmillan, New York, 1955, p. 892.

† There is nothing dreamy about the way he went about organizing the rebirth of Irish literature and theater, however. This side of his life is as surprising as his energetic promotion of his own literary career.

Here is fresh matter, poet,
Matter for old age meet;
Might of the Church and the State,
Their mobs put under their feet.
O but heart's wine shall run pure,
Mind's bread grow sweet.

That were a cowardly song,
Wander in dreams no more;
What if the Church and the State
Are the mob that howls at the door!
Wine shall run thick to the end,
Bread taste sour.

In this poem no 'position' is actually taken, though a vision of ideal order has been arranged side by side with a nightmare of mob violence and official repression. The poet's imagination encompasses the range between these opposites; hence he cannot commit himself to either.

Even Yeats's apparently topical poems are not really that. A brilliant example is 'Easter 1916,' which celebrates the heroes of the Easter Rebellion in Dublin. Being a true Yeatsian poem, it cannot rest content with a single note, even of eulogy. An act of heroism has transformed what had seemed to the poet a shabby people who 'but lived where motley was worn' into a nation in which 'a terrible beauty is born.' The sacrifice has meant for these countrymen of his, and for the poet himself, a marvelous rebirth of a sort. So far we may consider the poem a glorification of Irish nationalism and its struggles.

But in the second half of the poem there comes an important turn. The poet presents a new image, outside the political and specifically Irish context altogether, for his theme of transformation through sacrifice.

Hearts with one purpose alone
Through summer and winter seem
Enchanted to a stone
To trouble the living stream.

The enchanted stone appears at first to symbolize precisely the point that, all surface impressions to the contrary, the capacity for greatness and beauty had always been present in his countrymen's hearts. But something curious now makes itself felt. As the image of the stone in the midst of transitory nature is developed, the nationalistic theme is left behind. In the notion of hearts 'enchanted to a stone' the poet finds an unexpected meaning, and yet a meaning logical as his figure is sound:

> Too long a sacrifice
> Can make a stone of the heart.

The enchanted stone may be nothing but a dead weight, unaffected by life's changing realities. And the poet must remind himself harshly that consolatory euphemisms should not be substituted for the word 'death.' These men have *died*. In the same realistic mood, we must face the possibility that they died for the wrong reasons.

> What is it but nightfall?
> No, no, not night but death;
> Was it needless death after all?
> For England may keep faith
> For all that is done and said.

No matter, the poem concludes, we know their intention. The meaning of their sacrifice remains the same, and their names will always conjure up for us a 'terrible beauty.' But meanwhile we have been warned of the arbitrary character of faith, of the tremendous gap between man's desires and his capacities, his will and his fate. The poem is all the more honest and convincing because it refuses, as Yeats always did refuse, to be dogmatic. It is saved from dogmatism by the way it turns on a single image which, followed with strict integrity, forces the speaker to shift the ground of his thought and include the possibility that his heroes may have been wrong. The play or dialogue of warring opposites in Yeats's work almost always transcends the original motives of the poems.

The audacity of this poem, as of the later 'Church and State,' is characteristic of Yeats. In the deepest sense he believed in nothing yet spoke for belief. And speaking for it, he yet detested the thought of vain causes and idealisms that can make a man false to himself. This provides a subtle clue to his search for definitive images of 'the modern mind's discovery of itself,' and to his rejection of the claims of current religious, ideological, scientific, and social systems. It helps explain, too, his enduring fascination with the occult, with its proliferation of malleable images charged with psychological suggestiveness and relatively free of set doctrinal associations.

Modern poetry as a whole tends to be tragic in its assumption that we are at a cultural dead end, in which myriad values at cross-purposes, with modern political values the most virulent of all, are choking each other to death. The major poetic situation is the struggle of a heroic sensibility, or Self, to free itself from the condition of living death imposed by this murderous predicament. Clearly, the most elementary way to gain such freedom is to insist on the priority of instinct and emotion over all logical and systematic thought and over the demands of society. In many poems Yeats fastens on the sexual act and the mystery of sexuality as the ultimate sources of meaning. When, overwhelmed by the horrors of Nazism, Thomas Mann, expert *par excellence* on that death wish which so preoccupies our poetry, wrote that in our day 'the destiny of man presents its meaning in political terms,' Yeats set down what was, in context, a brutal, contemptuous reply in his little poem 'Politics':

> How can I, that girl standing there,
> My attention fix
> On Roman or on Russian
> Or on Spanish politics?
> Yet here's a traveled man that knows
> What he talks about,
> And there's a politician
> That has read and thought,
> And maybe what they say is true
> Of war and war's alarms,

But O that I were young again
And held her in my arms!

The closing lines echo the old folksong, 'Oh, Western wind, when wilt thou blow,' and serve a liberating function like that of the stone in the earlier poem. Yeats's reply to Mann suggests not paltry and callous lechery but absorption in the sexual mystery of annunciation symbolized in 'Leda and the Swan,' 'The Second Coming,' and many other poems and plays. It is this mystery rather than politics which has everything to do with man's destiny; as the poem 'Byzantium' implies, it is at the heart of all human creativity. For Yeats, poetry is intrinsically 'shameless' and 'irresponsible' in the manner of 'Politics'; it is in the domain of paganism: of beast-images, of forbidden divinities, of the life-force. Poets must not desert the female or kinship principle they celebrate in favor of Plato's Golden Lie that the State is the new order of the family, and hierarchy the new order of the heart. Their sympathies must lie, not with 'pious Aeneas' but with his enemy Turnus and the other 'unconsenting spirits' relegated to the nether shades.

Throughout his career Yeats sought to re-embody the free unconsenting spirit through the traditional symbols of myth and folklore. His fundamental attitude is clearly projected in the play *On Baile's Strand*. Cuchulain, the heroic, untrammeled warrior whose services have always been given spontaneously and generously—out of love—is persuaded to betray his own nature by swearing unquestioning allegiance to Conchubar the king. The result is tragedy without end: he slays his own son unknowingly, though every instinct forbids him to do so. Thirty-four years after this play, Yeats's poem 'Lapis Lazuli' (1938) maintains stubbornly the independence of art and the priority of its concerns to those of the State. To alter Mann's language and reverse his thought, 'the destiny of man' here 'presents its meaning' only through the poetic symbol, which preserves intact the creative power of the race.

The time of 'Lapis Lazuli' was that crucial moment when it seemed clear that all peace efforts were going to fail and that, barring a miracle, the new world war must come. It seemed to many anxious people that all effort should now become political, for only thus could the miracle be brought to pass. Yeats presents their position accurately but unsympathetically:

> I have heard that hysterical women say
> They are sick of the palette and fiddle-bow,
> Of poets that are always gay,
> For everybody knows or else should know
> That if nothing drastic is done
> Aeroplane and Zeppelin will come out,
> Pitch like King Billy bomb-balls in
> Until the town lie beaten flat.

The arts are not playthings to be set aside when crisis strikes. For Yeats the word 'gay' implies morale and the wisdom of the heart. In this light, Shakespeare's tragic characters—Hamlet, Lear, Ophelia, Cordelia—are gay:

> Gaiety transfiguring all that dread.
> All men have aimed at, found and lost;
> Black out; heaven blazing into the head. . . .

To be human is to play on the same tragic stage, and to play one's given role to the end. No more than the literal actors on the Shakespearean stage can common humanity 'break up their lines to weep.' The artist pursuing his craft becomes the symbol of man's indomitable creativity.

> No handiwork of Callimachus,
> Who handled marble as if it were bronze,
> Made draperies that seemed to rise
> When sea-wind swept the corner, stands;
> His long lamp-chimney shaped like the stem
> Of a slender palm stood but a day;
> All things fall and are built again,
> And those that build them again are gay.

In the final image of the poem, a carving in lapis lazuli, three Chinese figures, one of them playing a musical instrument for the other two, climb a lofty slope while a long-legged bird, 'a symbol of longevity,' flies above them. Yeats imagines them finally pausing at their 'little half-way house' to stare upon 'all the tragic scene' and listen to 'mournful melodies' while

> Their eyes mid many wrinkles, their eyes,
> Their ancient, glittering eyes, are gay.

Art becomes, in 'Lapis Lazuli,' not merely man's chief consolation in his tragic progress toward what is at best only a 'half-way house.' It becomes the prime carrier of civilization, the tireless opponent of chaos. The artist, with his dreams and his 'gaiety,' is thus the most practical and indispensable of men.

2. A RETROSPECT: THE HERE AND THE THERE

The faith that the nature and methods of art will guide us more surely to the truth of man's condition than any other approach has many facets. Nothing could be more inaccurate than to conceive of this kind of aestheticism as a mere 'escape,' or as a trifling absorption in 'lovely' effects of one kind or another. Long before he could have been fully aware of his ultimate directions, Yeats had been experimentally juggling opposites, particularly the world of the 'real' and the world of imagination, the worlds of the Here and the There. He wrote on conventional subjects, yet through them was forever engaged in this balancing and blending and distinguishing. The preoccupation brought him to uneasy revelations that revived old themes and symbols and gave them new settings.

'The Stolen Child,' originally published in 1886, is an interesting example, a liquidly delicate poem on the luring away of a child by faeries. The primary elements of this familiar situation of folklore are presented: the supernatural beings and the living child they entice away. But none of the familiar denouements occurs. Yeats does not tell us whether the child dies, is replaced by a changeling, or returns the 'next day' an old man. Against the warm, comforting associations of landscape and of the home the child abandons, we see the faery world bathed in a sinister light.

At the beginning we find the 'flapping herons' and 'drowsy water-rats' and hoarded 'stolen cherries' of that world only vaguely disturbing. In the second stanza there is something more troubled and furtive in the picture of the faeries' moonlight revels, 'mingling hands and mingling glances,' on the 'dim grey sands.' These apprehensions are brought to a climax in the third stanza as the faeries tell how they bring 'unquiet dreams' ('*evil* dreams' in the poem's first version) to the slumbering trout while the ferns

> drop their tears
> Over the young streams.

The image, so reminiscent of Blake, prepares us for the pathetic seduction of the 'solemn-eyed' child from his home at the end of the poem. He does not know that the faery refrain is as true for them as for him: '*the world's more full of weeping than you can understand.*'

The ambiguity of this refrain suggests a new turn on an old Romantic motif: the pathos of the unattainable. Yeats adds something hinted at but never developed in Blake's 'Ah! Sun-Flower' and in a few other poems. The ultimate frustration of the Romantic ideal becomes the possibility that, if we *were* allowed to pass over to the There, we should not escape the sorrows of the Here, but merely find them eternalized. Keats does not question his blissful state for the brief time that he is one with the nightingale, nor does Coleridge question the delight that would be his could he but once again recapture his vision of the 'damsel with a dulcimer.' But 'The Stolen Child' may actually be considered a complaint against the dream of perfection itself. That dream is deceptive; it prevents realization of the attainable; it calls into question the value of everything man plans or does.

The complaint is made explicit in another early poem, 'The Man Who Dreamed of Faeryland.' The hero of this poem is an ordinary person who might have found measurable, if mediocre, pleasure in a commonplace love and marriage, or in money making, or in taking revenge on his enemies. Instead, each time he reaches for one of these satisfactions he is tormented by the dream of perfection. Even after his death he is so tormented that he finds 'no comfort in his grave.' Everywhere insignificant bits of mortality—a pile of tiny fish at a market, a clump of knot-grass, some worms—have sung to him of an existence entirely unlike the drab and paltry one they themselves represent. But of what use has the dream been to one who is in any case one of 'those lovers that no lovers miss'?

In 'The Lake Isle of Innisfree,' the poet begins by toying whimsically with the idea of an Earthly Paradise. There *is* such an island, and he had dreamed, he elsewhere tells us, of imitating Thoreau and going to live, once he had 'conquered bodily desire,' on this island whose name so happily suggests freedom and inwardness. The opening rather blithely parodies Thoreau's prescription for the simple life in the woods. He will use only clay and wattles for his cabin, will plant exactly nine bean-rows, will have the music of honey bees around him—no other kind. Never mind why these preferences! But even more than in 'The Stolen Child,' the tone grows progressively more serious until, in the closing stanza, it conveys a really somber picture of the speaker as he stands on the 'pavements grey' of the Here, haunted by an inward image of his deprivation: 'I hear it in the deep heart's core.' Like 'The Man Who Dreamed of Faeryland,' this is not only a Romantic poem but also a criticism of the Romantic dream itself.

Perhaps the most beautiful of the earlier poems on this theme is 'Who Goes with Fergus?' Like the faeries summoning the child, still uninitiated into the promise of his mind and body, to 'the waters and the wild' of their own eerie existence, the speaker here seems to be calling attention to the dilemma of those who would escape into the region of dreams. Ostensibly he seeks to lure the youth and the maiden into this region, over which Fergus, the great king who has forsaken his former earthly power, now reigns. Actually, he is warning them.

> Who will go drive with Fergus now,
> And pierce the deep wood's woven shade,
> And dance upon the level shore?
> Young man, lift up your russet brow,

> And lift your tender eyelids, maid,
> And brood on hopes and fear no more.
>
> And no more turn aside and brood
> Upon love's bitter mystery;
> For Fergus rules the brazen cars,
> And rules the shadows of the wood,
> And the white breast of the dim sea
> And all disheveled wandering stars.

In Fergus's realm all should be calm and joyous as in a woven hanging. It is the realm of art as well as of the dream, where youth and maid need 'brood on hopes and fear no more.' But the imagery of escape becomes increasingly disturbed. 'White breast of the dim sea' and 'disheveled wandering stars' suggest no diminution of desire or of its frustrations, but only their endless continuance.

Very early, then, Yeats begins to use the method of setting interpenetrating opposites against one another as a deliberate way of discovering the character of the human predicament and of exploring the challenge it offers. As one reads his *Autobiography* and other writings, one is recurrently struck by his almost professionally practical attitude toward the uses of supernatural symbolism. Besides folklore, he was interested in theories of the occult from Rosicrucianism to spiritualism and mystical idealism of every sort, including that of Plato and Plotinus. His attraction to these cults and doctrines had many motivations, but one was overriding: a belief that they provided valuable clues to the unconscious life of mind and spirit and therefore to the sources of creative imagination. He sought a kind of antiscientific science whose touchstones were the 'truths' of myth and art, a science that would therefore—from a poet's standpoint, at least—go beyond the materialistic thought systems prevailing in his youth and the vague bodiless religiosity that shuddered away from them. He wished, he wrote, to be able to 'hold in a single thought reality and justice'—the difficult 'reality' of experience and the 'justice' of pure vision.

'Pure vision' in Yeats is strangely related to ordinary experience.

The world of symbols is not a humane or humanly ordered world, but men in their animal lives as well as in their aspirations are as it were its raw materials. As we have already seen, it is charged with the sexual principle. (The interpenetrating cones or gyres by which Yeats diagramed the great cycles of thought and personality are a sexual abstraction in themselves.) Yeats reverts again and again to the great paradox and mystery of our conscious life:

> But Love has pitched his mansion in
> The place of excrement.

A list of his most famous poems calls up a series of vibrant, archetypal symbols revolving about the sexual mystery: the rape of Leda; a Sphinx-like beast 'moving its slow thighs' over the desert as the annunciation reordering man's destiny; an old whore shrieking beautiful obscene profundities at a doctrinaire priest; an Earthly Paradise in which the great sages and heroes of tradition take their whimsical ease while the New Testament Innocents 'relive their death' again and again and 'nymphs and satyrs copulate in the foam.' In all these instances pure vision is inseparable from its physical origins:

> Those masterful images because complete
> Grew in pure mind, but out of what began?
> A mound of refuse or the sweepings of a street,
> Old kettles, old bottles, and a broken can,
> Old iron, old bones, old rags, that raving slut
> Who keeps the till. Now that my ladder's gone,
> I must lie down where all the ladders start,
> In the foul rag-and-bone shop of the heart.

So wrote Yeats within a year of his death at seventy-four, still very much engaged with the dual principle of human consciousness, the Here and the There. At about the same time he observed that to him all things seemed 'made of the conflict of two states of consciousness, beings or persons which die each other's life, live each other's death. That is true of life and death themselves.' He had been thinking in this way for many years, pushing into the heart of life by means of this interplay of opposites: 'two cones (or whirls),' he called them, 'the apex of each in the other's base.' His early poems hint at this conflict and interplay—the youth and the maiden of *this* life, and the inhabitants of Fergus's world in *that* life, partake of one another's destinies, for example. But as Yeats grew older he used larger canvases, with bolder and more intimate detail. Thus, in the famous 'Sailing to Byzantium' the speaker is an old man between two worlds. Or rather, he is deep within this world, which has all but rejected him and which he now wishes to repossess in a new way—by becoming part of a world of pure creativity in which the fleshly is transformed into the eternal. In four stanzas of eight lines each, the poet contrasts the two 'countries': the sensual realm of 'fish, flesh, or fowl,' of 'the young in one another's arms' and the raging life cycle; and the world of 'unaging intellect,' of the 'artifice of eternity,' symbolized by 'the holy city of Byzantium.' In *this* world stands an old man with his heart, still 'sick with desire,' 'fastened to a dying animal.' In *that* stand the 'sages' beyond death in 'God's holy fire,' whom the speaker implores to teach his soul to sing louder than the 'sensual music' by which he is here surrounded. Two worlds, two kinds of music, two sets of inhabitants, and the speaker between the two, seeking to make them one in his own person. It is man who has created the monuments of his soul's magnificence, but it is these monuments—his great works of art and thought, his spiritual creations, perhaps even God himself—which are needed now to carry him beyond the desperate moment in which he faces his own mortality.

A great deal can be 'learned' from 'Sailing to Byzantium' about attitudes toward death, sex, old age, and art. But whatever we thus learn is incidental to the terrible, blazing confrontation of the two spheres of being, each remote from the other yet inseparable from it. Yeats does not argue with or attempt to explain the human condition, nor does he subordinate to any specific doctrine his poem's anguished prayer for an ideal real enough to encompass and transform the speaker's experience and predicament. The poem comes close to pure symbolism, in the free play it allows thought and feeling over images of the widest possible relevance.

3. PROPHETIC YEATS

The relation of men to the great cycles of cultural history is another phase of this duality. In Yeats's later work especially the relationship assumes great importance. Do these cycles, in some measure, take their meaning from man himself, or is man merely the passive instrument of an indifferent deity or creative principle? Some of Yeats's finest plays deal with this theme, and in many works he uses as central symbols sacred events of myth and religion in order to present it as suggestively as possible.

The sonnet 'Leda and the Swan,' written when Yeats was fifty-eight (about four years before 'Sailing to Byzantium'), rivets attention on one such event: the ravishment of the girl Leda by the god Zeus in the shape of a swan. It begins with the full shock of the swan's swooping attack upon Leda, and the first eight lines linger over the sensual details of her surrender to the god's power. She feels 'the strange heart beating' against hers—'strange' because it is the heart not only of another being but of one at once more bestial than she and more divine—a 'feathered glory.' To make vivid this moment in Western mythical history Yeats considers the scene as its human participant must have felt it in all its physical immediacy and mystery. In the sestet he reminds us of the mythical events subsequent to this union: the birth of Helen, the Trojan War, the murder of Agamemnon. The poem ends asking if Leda's intelligence as well as her womb was impregnated by the god. Is she, the passive human recipient of the seeds of the future, now charged with the god's divinity in her own right? Yeats does not answer; he merely asks.

> Being so caught up,
> So mastered by the brute blood of the air,
> Did she put on his knowledge with his power
> Before the indifferent beak could let her drop?

In this concluding passage, Yeats lets the poem fall from the present to the past tense. He has made the ancient scene burst upon our sight and our other senses, has made us *realize*, through the way it is enacted before us, the impact of that pagan annunciation which began the pre-Christian phase of our civilization. Now he lets it slip back into the recesses of the most dimly imagined world of ancient myth. The words 'let her drop' at the very close suggest also this final release of the vision he has conjured up for us. As in 'Sailing to Byzantium,' two worlds have been set face to face symbolically, and the great unanswerable questions of philosophy and religion have incidentally been brought to our attention.

Another poem that parallels this vision of a great creative moment is 'The Second Coming,' which attempts to give us a symbol directly relevant to our own era. Yeats 'believed' that we were approaching the end of another 'Great Year,' or two-thousand-year cycle, in this century. The Christian Era draws to a close, and a new annunciation is at hand, foreshadowed in the modern political situation.

> . . . as my sense of reality deepens [he wrote in a letter in 1936], and I think it does with age, my horror at the cruelty of governments grows greater, and . . . to hold one form of government more responsible than any other . . . would betray my convictions. Communist, Fascist, nationalist, clerical, anti-clerical, are all responsible according to the number of their victims. . . . If you have my poems by you, look up a poem called *The Second Coming.* It was written some sixteen or seventeen years ago and foretold what is happening. . . . I am not callous, every nerve trembles with horror at what is happening in Europe, 'the ceremony of innocence is drowned.' *

In another letter, he defined modern politics as 'nothing but the manipulation of popular enthusiasm by false news.' By manipulated news, he said, he meant 'more than the manipulation of the news of the day.' He meant 'something that goes deeper,' something 'which I come up against in all my thoughts whenever modern interests are concerned.' The danger was that all traditional lines of value and communication, the whole heritage of man's

---

* *Letters*, p. 851.

best creativity, would be destroyed by a 'manipulation' so violent and ruthless that neither the old beauties of life nor the old capacity to resist and 'to keep one's well pure' could survive much longer:

> Turning and turning in the widening gyre
> The falcon cannot hear the falconer;
> Things fall apart; the centre cannot hold;
> Mere anarchy is loosed upon the world,
> The blood-dimmed tide is loosed, and everywhere
> The ceremony of innocence is drowned;
> The best lack all conviction, while the worst
> Are full of passionate intensity.

'The Second Coming,' one of the truly prophetic poems of our age, 'foretold' not only the spread of totalitarianism in its new forms but the Second World War and the rise of every imaginable destructive force. It marks the culmination of a drift sensed first by poets many years ago, and perhaps it expresses the death wish of modern culture. The images with which it begins, however, say nothing of this sort. Like those in the opening of 'Leda and the Swan,' they are immediate and physical. But the succession of images pounding out the failure of control and responsibility, of authority and meaning, pronounces our doom. Another series of images follows, with the further pronouncement that a new era, a second coming with its own incarnation and revelations, must surely be at hand. What shape will it take? Out of the recesses of the spiritual world a figure emerges. Like the rape of Leda it comes into monstrous close-up in the speaker's imagination and seems to break the invisible film separating the two worlds—a Sphinx-shape out of the pre-Christian darkness, indifferent to man, accompanied in its dreadful progress by shrieks and shadows:

> somewhere in sands of the desert
> A shape with lion body and the head of a man,
> A gaze blank and pitiless as the sun,
> Is moving its slow thighs, while all about it
> Reel shadows of the indignant desert birds.

The image drops away, back into *spiritus mundi*, the storehouse of the world's phantasmagoria. We return to the poet's thoughts about history and its cycles and to the question which evokes such images: Now that the old slumbering meanings are being shaken to life again by disorder and savagery and this great nightmare symbol begins to arise out of the wreckage, what 'Second Coming is at hand'?

> And what rough beast, its hour come round at last,
> Slouches towards Bethlehem to be born?

The organizing system for Yeats's poetic symbolism is provided in that surprising, delightful, somewhat makeshift book *A Vision* (1925; revised edition, 1937). Behind *A Vision* lies the occultist experience, reading, and thinking of the poet and his wife. Her efforts at automatic writing shortly after their marriage in 1917 led to the conscious formulation and construction in images of the themes and diagrams around which the book is built: the cycles of history and of individual personality; the relations between the wheel of time and timelessness, between physical universe and pure spirit; the opposition of Christian and pagan-Renaissance values; the 'dreaming-back' by the soul after death of its worldly experience; the new applications of the ancient concept of the Great Year—the two-thousand-year cycle within which a dominant mode of civilization is born, flourishes, and dies; and the basic symbol of interpenetrating gyres or vortexes, forever at war and forever passing through regular phases in their relation to one another.

How many of these ideas Yeats believed in unreservedly is open to question, especially since we cannot be sure he believed unreservedly in *anything*. Interestingly, he begins his introduction to *A Vision* with the observation that, as a result of the 'incredible experience' it represents, 'my poetry has gained in self-possession and power.' Also he tells us (possibly without intentional humor) that when he offered to spend the rest of his life interpreting the messages received through his wife's automatic writing, the spirits replied: 'No, we have come to give you metaphors for poetry.' (These spirits, incidentally, were demanding, pedantic, even petulant. For instance, 'they asked me not to read philosophy until their exposition was complete,' and sent flashes of light or struck chairs violently when they disapproved of the Yeatses' behavior. On the other hand, they quite sentimentally filled the house with the smell of roses when a son was born there.) And he ends his introduction with these words:

> . . . if sometimes, overwhelmed by miracle as all men must be when in the midst of it, I have taken such periods [the Great Years] literally, my reason has soon recovered; and now that the system stands out clearly in my imagination I regard them as stylistic arrangements of experience comparable to the cubes in the drawing of Wyndham Lewis and to the ovoids in the sculpture of Brancusi. They have helped me to hold in a single thought reality and justice.*

A Vision has the reputation of being merely schematic, and fantastically so. In fact, though, it is a storehouse—in addition to its schematizations—of wit, verse, and personal speculation of a quite elegant order. It is full of passages absorbing in themselves and illuminating of Yeats's poetry as a whole. For instance:

> A civilization is a struggle to keep self-control, and in this it is like some great tragic person, some Niobe who must display an almost superhuman will or the cry will not touch our sympathy. The loss of control over thought comes towards the end; first a sinking in upon the moral being, then the last surrender, the irrational cry, revelation—the scream of Juno's peacock.†

Out of the organized subjectivisms of A Vision and his brooding over their implications came the rich art of the later Yeats. He had developed a type of symbolic thinking that was free and hypothetical, yet emphatic and concrete, and he was enabled thereby to encompass great issues without being swamped in

* William Butler Yeats, A Vision, Macmillan, New York, 1956, p. 25.
† Ibid. p. 268.

partisanship. ('I never bade you go,' he wrote in 'Those Images,' 'to Moscow or to Rome.') A *Vision* brought to fruition his life-long search for a supernaturalism and for intellectual points of reference that would not commit him to any established religion or philosophical school. It provided the necessary exotic themes and images—he called them his 'circus animals'—which, because largely and primarily aesthetic, allowed him great latitude of thought and statement without risk of outraging the public or incurring censorship. (Even his aristocratic ideals are basically aesthetic in conception.) His humor, too, was enriched. We find many effects like that in 'Crazy Jane on the Mountain'; here, amidst the painful realization of the loss of heroic meanings in the modern world, there is suddenly called up the vision of the mythical warrior-king Cuchulain and his queen, 'great-bladdered Emer.' (The allusion is to a contest in which Emer clearly demonstrated her superiority to certain other mythical ladies.) The whole of 'John Kinsella's Lament for Mrs. Mary Moore' has the same kind of bawdy, tragic-hilarious humor.

The 'system' helped Yeats to see also his own personality and the relationships between science and religion as elements to be manipulated by art. In 'Sailing to Byzantium' the poet uses himself in his old age as such a symbolic and dramatic element. In his play *The Resurrection* he converts in a remarkable way the religious attitudes represented by his characters into aspects of the great oppositions defined in A *Vision*. Christ resurrected is but the fusion of pure physicality and pure spirituality mysteriously embodied. It is not the New Testament Jesus, but Dionysus re-born who ushers in a new phase of history. Greek disciple and Hebrew are confounded, while the Syrian, bearing within himself the memories of the 'fabulous formless darkness' before Greek civilization, recognizes the truth. The conception is similar to that of D. H. Lawrence's *The Man Who Died*: Christ paganized and 'revised' so that he now becomes one of those archetypal beings, 'created out of the instinct of man,' which, says Yeats in his *Autobiography*, may be 'the nearest I can go to truth.' In the play *Calvary*, the primal forces of the world are indifferent to the Crucifixion. 'God has not died for the white heron,' the musicians sing at the beginning of the play; and at the end: 'God has not died for the birds.' Lazarus reproaches Christ for not letting him die in peace; Judas is permitted to justify himself and to best him in debate; while the Roman soldiers who would like to comfort him are unconcerned about his mission. Similarly the poem 'News for the Delphic Oracle' mingles Christian, pagan, and historical symbols, subordinating them to a purely aesthetic pattern. Its deliberately cruel gaiety mocks any scheme of value that exalts morality, religion, or good will above the impersonal design of art and its sexual source in the life-force.

And yet behind all this was a very excitable, emotional, and morally responsive human being. The deep and passionate innocence of his childhood, described in the 'Reveries' section of his autobiography, never left him. It was in part what enabled him to use his 'system' and his supernaturalism without losing sight of his objectives: to speak fully out of his own nature and to discover the right images for the awakening modern consciousness. Many biographical contrasts underlie his feeling for the inter-relationship of opposites: those between his childhood slowness of book learning and his absorption in the small, magical domain of his maternal grandfather on the one hand, and his active curiosity and imagination on the other; between the mercurial articulateness of his father, the artist-intellectual, and the powerful silences of his mother and her family; between his devotion to the Irish countryside, its speech and lore, and later to its desire for independence, and his participation in the more cosmopolitan artistic and literary life of London; and between his romantic needs and his difficulties in love. Yeats's summary of his life in 'Dialogue of Self and Soul' is a painful one. Some method of transcendence was demanded if he was to rise superior to his memories of

> The ignominy of boyhood; the distress
> Of boyhood changing into man;
> The unfinished man and his pain
> Brought face to face with his own clumsiness;
> The finished man among his enemies . . .

The answer lay in devices for changing attitudes and feelings into their opposites, and the ecstatic saints, fools, beggars, and wicked old men of his poems and plays are a singing chorus of liberation. They have 'cast out remorse'—the 'conscience' of conventional systems of morality and loyalty—and have discovered imperviousness, unsentimentality, *self*-redemption. They are

> blest by everything,
> Everything we look upon is blest.

In these transpositions Yeats found ways to meet the profoundest needs of the modern mind with absolute courage and joy. The freedom the system helped him find enabled him to use it without becoming its creature. He could always, and did, change the particular symbols, re-explore their implications, try out this solution and that, and if need be discount them entirely:

> But hush, for I have lost the theme,
> Its joy or night seem but a dream;
> Up there some hawk or owl has struck,
> Dropping out of sky or rock,
> A stricken rabbit is crying out,
> And its cry distracts my thought.
>
> ('The Man and the Echo')

THREE

Ezra Pound: The Poet as Hero

> And Kung said, 'Without character you will
> be unable to play on that instrument
> Or to execute the music fit for the Odes.
> The blossoms of the apricot
> blow from the east to the west,
> And I have tried to keep them from falling.'
>
> (Canto 13)

1. AUTHORITY

Excitement attends almost all Ezra Pound's prose and poetry— the excitement of the man himself, his urgency and cantankerousness and virtuosity. Also, he has *authority*. In part this is the irritating authority of the self-appointed leader, yet it is indisputable. One sees it in the reminiscences of his oldest friends, still full of mingled admiration and resentment. 'An uncomfortably tensed, nervously straining, jerky, reddish brown young American,' says Wyndham Lewis, describing Pound's arrival in London in his midtwenties. 'He had no wish to *mix*; he just wanted to *impress*.' For the British, as for his own countrymen, he was 'an unassimilable and aggressive stranger.' Still, the authority was there despite the hostile response; he stood for the most rigorous poetic dedication, and the best writers were likely to recognize this fact. William Carlos Williams records one such recognition:

> He knew of Yeats slightly while in America but to my knowledge did not become thoroughly acquainted with Yeats' work until he went to London in 1910. There a strange thing took place. He gave Yeats a hell of a bawling out for some of his inversions and other archaisms of style and, incredibly, Yeats turned over all his manuscripts to the moment to Pound that Pound might correct

49

them. . . . Yeats learned tremendously from Pound's comments. . . .*

Pound's criticism has a self-confidence that convinces, or repels, by main force. It is passionate lecturing, and impresses by its air of knowledge realized in experience. Behind it lies the absolute conviction that the poet—especially Pound himself—is a hero bearing the task of cultural salvation on his shoulders. His seriousness is unmistakable; he speaks of 'our' problems. 'We appear,' he writes in his essay on Cavalcanti (Dante's friend and fellow-poet), 'to have lost the radiant world where one thought cuts through another with clean edge, a world of moving energies . . . magnetisms that take form, that are seen, or that border the visible, the matter of Dante's *Paradiso*, the glass under water, the form that seems a form seen in a mirror.' Pound was precocious in early defining his proper aims and in rediscovering principles of practice from his studies of Romance literature, particularly of Provençal and Italian poetry. Very soon he was applying the religion of art to political and historical theory:

> Has literature a function in the state? . . . It has. . . .
> It has to do with the clarity and vigour of 'any and every'
> thought and opinion. It has to do with maintaining the
> very cleanliness of the tools, the health of the very matter
> of thought itself. . . . The individual cannot think and
> communicate his thought, the governor and legislator
> cannot act effectively or frame his laws, without words,
> and the solidity and validity of these words is in the care
> of the damned and despised *litterati*. When their work
> goes rotten—by that I do not mean when they express
> indecorous thoughts—but when their very medium, the
> very essence of their work, the application of word to
> thing goes rotten, i.e., becomes slushy or inexact, or exces-
> sive or bloated, the whole machinery of social and of

* *The Selected Letters of William Carlos Williams*, ed. John C. Thirlwall, McDowell, Obolensky, New York, 1957, pp. 210-11. See also Yeats, *Essays*, p. 178.

individual thought and order goes to pot. This is a lesson of history. . . .*

But Pound's authority derives mainly from his verse. Even among the relatively imitative and 'soft' pieces of his early twenties, we shall find work of distinction. Singing lines, often brilliantly compressed, mark the early pages of *Personae: The Collected Poems*. The young poet, seeking his continuities with a British and a European past as well as with his native American one, is moving toward some new fusion of melodic, visual, and intellectual elements. These poems are both exercises and momentary culminations, such as we find in 'Ballatetta,' a graceful blending of Provençal and Romantic idealism; in the vigorously colloquial 'Cino' and 'Marvoil' and the mystical 'The Tree'; or in 'Portrait d'une Femme,' a compassionate yet satirical counterplay of matter-of-fact truths and imagined values. Ballad, sestina, *planh*, imitations of Villon and Browning—all these and similar efforts point up the poet's desire to repossess aspects of the consciousness of the past and to locate his own place in the tradition.

Then, rather suddenly, he is there. Among the poems of Pound's 1912 volume *Riposte* we find two of the most striking lyric poems of the century, 'The Return' and 'The Alchemist.' Of the former Yeats wrote that 'it gives me better words than my own.' In this poem he saw that same baffling, shifting relationship of waking mind to dream vision which he himself was forever seeking to interpret.

'The Return,' indeed, is a superb realization of 'the radiant world where one thought cuts through another with clean edge.' The hero-gods of the ancient past, who 'exist' for us only through literature, 'return' without confidence:

> See, they return; ah, see the tentative
>
> Movements, and the slow feet,
>
> The trouble in the pace and the uncertain
>
> Wavering!

* *The Literary Essays of Ezra Pound*, ed. T. S. Eliot, New Directions, New York, 1954, p. 21.

The 'falling' rhythmic movement here is an organic aspect of this imagined picture. The extra light syllables break up the natural gallop of the dactyl, and there is further interruption by the bunching of accented syllables in 'ah, see' and 'slow feet' and by the iambic foot with which the third line begins. These modulations give an effect of startled wonder at the very start, immediately corrected by a slowing down of the rhythm which suggests a sympathetic, pitying identification with the shades that is both muscular and psychological.

But 'they' *are* returning. The next stanza elaborates on their timidity and unsureness. However, it also accelerates the speed with which the hero-figures come into focus. Greater sharpness is gained, too, by the addition of dramatic details and vivid similes, whereas the first stanza concentrated almost entirely on generalized impressions of hesitant motion.

> See, they return, one, and by one,
> With fear, as half-awakened;
> As if the snow should hesitate
> And murmur in the wind,
>   and half turn back;
> These were the 'Wing'd-with-Awe,'
>   Inviolable.

In that last pair of lines we are swung sharply around, our attention thrust directly at the living past. Then the next stanza recovers the old sense of heroic being; in three swift, unbroken exclamations a whole world is repossessed:

> Gods of the wingèd shoe!
> With them the silver hounds,
>   sniffing the trace of air!

Finally there is the inevitable slipping away of the vision. Not at once, for the keener awareness is maintained through four more lines. But now the past tense is emphasized, and the song becomes a lament:

> Haie! Haie!
>> These were the swift to harry;
> These the keen-scented;
> These were the souls of blood.

As the poem ends, the wavering movement returns and we again see the hero-gods as they have become. The only reality left us is our awareness of the gap between vision and fact.

>> Slow on the leash,
>>> pallid the leash-men!

'The Alchemist' is a triumph of rhythmic 'scoring' equal, as a piece of incantation, to the dramatic conjuring of 'The Return.' This 'chant for the transmutation of metals' calls upon the female principle in all things to bring the gold to birth. It does so by invoking the names of goddesses, heroines of myth and literature, and historical personages, and with them the four elements and the realms of Paradise, Hades, and the physical universe. Images of light and burning, and of the life-force, project the alchemist's desire to see the transmutation take place. As the poem progresses, we see re-created before us the mystic unity of thought and being, imagination and sense: the world seen through medieval eyes. But the range of awareness and of reference is also the poet's own. In the self-hypnotic prayer of his alchemist we can see his own desire to 'transmute metal,' to employ in his poetry both the heritage of the whole past and his own immediate consciousness of the present, transforming them into aesthetic gold:

> Selvaggia, Guiscarda, Mandetta,
>> Rain flakes of gold on the water
> Azure and flaking silver of water,
> Alcyon, Phaetona, Alcmena,
> Pallor of silver, pale lustre of Latona,
> By these, from the malevolence of the dew
>> Guard this alembic
> Elain, Tireis, Allodetta
>> Quiet this metal.

Imagism, a much-publicized phase of the fight of Pound and others to make organic form the aim of the best poets and the expectation of their best readers, is foreshadowed and surpassed in this passage. Pound's emphasis on the single image as 'an intellectual and emotional complex in an instant of time' * is an aspect of his concern that the image, rather than some vague 'thought,' be recognized as the heart of poetic experience. From the pulsating centers called 'images' the poem will gain its form; rhythm, sense-effect, and structure must correspond to their guiding insight and emotion. It is characteristic of Pound that he should have taken the lead in this movement and that he should very soon have outgrown it and advanced to more complex problems.

Pound's experiments with translation added enormously to the authority of his tone and style. From the start translation afforded him the chance to sink himself into the poetry of the past and of other languages and societies. Responsive to tone and nuance, he could recover the sensibilities of others and find a voice for himself through them. His translations have the same basic virtue as his other poetry: intuitive grasp of the shape and emotional essence of his subject. Even if we do not know his originals, or are not equipped to read them, he convinces us that he has captured this shape and essence, has glimpsed 'the form in the air' and approximated it through the 'sculpture of rhyme.' An obvious instance is his famous rendering of the Anglo-Saxon 'Seafarer.' Here Pound cultivates a heavy, lurching, even clumsy, pounding of sound. He makes certain repetitions of consonants and phrasing that the original does not have, to stress the function of the alliteration as a major structural aspect of the Old English poem's rhythm. The effect is 'barbaric' and elemental, rhythmic as galley rowers are rhythmic; at the same time it underscores the rigors of seafaring life. While Pound actually stays very close to a literal translation of the text, he makes it a modern poem with archaic overtones. A sailor today would not quite feel the same way as 'the seafarer' does, though he would grasp the feeling readily enough.

Even more ambitious is his work with Chinese texts, notably

* Ibid. p. 4.

with the Fenellosa manuscripts. Asked to put into poetic form the scholar's prose-translations of Chinese poems in Japanese ideogram, Pound—working with Fenellosa's notes and educating himself in the process—accepted the challenge. Despite his initial ignorance of his materials and his mistakes, writes Hugh Gordon Porteus, Pound was able to grasp 'the great virtue of the Chinese language'—namely, the way in which its written characters 'contrive to suggest by their graphic gestures (as English does by its phonetic gestures) the very essence of what is to be conveyed.' * The ideogram itself, a stylized picture or 'graphic gesture' that has become the concrete manifestation of a sound and a concept, seemed to Pound the symbol *par excellence* of true communication, the kind that has not lost itself in abstraction. Because of it the poems of *Cathay* are by their very nature 'imagistic.'

In *Cathay* and elsewhere the word 'adaptation' may be more appropriate than 'translation.' The latter term often conceals a literal unraveling of a text which destroys what it should reveal. If the original poet were alive today, writing in *our* language and with *our* experience behind him, how would he do this poem? This is the problem Pound sets himself in his translation-adaptations.

One of Pound's major adaptations is his *Homage to Sextus Propertius* (1917). His treatment of the subtle and difficult Roman poet of the first century B.C. is based on passages from the original elegies. Pound rearranges them freely, playing on sound and association from his own standpoint as well as from that of the original text. His aim was to make an original modern poem out of the light that Propertius' sensibility and his own seemed to cast on one another. The *Homage*, he wrote, 'presents certain emotions as vital to me in 1917, faced with the infinite and ineffable imbecility of the British Empire as they were to Propertius some centuries earlier, when faced with the infinite and ineffable imbecility of the Roman Empire.' † He thus identifies himself with the

---

* Hugh Gordon Porteus, 'Ezra Pound and His Chinese Character: A Radical Examination,' in *Ezra Pound*, ed. Peter Russell, Peter Nevill Ltd., London, 1950, p. 215.

† *The Letters of Ezra Pound*, 1907-1941, ed. D. D. Paige, Harcourt, Brace, New York, 1950, p. 231.

speaker in the poem, who is 'not only Propertius but inclusive of the spirit of the young man of the Augustan Age, hating rhetoric and undeceived by imperial hogwash.' Pound was thinking of the war-rhetoric of his own moment and rejoicing in the weapons the ancient poet—'tying blue ribbons in the tails of Virgil and Horace' and 'touching words somewhat as Laforgue did'—had handed down to him:

> Out-weariers of Apollo will, as we know, continue their
>   Martian generalities,
> We have kept our erasers in order. . . .

Pound thus uses Propertius both to attack the rhetorical sham of the Great War and to restate certain artistic principles in a larger context than before. It is clear not only from the *Homage* itself but from his other writings of the time that Pound viewed the classics as rekindlers of energy rather than as inert, soporific emblems of 'education.' 'You read Catullus,' he has observed, 'to prevent yourself being poisoned by the lies of pundits; you read Propertius to purge yourself of the greasy sediments of lecture courses. . . . The classics, "ancient and modern," are precisely the acids to gnaw through the thongs and bulls-hides with which we are tied by our schoolmasters. . . . They are almost the only antiseptics against the contagious imbecility of mankind.' * The twelve poems of the *Homage* are thus intended, not only as a faithful rendering of the Propertian spirit but also as a counter-thrust against political and academic jargon and deception. 'There was never any question of translation, let alone literal translation. My job was to bring a dead man to life, to present a living figure.' †

That living figure, the Propertius who speaks in the *Homage*, foreshadows the protagonist of Pound's 1919 sequence, *Hugh Selwyn Mauberley*. Like Mauberley, he speaks for the true lyric tradition as opposed to the pretentious ponderosities of the day. He is a delicate ironist and a devotee of Aphrodite rather than of Calliope, Muse of History. And he intermingles proud self-

* Ibid. p. 113.
† Ibid. pp. 148-9.

assertion and self-belittling much as does Mauberley, who typifies the modern poet. In his quick shiftings among moods and styles, too, he resembles the speakers in *Mauberley* and in the *Cantos*. To illustrate: Poem I, which in many ways parallels the opening 'Ode' of *Mauberley*, begins with an entranced musical note, invoking the ghosts of the great Melic lyric tradition, then breaks off to jeer at the 'Martian generalities' of would-be heroic poets. Next, Pound-Propertius jauntily prophesies that he will have 'a boom after my funeral' and that all the 'devirginated young ladies' will then love his work. But in the midst of this buffoonery, mythical allusion is woven into the poem's fabric in the purest evocative fashion. At last the opening poem ends on a graceful, serious note caught up from its opening theme:

> Stands genius a deathless adornment,
> a name not to be worn out with the years.

In their final effect, all these shiftings make for a structural triumph revealing a complex sensibility. We must remember that Pound's adaptation is intended not as an exercise in translation but as a new work fully expressing Pound himself. He sets out to do deliberately what Yeats, through his 'revision' of Arnold's 'Dover Beach' in 'A Dialogue of Self and Soul,' did unconsciously: to bring the sensibility of the past into contemporary focus. The images by which this sensibility unfolds itself also define an ideal poetic personality and provide a symbolic argument made all-encompassing by the quick shiftings of the tone. In poems VI and VII we reach the subjective center of the sequence. These plunge into deep erotic passion, the former poem drunkenly linking the themes of love and death (but also indulging in some wry speculation concerning the duration of Cynthia's mourning were her lover to die suddenly) and the latter rejoicing lustily in the 'couch made happy by my long delectations' and idealizing the mistress as a Provençal *sirventes* might. Around the passionate center made by these two poems swirls the rest of the sequence, recapitulating its major 'public' and aesthetic themes but also toying repeatedly with the motifs of jealousy and fidelity. Finally, at the very end, the poet puts all worldly cynicism aside, 'taking his stand' with Varro, Catullus, and all other Dionysian poets. They are worshippers, not of Mars, but of Aphrodite—singers in the old way of their mistresses' beauty and their own desire, 'bringing the Grecian orgies,' as the first poem had said, 'into Italy.' And into England and America, for that matter.

2. MAUBERLEY: ALIENATION OF THE CITIZEN-ARTIST

From the early poems, translations, and adaptations, we can see that the vast excitement of Pound's work is rooted not only in his own personality and abilities but in those artistic and intellectual revolutions which marked the first third of this century. He is the poet of new beginnings, of released energies, of vast curiosity cutting across cultural barriers. And tragically, the psychological symptoms of prolonged social crisis, that crisis which culminated in two wars as well as in the Fascist system he has defended, have found expression through him also. He is an epitome of a para-doxical era: a fighter for creative freedom and sanity who found himself, in old age, committed to a mental hospital 'in a paranoid state of psychotic proportions' and only thus escaped trial for treason against the United States on behalf of Mussolini's gov-ernment.

No layman can do more than speculate on the psychological causes of Pound's strange and frightening duality of spirit. Pound is hardly our only example of moral and intellectual as well as emo-tional hypersensitivity at bay. Many of his peers and near-peers, Yeats for instance, have faced the same problems. But Yeats found saving symbols and masks and friends to keep him from running head-on against the world. Pound, like Wilde and Lawrence and Joyce a self-exile, never heeded Yeats's whimsical warning to his 'dear Ezra' to steer clear of naked politics.* One explanation we might offer is that Pound has committed one kind of fundamental Romantic error. He has tried to politicalize an aesthetic slogan, the slogan that it is the poet who protects the 'whole machinery

* A Vision, pp. 26-7.

of social and individual thought and order' against catastrophe
through his heroic tribal role as purifier of the language—its clarity,
precision, and vigor. In his work we see the poet as citizen refusing
to accept the alienation thrust on him as artist; the craftsman meets
the challenge of cultural crisis by teaching the world the 'secret'
behind craftsmanship—its ideal of integrity. Here is one key to
Pound's duality, a key to insight into his work. In *Mauberley*, for
instance, as we shall see, the poet-protagonist first fights to re-create
society in his own image and then, under pressure of the unequal
struggle and his own self-knowledge, splits in two psychologically.

The basic political and social ideas which have entered into
Pound's image of the good life and to which he has tried to ac-
commodate his aesthetic methods are fairly easy to locate. He
starts with self-evident premises, such as that the status and integrity of letters are vitally related to the condition of society—
a relationship (as *Mauberley* tries to show) almost totally discounted since the eighteenth century. We need to look at certain
moments in the historical past to find models of another way of
life; thus, in *Canto* 13 we see Confucius explaining:

> . . . when the prince has gathered about him
> All the savants and artists, his riches will be fully employed.

The medieval detestation of usury furnishes another model attitude, and who so gross as to defend usury as a public good? So
does the behavior of certain Renaissance figures and institutions,
and so does the distrust of bank-profiteering expressed by Jefferson, Adams, and other American Founding Fathers. One of
Adams's comments on the subject is emphasized and repeated in
the *Cantos:*

> Every bank of discount is downright corruption
> taxing the public for private individuals' gain. . . .

The 'social-credit' theories of Gesell and Douglas, and the policies
of Mussolini's government in its reorganization of credit financing
and public works, appeared to Pound the logical culmination of
past creative thinking concerning social problems. His *Jefferson*

and/or Mussolini * presents fascinating (and fantastic) correlations of aesthetic and political-economic means and ideals. One quotation from its preface will demonstrate his confusion of these spheres of activity:

> By October 6, 1934 we find Mussolini putting the dots on the 'i's.'

> That is to say, finding the unassailable formula, the exact equation for what had been sketchy and impressionistic and exaggerated in Thomas Jefferson's time and expression.

'Sketchy and impressionistic and exaggerated'—these are familiar enough words, when applied to the writers against whom the most serious and accomplished modern poets waged their successful revolution in the decades after 1910. And the problem of 'finding the unassailable formula, the exact equation,' will also strike a familiar chord, particularly when we remember that the preface in which these words appear was originally a letter sent in 1934 to T. S. Eliot, then editor of *The Criterion*. Fifteen years earlier Eliot had used similar terminology in discussing the problems of finding in any given piece of work the right 'formula for poetic expression of a particular emotion.' †

But Eliot had been talking about art—poetic art, to be exact— and Pound was simply translating the language of artistic criticism into that of socio-political theory in rather naïve fashion. His whole book, indeed, is colored by aesthetic-centered thought, though its ostensible theme is ideological. Thus he compares the 'artifex' of Mussolini's 1933 speech in Milan with the sculpture of Brancusi, and he talks of Jefferson's exaggerated 'verbal manifestations,' and of how 'the fascist revolution is infinitely more INTERESTING than the Russian revolution because it is not a revolution according to preconceived type.' Again, to show why the American system has in his opinion gone astray, he begins his

* Ezra Pound, *Jefferson and/or Mussolini*, S. Nott, London, 1935; Liveright, New York, 1935.
† Eliot, op. cit. pp. 124-5.

explanation with an observation on *metrical* technique; and he defends Mussolini's methods as not unscrupulous but creative: 'the opportunism of the artist.'

Pound's political and economic attitudes, however eccentric, have had their hard meanings and consequences for him in the real daily world. He has revolted his contemporaries as often as he has taught them the difficult demands of a principled art. For our purposes the real question is not whether or not Pound's specific *ideas* are defensible in themselves but whether or not they (and his 'paranoia') have subverted his art. Their effect on his poetry after the honest self-examination of *Mauberley* raises subtle problems. The *Cantos* are as wrongheaded as they are brilliant. He has shot tendentiousness into them almost at will and has indulged his compulsion to be a professor-without-appointment insufferably. But the *Cantos are* a success, though very nearly a pyrrhic one. They come close to disaster; only the creative *'direction of his will,'* to use Pound's phrase in comparing *Il Duce* with Confucius and with Dante, saves them from it in the long run.

Probably disaster or near-disaster has been Pound's special risk from the beginning: the condition of his unique drive and influence. If we are to take some of his statements at face value, he seems to have set himself the task not only of living by what he called 'vision of perfection' himself, but of revolutionizing the taste of one nation—or perhaps two—through his literary activities. Despite his striking achievements, he alienated many confederates and grew much disturbed over his 'failure' to bring about a cultural revolution. Out of his brooding self-analysis grew the two-part sequence *Hugh Selwyn Mauberley*, the first part dated 1919, the second 1920. 'A Farewell to London'—and to the United States as well—it presents the now-mature poet at the crucial point of rejecting the culture he has failed to change and at the same time, obliquely and almost 'secretly,' rejecting himself in a social role and seeking, through gestures of withdrawal and through the most unyielding irony, to redefine himself in all his relationships. Pound has said that *Mauberley* is merely a sort of simplification of the *Homage*, for readers without sufficient literacy to follow what he was doing in the earlier work. That is partly true, and partly a joke. It may also be an attempt to conceal the confessional aspect of the later sequence.

Mauberley is a quasi-fictional but basically autobiographical account of a young American poet's effort to find himself within the English literary tradition and at the same time to affect the tradition himself. Like Propertius, he is a bold critic of current pomposities, a lover of the Beautiful for its own sake, and above all a conscientious craftsman. But he is a more troubled and introspective figure than Propertius by far. Even more than the *Homage*, *Mauberley* is constantly varied in mood and tone: now polemical, now richly self-revealing or lyrical, now cold and polished, now scholarly in its allusiveness, now relaxed and bawdy or jeering. The title of the opening poem, *E. P. Ode pour l'Élection de Son Sepulchre* ('Ezra Pound, Ode on the Occasion of Choosing His Burial-Place'), echoes the sixteenth-century poet Ronsard, as the French in the closing stanza echoes the *Grand Testament* of the fifteenth-century poet Villon. The echoes associate the speaker with the lyric traditions of pre-modern Europe. They also suggest he is pondering his own self-exile and symbolic death, and comparing his own dedication to his art with that of the masters of the past. The 'Ode' as a whole raises the question whether he has, literally, exiled and sacrificed himself to no purpose—failed—or whether he has triumphed in his own fashion. Pound's vigorous denial that Mauberley is Ezra Pound * is justifiable enough in its way; *no* created speaking-character, even when called 'I,' is identical with its creator. The distinction, however, does not obviate the fact that Mauberley is *one* psychological image of 'E. P.'—an aspect of his self-awareness. We shall not be far wrong if, following the lead of the first poem, we call the speaker 'Mauberley-Pound.'

Mauberley's 'story' may be retold briefly, if with some inevitable oversimplification. For three years, the opening 'Ode' tells us, he has sought to revive the classical spirit of poetry in obstinate Britain. This was his Odyssean mission, and, wishing to perform it in a modern way, he has held before him as a contemporary

* Pound, *Letters*, p. 180.

model of the Grecian ideal the precision and formal perfectionism of Flaubert. But he has been more like Capaneus, who defied Zeus and was struck down, than like Odysseus; or if like Odysseus, he has been a variant one, less shrewd, who allowed himself to be tricked by the Sirens and then forgotten.

As in the *Homage*, though, the confession of error is tempered by its ironic tone, by the way in which the speaker allies himself with Grecian heroes and great writers, and in the ensuing four poems by the wholesale Propertian assault on the degraded state of contemporary civilization. Ugliness, crudeness, and mass production, the second and third poems say, are what is now demanded. The heritage of pagan myth, of Classical art and thought, and even of primitive Christianity is now washed away by a mushy, formless, leveling secularism. The decay of value has already, Poems IV and V insist, betrayed the youth of the world into mass slaughter. The civilization professes faiths it no longer understands and traditions it no longer cares to preserve save as rhetorical incentives in war:

> Quick eyes gone under earth's lid,

> For two gross of broken statues,
> For a few thousand battered books.

The succeeding seven poems shift to a historical review, with cinematic close-ups, of the modern literary scene since the 1880's. When Pound was born (1885), poetry and the other arts were already on the defensive in England, the alienation of the artist having reached a sort of dead end after a century or more of deterioration in his status. 'Painters and adulterers'—society had come to regard the two terms as virtually synonymous, and the Muse herself seemed reduced to beggary and whoredom. Some of Yeats's fellow poets of the 'nineties are summoned up as admired figures who remained true to the tradition of craftsmanship despite neglect and 'failure' like Mauberley's own. A Mr. Nixon, very possibly modeled on Arnold Bennett, advises the young poet to 'give up verse, my boy,' for 'there's nothing in it.' At the very end of the 1919 portion of the sequence, the poem 'Envoi,' modeled on Waller's 'Go, lovely rose' but thoroughly 'modern' in its rhythmic variations and in the character of its thought, reasserts his creed of Beauty. It symbolizes the poet's intention to continue along the chosen path of dedication to craft in the old sense despite every disillusionment and defeat.

The 'Envoi' serves as a kind of purgation of forensic ambitions and rhetorical warfare. The second part of the sequence, *Mauberley* (1920), departs decisively from that arena, becoming almost entirely subjective. Though the early themes are still echoed, it is the personal counterpart that is the theme. Where in the opening 'Ode' he had stressed his conflict with an unresponsive world, in the first poem here he stresses the limited, if genuine, character of his own skill. In the second poem he reviews the three 'wasted' years, seeing them as a time of drifting amid 'phantasmagoria.'

> Drifted . . . drifted precipitate,
> Asking time to be rid of . . .
> Of his bewilderment; to designate
> His new found orchid. . . .
>
> To be certain . . . certain . . .
> (Amid aerial flowers) . . . time for arrangements—
> Drifted on
> To the final estrangement. . . .

Entranced in his dream, he had ignored or neglected the real possibilities of poetry and of life, and had not yet discovered the true implications of his vision of perfection ('orchid'). The language suggests a relationship between this failure and one in love or in sexual experience; he had not yet learned the lesson Apollo read to Propertius.

It is as if the poet were saying that behind his attempt to 'conquer' Britain through art and argument—that manifestly quixotic and presumptuous task he had set himself—had lain a suppressed recognition of his inadequacies as artist and as man. Mauberley had avoided the simple, crucial issues of his own life in favor of enterprises so grandiose they would hide his privately feared inadequacies. Usually so cocksure, Pound came closer in these poems of *Mauberley* (1920) than almost anywhere else in his work to opening up to himself and to the world the terrible uneasiness behind his sense of persecution and his epic declaration of purpose:

> By constant elimination
> The manifest universe
> Yielded an armour
> Against utter consternation. . . .

Yet even in these five poems, breakdown and retreat behind verbal armor are not the poet's *final* answer. As many other poets have done, he uses the semblance of disorder to help himself get his bearings. Irony toward the age and its demands continues simultaneously with the new turn of the sequence, though the language has become indirect and inward. Mauberley-Pound had not believed in his exclusion from the world of letters before, and he does not believe in it now. As he develops the imagery of the poet-wanderer's drift into escape and (in Poem V) of his continuing vision—however self-defeating—of Beauty, the sheer brilliance of the writing, together with the fact that he has *not* after all 'given up verse,' is qualification enough of the self-doubts he has expressed.

> Tawn fore-shores
> Washed in the cobalt of oblivions. . . .

and:

> The sleek head emerges
> From the gold-yellow frock
> As Anadyomene in the opening
> Pages of Reinach.

That image of the modern mind which Yeats sought has, clearly, several manifestations in the personality of Mauberley-Pound. He is an Odysseus with an epic cultural mission; a prophet whiplashing a decadent social order; a creative dreamer lost in reverie, heir to the best in the entire poetic tradition. And he is also the exposed and vulnerable sensitive spirit who doubts himself, undercuts his self-respect by questioning his own motives, but then—like Yeats—accepts the burden of the Self, the whole bundle of failures, delusions, limitations, and comes up surprisingly tough and springy at the last. In this multiple image Pound closes off all possibility of reconciliation with a world which cannot respond to him on *his* terms and which he will not serve on *its* terms.

3. Some Notes on the 'Cantos'

The composition of *Mauberley* and the *Cantos* began about the same time. The two works have basically the same protagonist and similar perspectives, but the two segments of the former sequence were completed by 1920, while the *Cantos* has been a work in progress for more than forty years.* As the *Cantos* developed, it became clear that the work would be a complex proliferation involving many more motifs, characters, and clusters of ideas than *Mauberley*. The similarity and difference between them is well illustrated by the opening poem of each sequence. Although in both instances the protagonist identifies himself with Odysseus, in *Mauberley* the identification is clearly figurative while in *Canto* 1 the speaker seems literally to be the Odysseus of Homer until we approach the end of the poem. *Canto* 1, indeed, is a compressed translation of Book XI of the *Odyssey* (the 'Nekuia' or 'Book of the Dead'), one of the most brilliant translations from Classical literature in the English language. Pound employs certain Anglo-Saxon effects magnificently to catch the tone of primitive terror and the movement in Homer:

> Souls out of Erebus, cadaverous dead, of brides
> Of youths and of the old who had borne much;
> Souls stained with recent tears, girls tender,
> Men many, mauled with bronze lance heads,
> Battle spoil, bearing yet dreory arms,
> These many crowded about me; with shouting,
> Pallor upon me. . . .

* The first published canto appeared in 1919; volumes of cantos have appeared in 1925, 1928, 1930, 1934, 1937, 1940, 1948, 1956, and 1959.

And Anticlea came, whom I beat off, and then Tiresias
   Theban,
Holding his golden wand, knew me, and spoke first:
'A second time? why? man of ill star,
Facing the sunless dead and this joyless region?'

But Tiresias' question shows that the protagonist is not really
Homer's Odysseus after all. Odysseus summoned up the dead only
once. The figure repeating his invocation and experience in this
canto is Pound's actual protagonist, the 'I' of the *Cantos,* just as
the 'he' of *E. P. Ode pour l'Élection de Son Sepulchre* is the protagonist of *Mauberley.* Momentarily, in this first canto and at
various points thereafter, he wears this Odyssean mask; it is one
sign among many that he has now accepted the heroic role he was
uncertain he could manage in *Mauberley,* and without the self-
lacerating irony of that poem. Like the great epic heroes before
him, the 'I' of the *Cantos* must visit the dead and be guided by
prophetic voices from the past. Before the sequence is ended, he
puts on numerous masks to identify himself with many other
heroes of myth, history, and literature. Figures like Confucius and
Malatesta and John Adams speak out of their worlds as men striving to establish creative order. Thus they resemble Odysseus,
whose task it was to restore right order in his homeland and then
to carry its values to the hinterlands. Their active wisdom is like
that of Odysseus and also partakes of the procreative energy of
the life-force, which the Homeric hero so clearly symbolizes. In
Homer he is an almost impersonal embodiment of the cosmic
male principle Pound describes in *Canto 99:*

   . . . man's phallic heart is from heaven
      a clear spring of rightness. . . .

Women and goddesses are drawn to him inevitably, and when at
last he returns to Penelope it is the great bed carved out of living
oak which best symbolizes their reunion. In Pound as in Yeats this
tradition is combined with the more modern search for self-
definition and creativity. (It is appropriate for this reason among
others that Pound should have based his version of 'The Book of
the Dead' on a sixteenth-century Latin translation by Andreas

Divus. He thought that Divus had so captured the Homeric text as to provide a vital connection between it and the possibilities of modern English verse.)

From this beginning and from these implications extend the lines of thought and the underlying oppositions of value that hold the *Cantos* together. If the vivid repossession of the Homeric spirit in *Canto 1* symbolizes what the poem 'stands for,' it does not wholly provide its range of identification. Throughout the *Cantos* we experience moments of realization, each contributing to the fusion of values from various times and cultures. *Canto 13*, for one instance, presents with beautiful lucidity the Confucian spirit in a dialogue between Kung (Confucius) and his disciples. Rational discourse, anger, lyrical reverie, succeed each other; formal speech is played against the colloquial. The primal force of Odysseus' confrontation with the dead gave the poem one dimension; this canto adds a spirit of enlightened secularism and of philosophical nonconformism. Political, economic, and social dimensions are added elsewhere. And again and again we have passages in which, out of the materials of his wide reading and his longing to hold intact his vision of an Earthly Paradise, the poet brings the gods back to life:

> The light now, not of the sun,
> > Chrysophrase,
> And the water green clear, and blue clear. . . .
>
> Zagreus, feeding his panthers,
> > the turf clear as on hills under light
> And under the almond-trees, gods,
> > with them, *choros nympharum.* Gods. . . . .
> > > > > *(Canto 17)*

Pure, clear light and color, light especially, are inseparable from Pound's Paradise. He often returns to the picture just given when he wants the sense of divine beauty and tranquility. It sometimes seems he literally believes in Zagreus, the god of generation, who after dismemberment was healed in Hades and reborn as Dionysus. The condition of Zagreus resembles our modern plight and hope for reintegration. His name also suggests creative frenzy and sexual energy. So, then, Pound's Odyssean-Dantean hero must penetrate the hell of the modern world before he can reassert the wholeness that certain individuals and societies in the past knew. Associated with his search for prophetic truth and a right knowledge of the beautiful is that related sexual symbolism we have already noted. Pound seeks to restore the sexual mysteries that are the wellsprings of religion and art and that have suffered centuries of neglect because of the rise of 'usury' and commercialism. The sexual theme is the theme of self-realization and renewal:

> Hast thou found a nest softer than cunnus
> Or hast thou found better rest
> Hast'ou a deeper planting, doth thy death year
> Bring swifter shoot?
> Hast thou entered more deeply the mountain?
>
> *(Canto 47)*

By the same token the great crime of usury balks and blights the procreative cycle that is the source of all life's innocent cere-mony, all its joys and values. Pound uses the Latin term *usura*, which carries more of the medieval connotation of moral depravity than the modern English equivalent. The money-corruption Pound-Mauberley saw behind the alienation of the artist and his degraded status is the chief blight on the modern spirit.

> Usura slayeth the child in the womb
> It stayeth the young man's courting
> It hath brought palsy to bed, lyeth
> Between the young bride and her bridegroom
>   CONTRA NATURAM
> They have brought whores for Eleusis
> Corpses are set to banquet
> At behest of usura.
>
> *(Canto 45)*

In the 'Hell Cantos' (14-16) Pound uses the foulest images and invective he can think of to describe a civilization ruled over by this Usura. He includes as its representatives not only profiteers

and exploiters, but also a whole range of hypocritical moralists—
repressers of all that is instinctual—and 'perverters of language':

> the soil living pus, full of vermin,
> dead maggots begetting live maggots,
>   slum owners,
> usurers squeezing crab-lice, pandars to authority . . .
> and above it the mouthing of orators. . . .
>
> (*Canto 14*)

The poet is inspired by the procreative principle as Dante was
by the force of Divine Love, and there is a rough parallel between
the progression of the *Cantos* and that of the *Divine Comedy* (as
between that of the *Cantos* and that of the *Odyssey*). Just as Dante
summons up all his hatred and revulsion to depict the various pun-
ishments of the damned, so Pound hurls his disgust at the people
and conditions he considers the befoulers of life. We have spoken
before of poetry in its process of 'revision' over the generations by
what seems at times only a single poet. No one has a keener sense
of this process than Pound at his best, and one of the triumphs
of the *Cantos* is the way in which poets of the past are worked
into its fabric. Pound sometimes repossesses them through translation or adaptation, often with the kind of implied transference
of the speaking voice we observed in *Canto 1*. Sometimes he assumes another poet's tone or method, as in the Dantean 'Hell
Cantos.' Sometimes he creates a scene which puts the poets he
most admires completely within the context of thought of the
Cantos, yet at the same time brings out their unique qualities.
An outstanding instance is the portrait of William Blake in *Canto
16*. He is pictured running on the Purgatorial Mount, painfully
overcoming the road that winds about the mountain 'like a slow
screw's thread.' As he runs toward his own salvation, he keeps his
eyes full on the horror of the hell man has made for himself. The
picture has the sharp visual detail of Dante, though its effects are
developed 'presentatively,' in the post-Imagist manner. And it
interprets for us exactly the moral vision of Blake (the post-Renais-
sance poet whose sexual emphasis most resembles that of Pound
and Yeats):

And the running form, naked, Blake,
Shouting, whirling his arms, the swift limbs,
Howling against the evil,
        his eyes rolling,
Whirling like flaming cartwheels,
        and his head held backward to gaze on the evil
As he ran from it. . . .

The scope of the *Cantos*, as with epic structures generally, is
the whole of being, both real and imagined: the natural and the
supernatural, life and death, human experience and the dream
of the divine. Like *Mauberley*, the work has deep implications of
self-analysis for the poet himself, but it rarely invites our attention
to them. Rather, it centers on the clash and interplay of the modern Inferno and the ideal world. Its many 'voices' (the poets, the
heroes, the leaders, the thinkers), in contrast to Mauberley, can
and do say what Pound cannot say in his own right. Similarly
the shifting rhythms and styles of the writing broaden and deepen
Pound's scope immensely, and contribute to the poem's historical
and cultural inclusiveness. Published in 'installments,' as it were,
since 1919, the *Cantos* has been a gigantic experiment of a new
kind, its growth in time essential to its very nature. Each of its
larger units extends our range of consciousness concerning the relevance of the central perspective: a universal sensibility gauging
the depravity of a usury-ridden world and setting against it the
ideals of rational thought, rational economic practices ('rational'
in the view of such Social Credit thinkers as Douglas, Gesell, and
Pound), and a 'pagan' aestheticism. As each unit is developed, it
recapitulates the root-themes in a new context; ordinarily the
refocusing is not at first clear to the reader, but the pattern does
emerge.

The method Pound employs is an outgrowth of his preoccupation with sensuous presentation through the concrete image, the
precisely appropriate rhythm, and the ideogram—that is, with
communication that grows on the reader as a series of experiences.
The opening two cantos introduce fundamental motifs: first, the
inclusive sensibility that is the poem's hero, and its purposes; and

second, the ideal of creativity in action, whose patron deity is Zagreus. Succeeding cantos show the rich implications of these motifs. The Cid, for instance, adds chivalric overtones to the Odyssean hero, and the echoes of such poets as Sappho and Catullus further define the poetic tradition whose values the *Cantos* seeks to reassert. Pound's ingenuity in perceiving and delineating new dimensions, new aspects, is one of his most intriguing qualities throughout the sequence. Thus, his conception of sentimentality as a fraudulence of feeling and expression that destroys standards of value and therefore abets Usura is brought out with all his virtuosity at the beginning of *Canto* 30. The goddess Artemis is heard complaining (her song is a 'compleynt,' and the form and diction suggest medieval verse) that the soft-mindedness of our professedly humanitarian age prevents all correction of abuses and genuine purification of society. 'Pity,' she cries, 'spareth so many an evil thing' that 'all things are made foul in this season.' The result is that

> Nothing is now clean slayne
> But rotteth away.

Similarly, the rendering in English of Cavalcanti's *Donna mi prega* adds the Platonic idealism and intellectual eroticism of that poet to the ideal vision developed in so many facets in the course of the sequence.

If we think of each group of cantos as one of a number of hard centers around which the basic motifs are constantly in motion, while the whole work plunges cumulatively ahead, we shall have little trouble grasping the main outlines of what Pound is doing. Once we have these outlines, we are less likely to be thrown off by the many surface aspects that must confuse even the best-educated reader: the Greek and Chinese phrases, the allusions to books most of us would not in the normal course of things have read, the Joycean punning, and so on. To Pound the specific connotations of a given language seem often too idiosyncratic to be sacrificed. Even the *appearance* of letters and words has its idiogrammatic particularity, conveying something of value otherwise forever lost.

The major groups of cantos can readily be summarized. The first six or seven establish the basic axes. *Cantos 8-19* center on the Renaissance and its relation to the modern triumph of Usura. *Cantos 30-41* bring the origins of the United States, the economic and social views of the Founding Fathers (Jefferson, Adams, and Madison in particular), and the struggles over the form the American banking system and money-policies should take into the foreground. *Cantos 53-61* take up Chinese history (a motif foreshadowed in *Canto 13*), finding conflicts and ideals that parallel those of the Renaissance and of eighteenth-century and modern America and England in a civilization totally unlike that of the West. *Cantos 62-71* center on the figure of Adams again. *Cantos 74-84* (the 'Pisan Cantos') show the poet at the end of the war, in an American prison camp near Pisa, sizing up his life and achievement in the light of the various themes and ideals projected by the poem so far. (In this section, as elsewhere, a defense of the Fascist system is implied, its ideals and practices being compared with those of Adams on the one hand and of Confucian Chinese rulers on the other.) *Cantos 85-95*, called 'Rock Drill,' sum up the bedrock convictions and discoveries of the voyager-hero. *Cantos 96-109* ('Thrones') gradually prepare us for the protagonist's final encompassing vision of the secular-paradisal potentialities of man. At this writing the presumption is that there will be a final group of eleven poems.*

From this very elementary summary it will be clear that the structure of the *Cantos* has a rhetorical emphasis as well as a narrative organization. Its method of presentation, however, is based on Symbolist, Imagist, and stream-of-consciousness techniques: the juxtaposition of scenes, images, lyric passages, evocative moments of every sort without conventional transition, preparation, or formal consistency. Furthermore, while the 'argument' progresses on ever widening fronts and the protean protagonist wanders through every kind of experience, the poet deliberately inserts passages at certain intervals that are intended to recall the earlier sections and

* Many of the cantos not mentioned in this summary are transitional or recapitulate motifs already developed. *Cantos 72-73* have so far been withheld from publication.

suggest their connection with the motifs introduced later. He also sets passages that contrast sharply with the tone of everything around them in strategic places—as when he puts the calm discourse of Kung and his disciples just before the violent 'Hell Cantos'; or the vision of Circe's isle (*Canto* 39) in the midst of the first Jefferson-Adams-Madison group; or the incantation to all the goddesses (*Canto* 106) in the 'Thrones' group, which as a unit is devoted to bringing into a single focus the interpenetrating Occidental and Oriental motifs followed out in the *Cantos* as a whole.

Ezra Pound rarely achieves the kind of self-transcendence within a short space which is the mark of Yeats's greater genius as a dramatic lyricist. But he is unrivaled in sheer poetic courage, in breadth of conception, and in the intensity of his music and imagination at peak moments. No one has surpassed him in conveying the death throes of a civilization or in summoning up the radiance and frankness of the boldest creative spirit. The fact of Pound's commitment to a free imagination disciplined only by its own traditions and knowledge is surely more fundamental to his art than are the terrible distortions into which that commitment has at times misled him.

FOUR

T. S. Eliot and the Displaced Sensibility

1. 'DAMNATION ON THIS EARTH'

With the early poetry of Eliot, we find ourselves almost at home in the twentieth century—not domesticated in it but moving on its landscape with an uneasy familiarity. Eliot goes further than Yeats or Pound from the innocent world of ancient tragedy in which heroic man exerts his every energy toward the reshaping of Fate itself. His is the 'vulgarly' intimate daily world of the modern in which Baudelaire and other French poets of the last century lost and found themselves, a world for which the writings of Henry Adams, Henry James, and a largely forgotten poetic generation (that of E. A. Robinson, Henry Cabot Lodge, and Trumbull Stickney) had to some extent prepared the American mind. So profoundly has the self been violated by that world that no retreat into privacy except by way of artistic style seems open to it. Its inhabitants can no more protect their individuality with dignity than could the Little Jo of Dickens's *Bleak House* or the inmates of Chekhov's 'Ward Number Six.' The awakening of consciousness to brutal 'objective truth' in the middle and late 1800's has led, in Eliot's twentieth-century world, to new 'laws' of human reality. These laws reflect his sense of a mindless, snatching horror at the heart of life such as we have already noted in his 'Rhapsody on a Windy Night.'

Here is a vision of something pitiful but, often, vicious and pathological as well. The ironic self-demeaning of Yeats's 'Dialogue' and Pound's *Mauberley* has a drop of poisonous truth in it, and it is this truth that Eliot brings to the fore. His philosophical common man, Sweeney, explains the dwindled vision to a woman in 'Fragment of an Agon':

SWEENEY: Nothing at all but three things.
DORIS: What things?

SWEENEY: Birth, and copulation, and death.
That's all, that's all, that's all, that's all,
Birth, and copulation, and death.
DORIS: I'd be bored.
SWEENEY: You'd be bored.
Birth, and copulation, and death. . . .
That's all the facts when you come to brass tacks:
Birth, and copulation and death.

We will all, I think, recognize this reduction of the life cycle to all-but-nothingness as one of the great disheartening attitudes against which the age must contend. The colloquial flatness and overtones of 'sophisticated' exhaustion are reinforced by the various ways in which Eliot beats out his thought in wittily syncopated jazz rhythms throughout this highly stylized vaudevillian composition. He does the same sort of thing in *The Waste Land:*

O O O O that Shakespeherian Rag—
It's so elegant
So intelligent.

For Eliot the arts of the jazz musician and the English vaudeville performer represent a moral vigor still present, at least potentially, in the lower classes. His imitation of their tricks and turns becomes a sardonic commentary on what he has called, in his essay on the music-hall comedienne Marie Lloyd, 'the listless apathy with which the middle and upper classes regard any entertainment of the nature of art.'

But we should not ignore the sheer delight he takes in those tricks and turns for their own sake. So much has been made of the philosophical and theological convolutions of his work that the foundations of his appeal—evocative skill, aliveness to rhythmic overtones, bold dramatic portraiture, and joyous tomfoolery— have been obscured by a mist of critical commentary, some of it his own. His comic passages alone make up a broad gallery of essentially popular effects:

Apeneck Sweeney spreads his knees
Letting his arms hang down to laugh . . .
                    ('Sweeney among the Nightingales')

Reorganised upon the floor
She yawns and draws a stocking up . . .
                                        (Ibid.)

          Priapus in the shrubbery
Gaping at the lady in the swing.
                              ('Mr. Apollinax')

Madame Sosostris, famous clairvoyante,
Had a bad cold, nevertheless
Is known to be the wisest woman in Europe,
With a wicked pack of cards. . . .
                              (*The Waste Land*)

          Yes, I've seen her poetry—
Interesting if one is interested in Celia.
                              (*The Cocktail Party*)

Many of Eliot's most somber impressions are equally available
to the general reader. No one can more readily call up the dreary
associations of filth and fog common to all who know big-city life,
and the further psychological associations of hopelessness and
loneliness intertwined with them. Minor instances of Eliot's power
to evoke such associations may be seen in the imagery of 'Preludes'
and of 'Morning at the Window'; a major instance in the opening
stanzas of 'Prufrock,' or in 'Burnt Norton':

Men and bits of paper, whirled by the cold wind
That blows before and after time,
Wind in and out of unwholesome lungs
Time before and time after.
Eructation of unhealthy souls
Into the faded air, the torpid

> Driven on the wind that sweeps the gloomy hills
> of London,
> Hampstead and Clerkenwell, Campden and Putney,
> Highgate, Primrose and Ludgate . . .

Of course, it will be clear that neither the comic moments nor the evocations of dreariness are presented in isolation. Thus, in context, the lines from 'Sweeney among the Nightingales' point up a certain paltriness in contemporary man. And the impressions from the third movement of 'Burnt Norton' mingle echoes of Dante's *Inferno* with details of the London subway, casting for a symbolism far wider than a simple physical response would in itself ordinarily include. The 'time before and time after' phrasing will suggest a further intellectualization of the impressions. Nevertheless, the force and emotion of the poems is largely derived from the more elementary nature of their first impact.

Equally important is the complex of associations which gives unexpected psychological dimensions to Eliot's work. In 'Rhapsody on a Windy Night' there are signs of a perhaps abnormally fastidious sense of *smell*. *Stale* smells in particular make the author unhappy. Indeed, they so oppress him that one feels almost any physical experience or relationship carries with it a threat of possible revulsion. The 'smell of chestnuts in the streets' and 'female smells in shuttered rooms' are linked with the fetid odors of unaired corridors full of cigarette smoke and with the closeness of 'cocktail smells in bars.' The 'smell of steaks in passageways' in 'Preludes' and the unclean world of the prostitute sketched so economically in that poem, as well as other aspects of the shabby 'blackened' street, contribute to the impression that in the poet's scheme of sensations filth and disgusting smells are perilously associated with food, drink, femaleness—the world of the body and the physical life altogether:

> The sleek Brazilian jaguar
> Does not in its arboreal gloom
> Distil so rank a feline smell
> As Grishkin in a drawing-room.
>
>   ('Whispers of Immortality')

These are very nearly cloacal associations. There are many other instances, such as the constant juxtaposition in 'Prufrock' of impressions of evil, filth, and squeamish self-consciousness with the refrain

> In the room the women come and go
> Talking of Michelangelo

and with other allusions to women. The refrain is first introduced after the sinister opening stanza; it is followed by an extended figure of the fog as a great yellow cat, dirty and wet. Through such juxtaposings the protagonist's general revulsion from life and his sexual fears are suggested simultaneously. 'But in the lamplight, downed with soft brown hair!' he exclaims with a shocked realization of female animality in the midst of an erotic reverie on the whiteness and beauty of ladies' arms. The dismay is echoed in virtually all of Eliot's interior scenes in which women appear; all have their suggestions of actual or potential disgust. In his work woman—when not etherealized—is the essence of the physical; and for Eliot, though his poetic power depends to a great extent on vivid sense-evocation, the merely physical is a source of horror. It is not interchangeable with the condition of literal damnation, but is very nearly so. 'Hell,' he says in his essay on Dante, is (as opposed to Purgatory and Paradise) a 'state which can only be thought of, and perhaps only experienced, by the projection of sensory images.' When the hero of *The Family Reunion* tries to describe the terror surrounding the Furies, he treats it as a hyperphysical attribute of the infernal realm, present wherever they are:

> That apprehension deeper than all sense,
> Deeper than the sense of smell, but like a smell
> In that it is indescribable, a sweet and bitter smell
> From another world.

Yet it is also true that the world of Eliot's imagery has room for impressions of pure joy through physical sensation—impressions that suggest a dream of freedom from the burdens of ordinary experience. Almost always, though, they are bathed in nostalgia and regret for the irrecoverably lost. F. O. Matthiessen speaks of 'how often a sudden release of the spirit is expressed through sea-imagery which, with its exact notation of gulls and granite rocks and . . . sailing, seems always to spring from his own boyhood experience off the New England coast'; and of how Eliot uses an imagery of spring flowers and of adolescent girls—their beauty idealized—to express the 'stirring of desire against the memory of previous failure.'

> It is the loss of such loveliness in the failure of actual sexual experience to measure up to it that constitutes the emotional undercurrent of his flower-imagery. . . . Regaining the purified vision in later life is the theme particularly of the second and fourth poems in *Ash Wednesday*, and of 'Marina.' *

That bittersweet nostalgia is the natural counterpart of the motif of revulsion. Only rarely does the poet rise to a moment of transcendence over both kinds of feeling. His greatest success of this sort, probably, lies in that passage in *The Waste Land* in which he projects the ecstasy of ascetic self-mastery:

> The boat responded
> Gaily, to the hand expert with sail and oar
> The sea was calm, your heart would have responded
> Gaily, when invited, beating obedient
> To controlling hands . . .

Clearly, Eliot cannot resort, as do Yeats and Pound, to the world of self and body for the exaltation that will transcend man's tragic condition. His whole search, as a poet and as a thinker, has been for a higher order which will discipline his irritable excitability and his talent for critically negative and satirical delineation. Toward this end, he early set himself to the deliberate cultivation of a religious idealism and orthodoxy, and to Anglicanism as its most convenient institutionalization. Yet he remains intimately of this century, a poet of unresolved conflict, a recorder of physical

* F. O. Matthiessen, *The Achievement of T. S. Eliot*, 3rd edition, Oxford University Press, New York and London, 1958, p. 150.

sensation so intense it falls into ennui and revulsion, and of visions of beatitude with no reassuring perspective beyond the dream itself.

2. THE 'OBJECTIVE CORRELATIVE'

It is Eliot's *method* which marks him most inescapably as of this age. He wants to communicate the predicament of modern man in the midst of lost meanings. The intelligence that dominates his work is not an aggressive one like Pound's as we usually see it; rather it is like the ironically withdrawing and vulnerable spirit of *Mauberley* (1920). His poetry is in many respects narrative and dramatic, yet he rarely unfolds a situation or plot in a straight-forward manner. In his extremely interesting essay on *Hamlet*, written at about the same time as Pound's *Mauberley*, Eliot expresses the view that no emotion can be expressed accurately in art without an 'objective correlative,' which he defines as 'a set of objects, a situation, a chain of events which shall be the formula of that *particular* emotion; such that, when the external facts, which must terminate in sensory experience, are given, the emotion is immediately evoked.' * As a simple example of this principle, just one passage in Eliot's 'The Love Song of J. Alfred Prufrock' will serve. In stanzas 9 to 11, the protagonist does not say, 'I am afraid of mature sex, but I am also afraid of the emptiness of a life without it. I wish I had never been born.' If he did so, we should never come nearly as close to his true feeling as we do when he speaks caressingly of 'arms that are braceleted and white and bare' and then reminds himself with a furtive but shuddering recoil that in lamplight they are 'downed with light brown hair,' apologizes for betraying himself so, speaks pityingly (and self-pityingly) of 'lonely men in shirt-sleeves' and the smoke rising from their pipes as they look out of windows, and at last makes his sudden hopeless outcry:

> I should have been a pair of ragged claws
> Scuttling across the floors of silent seas.

* Eliot, op. cit. pp. 124-5.

The *Hamlet* essay, however, goes beyond this simple principle to a somewhat more subtle ramification. It examines Shakespeare's 'failure' to find a necessary objective correlative for the complex emotion of his play.

> Hamlet (the man) is dominated by an emotion which is inexpressible, because it is in *excess* of the facts as they appear. And the supposed identity of Hamlet with his author is genuine to this point: that Hamlet's bafflement at the absence of an objective equivalent to his feelings is a prolongation of the bafflement of his creator in the face of his artistic problem. Hamlet is up against the difficulty that his disgust is occasioned by his mother, but that his mother is not an adequate equivalent for it; his disgust envelops and exceeds her. . . .

> . . . The levity of Hamlet, his repetition of phrase, his puns, are . . . a form of emotional relief. In the character Hamlet it is the buffoonery of an emotion which can find no outlet in action; in the dramatist it is the buffoonery of an emotion which he cannot express in art. The intense feeling, ecstatic or terrible, without an object or exceeding its object, is something which every person of sensibility has known. . . . The ordinary person puts these feelings to sleep or trims down his feelings to fit the business world; the artist keeps them alive by his ability to intensify the world to his emotions. . . . Under compulsion of what experience he [Shakespeare] attempted to express the inexpressibly horrible, we can never know. . . . We should have to understand things Shakespeare did not understand himself.*

We shall not debate whether or not Eliot is right about *Hamlet,* for what is important here is the character of his interest in the play. *Hamlet,* he finds, is an 'attempt to express the inexpressibly horrible.' It is in the light of *this* finding that he formulates the problem of expressing emotion in poetry as one of discovering

* Ibid. pp. 125-6.

objective equivalents that will evoke a whole state of thought and feeling. An emotion, 'inexpressible because it is in *excess* of the facts as they appear,' may or may not be the maggot which is devouring Hamlet. It is obviously, though, the maggot in Eliot: 'The intense feeling, ecstatic or terrible, without an object or exceeding its object, is something which every person of sensibility has known.' And it would appear to be the maggot in the displaced modern man, who carries a burden of emotion without exact referent. The effort in modern art to strip away surface logic and story and to convey a subjective state through direct suggestion reflects the need to discover and define that emotion, to purge it of its murky turbulence and bring it into some ordered calm vision in the clear sunlight, as Eliot says Shakespeare did in *Othello*, *Antony and Cleopatra*, and *Coriolanus*. It is also the expression of a predicament and a kind of anguish—and on occasion of a hopeless and ironic throwing up of the hands.

In other words, Eliot's 'attack' on *Hamlet* is actually a defense of it, and, by implication, of his own work also. The problem of expressing the inexpressible—that impossible task arising out of the very nature of sensibility—becomes for him the essential problem of art. In his own work, Eliot is preoccupied with the very kind of failure he attributes to *Hamlet*. 'It is impossible to say just what I mean!' cry Prufrock and Eliot together. 'Portrait of a Lady' centers about a painful failure of communication, and the speaker is burdened with a guilt for which there is no adequate expression; he does not know who, morally speaking, he really is. 'La Figlia Che Piange' radiates the same sense of cruelty and remorse combined, the same baffled awareness of the ambiguities of sexual passion. After its almost sadistic intensity one needs to remind oneself that the same poet could write:

> I am moved by fancies that are curled
> Around these images, and cling:
> The notion of some infinitely gentle
> Infinitely suffering thing.

('Preludes')

Yet the feeling of these lines animates all of Eliot's work.

We may call Eliot's method of exposing this tangle of feeling *presentative*, or cinematic, as well as subjective. Impressions, voices, images, dramatic glimpses and poses provide a varied surface, but actually they are located with care in a cumulatively manipulated design. One startling consequence is that if we compare 'Prufrock' with Browning's 'Andrea Del Sarto,' another dramatic monologue in which a self-proclaimed failure tries to explain 'exactly what I mean,' 'Prufrock' emerges—from a psychological standpoint, and apart from other merits—as more *precise* than Browning's poem. The supposedly 'subjective' method gets us more convincingly close to the 'inexpressible' and at the same time gets the whole reality of Prufrock's predicament down in a way which Browning's approach does not allow. As Prufrock, in his reverie, imagines himself accounting for his behavior and character to the 'you' of the poem, he takes us over the landscape of his neurosis, exposes his most naked fears, and deprecates himself in the light of heroic literary tradition and of a satiric observation of his own social set. For Eliot the literal stage setting and scene of the traditional dramatic monologue is initially indispensable, but only to trigger the psychological mechanism which then moves the poem out into new dimensions.

A little more than a decade later, 'Gerontion' and *The Waste Land* had pushed much deeper into this structural method. The old man in 'Gerontion' is neither a completely realistic character susceptible of literal psychological analysis, nor does he symbolize a particular social class. He is an allegorical figure who represents the shrunken state of Western religious tradition and the morbid preoccupation of modern man with his own degradation. His memories include all memory, but with value and flavor removed. Art, love, and religion seem to him debilitated and perverted by a selfish secularism. *The Waste Land*, too, on a larger canvas, embraces the whole modern scene and tries to bring to bear upon it all the past and all the intellectual interests of its author. Both works presentatively convey an underlying humiliated bafflement. But, though Eliot is certainly an intellectual and a master of structural techniques, his primary power arises from his line-by-line music and intensity and 'magic':

> April is the cruellest month, breeding
> Lilacs out of the dead land, mixing
> Memory and desire . . .
>
> (The Waste Land)

These lines come at the very beginning of *The Waste Land* and illustrate a fact often neglected entirely—namely, that the poem builds into its total form and conception from a number of lyric and dramatic moments such as this one. Here Eliot plays on the familiar nostalgic associations of spring, but darkens and deepens them through the strong adjectives 'cruellest' and 'dead' and through the interruption of the lilting *r*'s and *l*'s and front vowels by the long *u* of the first line, the scattered stop-sounds, the sharp breaks in movement forced by the punctuation, and the contemplative effect of the two participial phrases. While he has not yet presented the great theme of death and resurrection, these lines definitely prepare us for it.

Consider 'Gerontion' from a similar primary standpoint. The poem begins:

> Here I am, an old man in a dry month,
> Being read to by a boy, waiting for rain.

The picture is a literal one; it implies blindness or near-blindness in the speaker, and a general impotence underlined by the phrases 'dry month' and 'waiting for rain,' though we do not yet know the importance of these details. But together with the next four lines they present a bleak picture of the last years of a sterile life:

> I was neither at the hot gates
> Nor fought in the warm rain
> Nor knee deep in the salt marsh, heaving a cutlass,
> Bitten by flies, fought.

'Hot gates' is the only phrase that raises any problem of explicit meaning, although I suppose an anxious reader would not be satisfied until he had learned just what war or wars Gerontion has *not* fought in: the Crusades? the Greek war of independence against the Turks? Eliot gives us a good many mysterious phrases to ponder if we expect precise denotation in our poetry, but the *connotations* of these lines are perfectly clear if their literal reference is not. Whole seminars have expired with delight at being reminded that 'hot gates' is a literal translation of the Greek place-name Thermopylae, but their lives might have been saved for another day's dying had they also been reminded that we need not forever be *translating* what a poet says into something else. The phrase 'hot gates' suggests danger, perhaps pain; the rest of the passage recalls the kind of engagement that entails discomfort, deadly action, and suffering. Whether the 'hot gates' are the gates of hell, or of a burning city, or of an engulfing sexual experience, or some particular combination of any of these is certainly less important than the impact of the phrase itself in the context of sound, color, and language in which the poet gives it. For Gerontion, the 'shrunken old man,' the images of these lines are conjured up in a dream of lost opportunities to live significantly.

In the ensuing lines, however, he shifts direction somewhat. The scene he describes, with his landlord, the 'jew' (the lower-case spelling suggesting his subhuman status), squatting on the window sill like an enormous carrion bird, can hardly be taken literally. Moreover, the ambiguous syntax suggests another impossibility: that the owner is physically inseparable from his house, and that both were simultaneously 'spawned' in an Antwerp cafe, 'blistered in Brussels,' and 'patched and peeled in London.' Still, it is easy enough to *visualize* all this, and visualization is all the poet asks for his implicit allegory to carry. When we ask ourselves what he must mean, the answer is there: The Western world is bereft of its heritage and hope because of the triumph of that commercial system supposedly initiated by Jews after the Middle Ages, a system that burgeoned with the rise of the wool trade and of the centers of commerce named in the poem. The mortgaged state of the modern spirit is cheerlessly imaged in a series of bleakly detailed lines and summed up in the one word 'merds.' Prufrock's cloacal horror in the face of life is now given historical dimensions.*

---

* Gerontion, though apparently the most sophisticated of lost souls, reflects his creator's conservative indifference to the dangerous dynamics of anti-

Moreover, at the opening of the poem tersely alliterative mono-syllables and stop-sounds, and the numerous relatively short lines, create an impression of a life choked off from fruitful meaning. In contrast, the second stanza summons up the open-souled readi-ness for revelation of true communicants. Gerontion would like to experience their ardor for 'Christ the tiger' (who comes to 'devour' our old selves so that we may be reborn), but cannot shake out of himself the sophisticated consciousness of perversion of all basic values symbolized by the suspect figures Silvero, Hakagawa, Madame de Tornquist, and Fräulein von Kulp. When these figures are presented the tone takes on a whispering irony. In the fourth stanza his tone again shifts, with overwrought, even hysterical effects: Gerontion argues anxiously against the notion that men can win through to redemption by their own efforts through study-ing history and other disciplines. He understands very well the assumptions of religious belief and the need for grace: 'These tears are shaken from the wrath-bearing tree.'

The two closing stanzas bring the poem to a point of great emo-tional intensity. The speaker expresses his baffled anguish that through no effort of his own can he regain the lost innocence which at first was spontaneously at one with divinity; simple love was long ago replaced by 'terror,' and then by 'inquisition' (intellectual inquiry as a substitute for faith). The poem ends in a whirl of self-depreciating and pessimistic images of defeat. Gerontion ac-cuses himself of merely seeking a last bit of titillation by indulg-ing in these religious 'deliberations.' He points out that the agents of death and decay, symbolized by the spider and the weevil, will not be halted by anything he can say or do, and he recalls the names of people once famous or notorious who are now 'whirled/ Beyond the circuit of the shuddering Bear/ In fractured atoms.'

As a 'presentative' sequence, the poem has given us, first, a landscape of pure negation, then an image of wondering faith, then some sinister close-ups of perverted value, then a paradoxical argument in the subtly, insinuatingly forceful manner of Jacobean

Semitism. It is a measure of the limitations of the genteel tradition that Eliot could not see Gerontion's stereotype of the Jew landlord as one more sign of the old man's degeneracy.

drama and Metaphysical verse, and at last a network of impressions of the speaker's tortured inability to put his soul in order. Eliot has, in his essay 'The Metaphysical Poets,' argued that the seventeenth-century writers on whose rhythms and rhetoric he here plays variations were the last poets before our century who did not 'dissociate' thought and feeling. We must, he has felt, regain that lost wholeness of theirs, their ability to see thinking as experience and thus—as he wrote of Donne—to become 'expert beyond experience.' Reading 'Gerontion,' we can see how crucial Eliot felt such a recovery to be; his 'presentative' method is a way of achieving apprehension of a total state of being and awareness. It is interesting that the sequence of effects in 'Gerontion' roughly parallels that of *The Waste Land*, which also gives us the negative modern landscape, the close-ups of lost possibility and perversion, the momentary visions of challenge and hope, and the agony of understanding without grace represented in the shorter work. Eliot's major poems are psychological journeys through many points within that agony or predicament.

3. 'THE WASTE LAND' AND 'FOUR QUARTETS'

A vast battery of commentary has all but blasted the essential Eliot out of sight. His intellectualized mysticism, his interest in theodicy and theology generally, and his philosophical tendencies loom up more formidably than they should because of all the attention given them. *The Waste Land* can, and in a sense *should*, be read as a Christian sermon in disguise, and *Four Quartets* as open religious contemplation. Yet neither work is finally a sermon or a devotion. Each explores a relationship between a speaker and his religious awareness *poetically*, in ways that create something more malleable than dogmatic doctrine. The result is a shifting design worked out of psychological ambiguities such as must engage the modern mind when it confronts issues of belief and morality. As Eliot himself wrote in 1924, 'The poet who "thinks" is merely the poet who can express the emotional equivalent of thought. But he is not necessarily interested in the thought itself.' * Eliot is, of course, speaking of the poetic process, not of any specific poet.

So the two major works are not so much direct religious expressions as journeys of a sensibility over the landscape of its own condition. This sensibility, the 'hero' of the poems, goes through many adventures, not in a narrative sequence but in a montage of images, memories, portraits and caricatures, dramatic scenes, and musings. Medieval legends contribute to the symbolism of *The Waste Land*. Their heroes sought a vision of divine grace, symbolized by Christ's blood held in the Holy Grail. Eliot's hero-sensibility wanders over the parched 'waste land' of a secularized existence, seeking to know itself. Like the Grail hero, he sees strange and vicious sights in a land whose blight is its punishment for the violation of ancient taboos. He inquires their meaning—a necessary prelude to revelation. Originally, success in this quest meant renewal of the land's fertility and of the impotent Waste Land king's reproductive powers. In *The Waste Land* the desired renewal is purely psychological or spiritual; at the same time the blight upon the modern soul is felt to be all but incurable.

When the poem was published in 1922, it was its uncompromising self-irony that appealed to readers. Its combination of a longing for positive values with an overriding mood of futility resembles that in *Mauberley*, though Eliot's poem shows tighter organization, greater power of sensuous evocation, and more effective use of emotionally charged archetypes. (Hence Pound's letter to Eliot in which he describes himself as 'wracked by the seven jealousies.' †) Like *Mauberley*, too, it was a post-war poem charged with nausea at the thought of the young men who had died, as Pound wrote, for 'a botched civilization.' The speaker in *The Waste Land* screams out to a fellow-botcher in the crowd of the damned:

---

* Eliot, op. cit. p. 115. Eliot's critical writings recur to this idea, or problem, constantly.

† Pound, *Letters*, p. 169. The whole sentence is interesting as a comment on certain differences between the two poets: 'I am wracked by the seven jealousies, and cogitating an excuse for always exuding my deformative secretions in my own stuff, and never getting an outline.'

> That corpse you planted last year in your garden,
> Has it begun to sprout? Will it bloom this year?

It is the great corpse of all the war dead, and the sardonic question is whether they—with all the figures of tradition who, like Jesus, died for mankind and then rose from the dead—have yet shown signs of a miraculous rebirth. The speaking sensibility may desire to feel a fresh and open faith, but cannot escape the bleak reminders that undercut its purpose.

The original epigraph for *The Waste Land*, we are told, was the climactic outcry of Kurtz in Conrad's *The Heart of Darkness*: 'The horror! the horror!' * The great tragic stanza, passionate and bizarre, that concludes 'The Burial of the Dead' (Part I of Eliot's poem) epitomizes the motives behind this first choice. Contemporary London becomes an 'unreal city' over whose hellish streets zombie-like mass-men move without will, past the church that *might* mean salvation could they but stop and consider. The grotesquely casual question about 'that corpse you planted last year in your garden' is shouted over the heads of this procession, as is the warning that follows about the 'Dog' tearing open a grave. The warning echoes both the New Testament and Webster's hysterically morbid play *The White Devil*. These characteristic echoings are not essential to our understanding, but they do extend our range of associations and of feeling. To them are added three fierce phrases from Baudelaire: 'hypocrite lecteur—mon semblable,—mon frère!' You and I, the speaker is saying to his 'own image'—the 'hypocritical reader' who may think himself outside what the poem presents—are in the horror together; we are 'brothers,' to each other and to those walking corpses in that awful procession.

The speaker arrives at this climactic realization early in the poem, but not without complex preparation for it. We first have met a disturbing image of April as 'the cruellest month,' a time of painfully quickened sentience, memories of the past, and bringing to birth out of the death that was winter. The ensuing monologue of

---

* Grover Smith, Jr., *T. S. Eliot's Poetry and Plays*, University of Chicago Press, Chicago, 1956, p. 68. See also Pound, *Letters*, pp. 169ff.

Marie illustrates the sterile implications of the phrase 'a little life with dried tubers.' For her, life's challenge is reduced to the pursuit of comfort, punctuated with moments of physical intensity: the thrill and risk of a sleigh-ride in childhood, for example, with its overtones of sexual excitement:

> And I was frightened. He said, Marie,
> Marie, hold on tight. And down we went.

Her monologue is interrupted by the thundering voice of a prophet or preacher—one of several *personae* or dramatic roles adopted by the poet-speaker in the poem. It castigates Marie and her whole modern milieu (and ours) as 'stony rubbish,' picturing an unbearably desolate landscape as our world and grimly inviting us to come in 'under this red rock' (ultimately, a symbol of the church). The rock's shelter holds another terror, however: that of our recognition of our soul's peril and of the sacrifices needed for self-purification. 'I will show you fear in a handful of dust.'

The one alternative to the spiritual way offered by the non-religious life is romantic love. The poem leaps into an imagery of nostalgic yearning, love ecstasy, and disillusionment, all compressed into a few lines. There is a snatch of song from *Tristan and Isolde*, then a glimpsed moment of absolute entrancement, then the dreary afterbeat underlining the narrow limits of this secular alternative to true devotion. One is reminded of Dante's despair at the plight of the damned lovers in Hell, although of course Dante assumes their literal damnation. Though Eliot seems on the surface to be doing the very opposite of what Yeats does in the 'Dialogue of Self and Soul,' his nostalgic tone suggests that he regrets the *transience* of the romantic moment rather than its spiritual *unworthiness*.

The crucial passage that follows has a similarly unresolved character. It introduces Madame Sosostris, the fortuneteller, whose 'wicked pack of cards' are something like a Tarot pack. The pictures on them are the archetypal figures that dominate the poem: of divinity, of womanly beauty and suffering, and of sacrifice and resurrection. The thoughtless carrier of neglected meanings, she does not really understand these symbols. In our shallowness lies our damnation. This damnation can be understood as modern man's failure to realize his own meanings (which even in a secular context include concern and self-sacrifice for one another) as well as interpreted in the religious sense superimposed by the author and usually emphasized by his critics. Indeed, Eliot is very close to the aestheticism of Yeats, as his avoidance of overt didactic statement shows. In *The Waste Land* itself Eliot is careful never to mention Christianity. Actually, the poem derives its strength from the way its implied Christian, pagan, and private motives cast light on one another and from the ensuing fusion of symbols. Eliot wishes his poem to move within a moral and Christian context, but without loss of its own primary place to something 'above' or 'beyond' it. For example, Part V of the poem gives a key to the contents of the three middle parts in the message of the thunder: 'Give, sympathize, control.' Patently God's message, it comes *not* from the Bible but from the Hindu *Upanishads*. Part II, "A Game of Chess,' has to do with our lack of sympathy or love; Part III, 'The Fire Sermon,' with lack of control; Part IV, 'Death by Water,' with failure to give or sacrifice. The ascetic and devout aspects of this sequence are subordinated to a coloration of personal bitterness and sexual despair for which the Christian context may be but a mask.

Thus, in 'A Game of Chess' we first see a woman who, surrounded by luxury and by art-works (the main one of which celebrates the tragic yet beautiful fate of the ravished Philomela), is nevertheless reduced to shrieking frustration. The horror of her condition lies as much in her burning need for love as in any lack of religious faith. (That is why she is so much more convincing in her agony than are the characters of *The Cocktail Party*, who are made puppets of their presumed spiritual deficiencies.) In the squalid pub-monologue that follows, we see a lower-class counterpart: a tragicomic presentation of the brutalizing of a poor woman's life because of the grossest indifference to her as a person. The discoveries writ large in these two close-ups, which together sum up a whole social order, are examined more variously in 'The Fire Sermon.' Here, among many instances of uncontrolled or inappropriate lust, the central incident is most telling. The mechanical 'seduction' of the typist evokes a disgust, like that expressed in 'Rhapsody on a Windy Night,' for the inescapable physical compulsions of existence, its mindless and silent insistences.

Certain elements in the poem, then, do not altogether support its prophetic pretensions. It is perhaps for just this reason that Tiresias, the mythical prophet so important in *The Odyssey* and in the plays of Sophocles, is introduced at this point. Tiresias has been both male and female, and has walked in Hades 'among the lowest of the dead'—that is to say, has experienced everything possible to a human being. But Eliot's Tiresias does not condemn; he 'sees,' 'foretells,' 'foresuffers'; he knows all the pain and barrenness and banality of the human condition. Hence, his co-suffering and helpless role seems especially significant. Indeed, the incident related in 'The Fire Sermon' parodies the Grail motif and demeans *its* pretensions. The young man comes to the Chapel Perilous—to the room where the girl's drying underclothes are 'out of the window *perilously* spread'—and violates sacred mysteries of which both are quite unaware. Then, instead of receiving revelation, he gropes his way back down the 'unlit' stairs to the infernal darkness whence he came. Later in this section the voice of another victim of seduction is heard. This time the girl involved is fully aware of her loss, but she accepts the betrayal with a humility that makes her monologue one of the poem's most affecting sequences. In both passages, there is revulsion against the *grossness* of the physical: 'the young man carbuncular,' 'the broken fingernails of dirty hands.' (We could note many such parallel effects in Part III as the defilement of the Thames banks by lovers on summer nights, the rat 'dragging its slimy belly' on the bank of the canal, or the 'unshaven' homosexual Mr. Eugenides.)

Brief, elegiac, classical in form, Part IV ('Death by Water') serves a function like that of the stanza introducing the 'enchanted stone' image in Yeats's 'Easter 1916.' It maintains the tragic note and is consistent with the general thought of the poem: Phlebas must some day have died in any case; why not, then, in a greater cause than the 'profit and loss' of business or the simple physical awareness of 'the cry of gulls, and the deep sea swell'? But there is no explicitly modern note in this section, and the 'Grecian' aspect

suggests the godlike potentialities of man as the sculpture of
Phidias suggested it. The cabalistic phrasing of the second and
third sentences evokes a feeling of awe toward the sacred mysteries
behind man's existence. The passage, incidentally, illustrates Eliot's
great virtuosity. He preserves the poem's unity despite the variety
of elements involved: moments of pure lyricism, snatches of dialogue and satire, violent dramatic projections, and literary echoes
and burlesques.

It is most of all through this virtuosity that Eliot keeps the poem
from being swamped in doctrinal tendentiousness. A triumphant
example may be found in the brilliant summations in Part V: the
agony of the lost, parched-throated sensibility in the 'mountains of
rock without water,' the nightmare reversals in the vision of the
Chapel Perilous, and the imagery of the thunder's message. Among
all these symbols the emphasis on the modern neurosis far out-
weighs the apocalyptic effort. Nowhere in the poem, of course,
can the apocalyptic aspect be ignored. The 'red rock' and the
Church of St. Mary Woolnoth in Part I, and the parallel allusion
to Christopher Wren's beautiful Magnus Martyr in Part III; the
moment of revelation in Part V when the cock crows, the lightning
flashes, the rain falls, and the thunder speaks; and the continuing
symbolism of Grail hero and reborn god all imply Christian faith
and the real possibility of redemption. But their chief emotional
effect is to heighten our sense of predicament. No adequate mode of
action to meet the spiritual challenge is discovered in the poem's
imagery. Even the thunder's message reminds us that we can know
giving only through the abhorred body in 'the awful daring of a
moment's surrender' and *sympathy* only as a dream contrasting
with our locked-in pride. Eliot's failure to discover the action with
which to respond to the challenge is the great weakness of all his
work. In *The Waste Land,* the nearest he comes to success (apart
from the note of desperate humility struck at the very end) is the
buoyant imagery of ascetic self-control in the thunder's message—
an imagery that underlines the horror of life expressed throughout
the poem.

It is so, too, with *Four Quartets,* a group of poems begun with
'Burnt Norton' (1935) and completed by 'East Coker,' 'The Dry

Salvages,' and 'Little Gidding' in the early years of World War II. Here also no active 'correlative' can be found—only a kind of self-hypnotic mystical contemplation, falling far short of the total saintly renunciation of one's accidental commitments envisaged in 'Little Gidding':

> A condition of complete simplicity
> (Costing not less than everything)

Despondent at the inadequacy of his art to help him attain such a condition, the poet complains. 'Words,' he says, 'strain' and

> Crack and sometimes break, under the burden,
> Under the tension, slip, slide, perish,
> Decay with imprecision, will not stay in place,
> Will not stay still. . . .
>
> ('Burnt Norton')

The years of his poetic maturing (including the year in which he wrote *The Waste Land*) have been 'twenty years largely wasted, the years of *l'entre deux guerres*,' and of 'failure.'

> . . . one has only learnt to get the better of words
> For the thing one no longer has to say, or the way in
>   which
> One is no longer disposed to say it . . .
>
> ('East Coker')

London is still the dread 'unreal city,' the temporal life is still a 'waste sad time,' the spirit remains 'unappeased and peregrine,' and full maturity reveals no mellowing of the world's prospect but

> First, the cold friction of expiring sense
> Without enchantment . . .
> Second, the conscious impotence of rage
>   At human folly, and the laceration
>   Of laughter at what ceases to amuse.
> And last, the rending pain of re-enactment
>   Of all that you have done, and been. . . .
>
> ('Little Gidding')

So 'the horror' is still with us, and within us, whenever literal reality is looked at directly. It is still, in part, a social horror—dreariness and dirt of the world of the City, desolation of a world at War. The sexual horror has receded, perhaps, or been replaced by fears of old age and loss of creative powers (though the language still carries strongly sexual overtones). But *Four Quartets* is the most expansive of Eliot's works; there is more 'positive' projection in it than in *The Waste Land*. That is, there is more projection of the kind that is not immediately torn down by a sardonic blast or a disillusioned afterbeat. Yet its moments of visionary realization or mystical transcendence are tinged with a melancholy deeper than nostalgia as we ordinarily conceive it—a helpless regret for that which *never happened*. The irrevocably unattained makes for even more self-taunting dreams than the irrevocably lost.

The first of the *Four Quartets* wastes little time creating such a moment. A prefatory incantation of ten lines in which the unity of all time is stated and restated in various ways leads the way into it. The opening passage reads like an abstract argument until we realize its liturgical character; it must be intoned like the Lord's Prayer or one of the Psalms, and then its abstractions become a hymn of praise to the eternal oneness behind the diversities of past, present, and future. It is true that this incantation has an unorthodox, tentative character, which may, however, be interpreted as a note of humility, as though the speaker were reluctant to pretend to knowledge of the Absolute. He qualifies his assertions with 'perhaps,' advances a key proposition with a hypothetical 'if,' and proposes a conclusion in language ambiguous enough to allow room for the notion that what is said may be mere wishfulness.

> What might have been is an abstraction
> Remaining a perpetual possibility
> Only in a world of speculation.

So 'Burnt Norton' begins, with a curiously pragmatic incantation that mingles with its attitude of genuine devotion a skeptical diction and syntax at least half-belying the author's intention. (Note how the one word 'only' both limits the assertion of possibility and introduces the thought that it may all be mere 'speculation.') The passage fades into a moment of realization of what I have called the 'irrevocably unattained,' introduced through negatives of various sorts:

> Footfalls echo in the memory
> Down the passage which we did not take
> Towards the door we never opened
> Into the rose-garden. . . .

And then we are led, despite the poet's protest that he does not know 'to what purpose,' into the 'rose-garden'—led by a thrush whose annunciation of this paradisal moment he calls a 'deception.' The method, then, is to construct a beatific vision out of such ambiguous negatives. We penetrate into it for a glistening instant, amidst 'invisible' forms, 'unheard' music, 'unseen' sights:

> Dry the pool, dry concrete, brown edged,
> And the pool was filled with water out of sunlight. . . .

At last, there is the final paradox:

> Go, said the bird, for the leaves were full of children,
> Hidden excitedly, containing laughter.
> Go, go, go, said the bird: human kind
> Cannot bear very much reality.

Its primary meaning is that the reality which lies beyond experience is too dazzling for us to endure very much of it; we must retreat to the protection of our 'unreal' existence, in the Platonic sense. Still, the thrush does 'deceive' us about these matters, and he may be talking about reality as we ordinarily know it after all. We 'cannot bear very much' of that kind, either, if Eliot's interpretation of 'the horror' is an accurate one. Yet we need, and are able, to approximate for a moment a state of being which cannot be held beyond that moment—'in the rose-garden,' or 'in the arbour where the rain beat,' or 'in the draughty church at smokefall.' 'Only through time time is conquered,' but the conquest is transient and uncertain. Against this knowledge the poet seeks to construct, as did the mystics of the past, images of permanence and certainty. Thus he echoes St. John of the Cross, not only in such an image as 'the figure of the ten stairs' (on which the soul ascends to God) but also in the more despondent figure of a 'black cloud' that carries away the joy and lucidity of the seeker's vision. But he cannot altogether elude the acidic presence of that modern, skeptical realism against which he would struggle; the darkness he feels is in the nature of being as well as in the would-be believer's mind. Will grace be bestowed ultimately on him—'Will the sunflower turn to us?' The question in the crucial fourth part of 'Burnt Norton'—corresponding in brevity and poignancy to Part IV of *The Waste Land*, as the *Quartets* correspond in their general formal structures—goes unanswered. Eternal life or eternal death? There is an image of flashing light and revelation similar to the one in Hopkins's 'The Windhover,' but the confrontation of agonized questioning and mystical vision is not resolved here any more than in a typical Yeats poem.

Nevertheless the *Four Quartets* is in a significant way a struggle for affirmation, as the sequence of titles suggests. Burnt Norton, a deserted manor-house in Cotswold, may represent the whole problem of the continuing meaning of the past in the present and therefore in the future; so, too, it represents the interrelation of all time and the existence of a timeless present transcending our temporal one. East Coker, ancestral village of the poet's family, relates the special meaning of the past to the general questions posed in 'Burnt Norton.' The Dry Salvages, off the New England coast, ushers in the future (in relation to the English past); and Little Gidding, important in English history as a refuge for Charles I and as a place where the devotional life led to reported revelation, unites all these considerations in a glowing aura of devotional self-reassurance.

The weakest link in the sequence is 'East Coker.' It begins effectively, with a somewhat gloomily Elizabethan incantation on the theme of mutability, followed by a vision of the age-old dance of life. This is a ritual country dance celebrating marriage and all the phenomena of material existence: the 'living seasons,' the constellations, and also (inescapably, as we know from the revulsion of Eliot's earlier work)

> The time of the coupling of man and woman
> And that of beasts. Feet rising and falling.
> Eating and drinking. Dung and death.

Bogged down in the physical, the poet forces himself toward counterassertion. He employs an imagery of confusion (spring and summer flowers seen in late November, the imagination's leaping association of unlike things, the personifications in ancient myth and prophecy of astronomical phenomena) to suggest that experience teaches us nothing, and then he launches a somewhat prosy exposition of the same theme concluding that the 'only wisdom' man can hope for is that of humility. Almost everything in 'East Coker' after the opening section is weaker than its counterparts in the other *Quartets*. Despite the evident virtuosity, the rhythm of the longer-lined passages is more flaccid, and the diction too loose and easy. The image of Christ the surgeon in Part IV, and the effects surrounding it, seems almost trite as handled here; and the closing stanza of this part depends for its wit on a doctrinally sympathetic reading. Part V begins with a directness and candor that make it akin to Part I; but its second stanza, which brings 'East Coker' to an end, is a flat attempt to gain profundity in a way which will lift the poem out of its Slough of Despond. The obviousness of the attempt is its downfall.

Much more interesting, 'The Dry Salvages' finds in the river and sea powerful symbols for the expression of pessimism and of the poet's longing to turn it against its own meanings. The river is 'a strong brown god,' a primal reality ignored except as a problem for 'the builder of bridges.' Like the 'many gods' and 'many voices' of the sea, he can embody both the rankness of experienced truth and something beyond it, a double function the poet has also given the concept of time—that major theme on which the whole sequence plays. Part II makes the comparisons explicit:

> Time the destroyer is time the preserver,
> Like the river with its cargo of dead Negroes, cows
>   and chicken coops,
> The bitter apple and the bite in the apple.
> And the ragged rock in the restless waters,

> Waves wash over it, fogs conceal it;
> On a halcyon day it is merely a monument,
> In navigable weather it is always a seamark
> To lay a course by: but in the sombre season
> Or the sudden fury, is what it always was.

In contrast with the faltering effects of 'East Coker,' the phrasing and imagery of 'The Dry Salvages' are incisive, and its movement sure. Whatever the metaphysics, the poet's sense of subjective reality is given full play. From a starting point natural to his temperament he closes in on the basic predicament of the *Quartets:* that for most of us there are 'only hints and guesses,' only 'the unattended/ Moment, the moment in and out of time,/ The distraction fit.' The bitter fact of existence within time, with its connotations of an infinite extension of life's terrors and agonies, is measured in the plain but deep-stamped sensuousness with which the river god's (that is, the time god's) presence is asserted.

> His rhythm was present in the nursery bedroom,
> In the rank ailanthus of the April dooryard,
> In the smell of grapes on the autumn table,
> And the evening circle in the winter gaslight.

The Baudelairean 'damnation on this earth' is implicit in the details selected for this acknowledgment of the god's power. It is implicit as well in the descriptive passages on the everpresence of the sea: its 'howl' and 'yelp,' the 'whine in the rigging,'

> the torn seine,
> The shattered lobsterpot, the broken oar
> And the gear of foreign dead men. . . .

The time theme is a natural aspect of the contemplation of these data of destruction, as it is of Eliot's picture of the 'tolling bell' that

> Measures time not our time, rung by the unhurried
> Ground swell. . . .

In 'The Dry Salvages,' therefore, Eliot's familiar psychological bearings converge with his intended religious bearings. The tragic condition of man is stated in all its painfulness and perforce accepted—the symbolism of sea and river shows how inescapable it is. Then the acceptance is converted, in Part III, into the blander terms of Hindu thought in the supposed words of the god Krishna:

'Fare forward, you who think you are voyaging;
You are not those who saw the harbour
Receding, or those who will disembark.' . . .

We are thus prepared for the specifically Christian dimension, revealed in Part IV in the short, sad prayer to Stella Maris—which also accepts man's condition—on behalf of all who have to do with the sea and of their loved ones. So sure are the emotional premises which the foregoing sections have established that Eliot can afford an almost businesslike tone here as he issues clipped instructions to the Virgin which might, in part at least, sound comic in a different context. He is free also to be rather expansively confessional in the closing section, which sets severe limits on what man can foresee, create, or hope for. The firmness of the poet's control throughout this *Quartet*, however, .gives real weight to the qualified avowal, toward the end, that 'the hint half guessed, the gift half understood, is Incarnation.' If there is a lapse (forewarned in the passages echoing the message of Krishna) into a Tennysonian emphasis on the virtue of 'carrying on' for its own sake, his astringent truthfulness prepares us for the kind of affirmation 'Little Gidding' will make.

In this last poem of the sequence the intensification of feeling and technique is truly remarkable. The poem begins with impressions of 'midwinter spring': the glare of sunlight on ice and snow suggests a 'pentecostal fire,' a season of spiritual spring though 'not in time's covenant.' It also suggests the presence of illusion and so hints at the self-deception possible in the feeling that one has experienced grace; but for the most part the sharp beauty and the rich feeling of the passage conceal the latter implication. Nevertheless, the reader is warned that all who make the journey to this place where grace had been bestowed in the past must put aside 'sense and notion' and come in a state of prayer ready, as Gerontion would say, for 'wonders.' What communication comes is from the dead and 'tongued with fire beyond the language of the living.'

This precariously illogical method of affirmation is brilliantly sustained throughout the poem. In a sense 'Little Gidding' plunges into a mood more depressive even than the bleakest moments of 'The Dry Salvages.' Part II, for instance, consists of two movements of almost unrelieved darkness—a three-stanza song of death which states more fiercely the mutability theme introduced at the start of 'East Coker,' and a scene based in verse-form (though with modifications) and in tone and idiom on Dante's *Inferno*. This scene takes place on a London street after an air raid. The speaker, an inhabitant of the hell of his own civilization and personality, meets a 'familiar compound ghost,' a 'spirit unappeased and peregrine,' who sums up for him the utter frustration the future has in store for him unless grace, whose possibility is *just* allowed for, is experienced:

> From wrong to wrong the exasperated spirit
> Proceeds, unless restored by that refining fire
> Where you must move in measure, like a dancer.

The rest of the poem moves toward a program for reconciliation and affirmation. Part III descants on the need for a detachment which will yet not be indifference but will liberate us from too great immersion in particular times and places. It reassures us in the words of Juliana of Norwich:

> Sin is Behovely, but
> All shall be well, and
> All manner of thing shall be well

—*if*, that is, we are not lost in the issues of the day, or even in the old loyalties of history. We must 'purify our motives' by seeing in the causes of past and present only a 'symbol perfected in death'—an abstraction pointing perhaps to an ultimate Cause outside time and death. Part IV focuses, as in 'The Dry Salvages,' on the paradox of Christian faith, the acceptance of a torment devised by Love in much the same spirit as Hopkins's 'The Wreck of the Deutschland.' These motives, the deep dive into the heart of terror and the open-eyed search for faith in God, are recapitulated and combined with the other major lines of the whole sequence in Part V in a magnificent poetic peroration. We might *almost* forget that this peroration is the final, swelling bit of orchestration growing out of that initial rose-garden imagery, in 'Burnt Norton,' of the pathos of the illusion of beatitude. The frustration of man's need to grasp the ineffable is still the true theme of Eliot.

Perhaps we might take Mr. Eliot's religious concerns more at face value. Certainly the poet is serious about them. Not only *The Waste Land* and the *Four Quartets*, but most of his other mature work concerns the quest for vision and the despair of attaining it. The best of Eliot's plays, *Murder in the Cathedral*, has for hero the martyr Thomas à Becket, who seeks a way to live up to his great mission by divorcing his awareness of it from his own ambition for fame and canonization. The other plays use trappings of realistic and classical drama and comedy of manners, but essentially they are derivative dramatizations of the themes of the two great sequences. Yet as we have seen, the aestheticist tradition and the Baudelairean mood of oppression are both strikingly manifest in Eliot's work, and a certain ambiguity of emphasis always clings to it. Even when he seems to be absorbed in the specifics of Christian faith, Eliot interests us most as he explores the limits of sensibility and conveys the sense of what it is to be alive and thoroughly conscious today.

FIVE

Rival Idioms: The Great Generation

1. ROBINSON AND FROST

Among the poets born within the generation after Yeats's birth are various important figures whose achievement has been ranked by some with that of Yeats, Pound, and Eliot. Unrivaled as a generation of begetters of new forms and of new awareness in their art, they have produced a number of strong idioms we must remark as rivaling those of the three so far considered.

Cultural change—'mutability'—has itself, of course, long been a great poetic theme. Whatever challenges, insights, or liberations it has brought about, our poets have usually seen it tragically and nostalgically. Edwin Arlington Robinson, almost an exact contemporary of Yeats, found in it the ultimate mystery and the ultimate perspective. His nostalgia for a romantic and chivalric past, and for a lost American élite (its creed of *noblesse oblige* personified in the character of 'the man Flammonde'), is one of his dominant themes. So is his love for certain kinds of old people who embody in their frailty of body and toughness of spirit man's relation to time and change. Sometimes Robinson could think poetically with a hard, uncompromising candor. The early 'John Evereldown,' for instance, and the relatively late 'Eros Turannos' both bear down brutally on the theme of the power of sex to rule a life. The tone is tragic; to be driven by sexuality is seen as a defeat of the human spirit—a breakdown of what might once have been hoped for, and consequently a subtle token of mutability. Robinson early determined (see his 'Zola' and his 'George Crabbe') not to evade 'the racked and shrieking hideousness of Truth' but to seek 'the sure strength' with which it endows those who do not fear it. Still, truth to him seems necessarily marked by 'hideousness'; it is an evil to be endured with high-spirited grace and, if possible, subordinated by an almost secret asceticism:

'Let the men stay where they are,'
She said, 'and if Apollo's avatar
Be one of them, I shall not have to grieve.'
('The Tree in Pamela's Garden')

With the slightest of turns on the conventional dichotomy of the fleshly and the spiritual, the vote is ultimately cast against the former. Robinson's energy does not carry him as far as the revolutionary resolutions of Yeats and Pound. He gives us something like Eliot's root criticism of modern life and of worldliness, it is true, but nothing like his pursuit of visionary Christian consciousness. Robinson, like Hardy, keeps most of himself in touch with a past whose faiths and ways he is loath to relinquish. Just as he does not free himself from conventional blank verse and conventional rhyme, so also he is limited in his range of idea and feeling. He lacks the technical and intellectual daring of the great Romantics and Victorians, let alone of his own best contemporaries. Yet Robinson's idiom is his own. He speaks authentically for himself and his milieu. In thought, and he did 'think aloud' in his verse far more than was needed, he never outgrew the subdued meliorism of his youthful 'Credo,' with its kinship to 'Thanatopsis' and its next-door-neighborliness to Henley's 'Invictus.' That much-praised elegiac ode 'The Man Against the Sky,' though a product of his middle age, is hardly more than a slightly 'atribilious'—to use his own fine word—elaboration of 'Credo.' Its speculations project the soul sicknesses, and some of the philosophical puerilities, of the American 'nineties elsewhere expressed by such writers as Moody, Stickney, Lodge, and Adams. To these writers the breaking-up of a world was evident, but its aesthetic correlatives had not yet made themselves manifest.

The post-Wordsworthian rhythms of 'The Man Against the Sky' are for the most part as tiresomely portentous as the discussions following its publication about whether or not it was 'pessimistic.' It is a mark of Robinson's own naïveté that he should so vigorously have defended himself against this charge. 'I meant merely,' he wrote, 'through what I supposed to be an obviously ironic medium, to carry materialism to its logical end and to indicate its futility as an explanation or a justification of existence.' * Unfortunately, that *is* what he 'merely' meant, and the poem is largely an artfully complicated progression of schoolboy profundities:

> If after all that we have lived and thought,
> All comes to Nought,—
> If there be nothing after Now,
> And we be nothing anyhow,
> And we know that,—why live?

Why live indeed?—after such lines, what forgiveness? The answer lies (as it does with Robert Frost) in a sharp and poignant vision that penetrates further into truth than the poet's explicitly 'philosophical' expositions could ever do. Set 'Charles Carville's Eyes,' which first appeared in the same volume as 'Credo,' against the latter poem or 'The Man Against the Sky.' It is a poem to contemplate, not for what it tries to explain but for what it finds inexplicable. Here is the mystery of Charles Carville, whose sad, 'blank' eyes were at such variance with his 'glad' mouth and his 'whims' and 'theories' which went only half noticed because of the lie his 'melancholy face' gave to them. The mouth 'redeemed' the face and eyes, yet the latter had the last bleak word. This is the true, the unanswerable and intransigent Robinsonian irony.

From 'Charles Carville's Eyes' one might project an implication that personal will (the smiling mouth, the whimsical theorizing) and impersonal fatality (the 'insufficient face, forever sad') must be out of harmony with one another, now and until the end of time. The predicament is like that of Clavering, or Richard Cory, or Captain Craig, or Flammonde, each of whom 'fails' out of an excess of fineness or breeding that makes him more vulnerable than most. In all these instances, the inner man cannot make terms with the superimposed conditions of modern society; the wryness expresses the resistance to self-pity of a displaced élite. Robinson is scarcely a 'social' poet in anything like a Marxian sense. What he deals with is an ironic principle that cuts through all of life. Some of his best poems, such as 'The Sheaves' and 'As It Looked Then,' trans-

* *Selected Letters of Edwin Arlington Robinson*, Macmillan, New York, 1940, p. 93.

late this juxtaposition of the irreconcilable—the beautiful and the fatal, the illusion of meaning and the meaninglessly antihuman—into the most objective natural imagery. But the sensibility behind the poem is never far from that of Miniver Cheevy or Aunt Imogen or the protagonist of 'The Poor Relation'; self-pity is resisted, yet not entirely overcome. The humor and humanity of 'Mr. Flood's Party' almost conceal this fact, which the half successful 'Clavering' (like too much else of Robinson's poetry) does not. Despite some magnificent lines this is a complaint against the nature of things rendered mawkish by a crude mysteriousness, a series of hints and winks and nods of the sort that sometimes accompany a drunk's maunderings. 'Clavering,' though in part its endless parallelisms make it read like one of Lewis Carroll's parodies, is a serious dissent from the usual view that we have only ourselves to blame for our failures. Very early in his career Robinson rejected this view in unmistakable terms: 'My philosophy does not swallow this teaching . . . that a life is what we make it.'

Behind much of Robinson's work, in both its more successful and its less successful aspects, lies a deeply American obsession with the theme of failure: failure of a career, failure of a social class or a society, failure of a needed meaning to sustain itself—and, finally, the inevitable failure of life to resist death's encroachment. Remembering Eliot's motifs of sexual and spiritual failure and Pound's savage complaints at a culture's failure to realize itself, we see how much those poets have in common with Robinson after all. 'When we think of America,' said D. H. Lawrence in his introduction to Edward Dahlberg's novel *Bottom Dogs*, 'and of her huge success, we never realize how many failures have gone, and still go to build up that success.' But the truth is, we do realize it enough to have a poetry saturated with the theme and embittered at the triumph of a countertheory of material success that belies the whole need for emotional and aesthetic fulfillment. Robinson tends to interpret the problem as a universal one, implicit in man:

> Rarely at once will nature give
> The power to be Flammonde and live.

But if we substitute for 'nature' some word signifying the crucial emphases of our civilization, we shall not go far astray. Robinson defines the predicament as a cultural one in his 'Cassandra':

> I heard one who said: 'Verily,
>   What word have I for children here?
> Your dollar is your only Word,
>   The wrath of it your only fear.
>
> 'You build its altars tall enough
>   To make you see, but you are blind;
> You cannot leave it long enough
>   To look before you or behind. . . .
>
> 'Your dollar, Dove and Eagle make
>   A Trinity that even you
> Rate higher than you rate yourselves;
>   It pays, it flatters, and it's new.
>
> 'And though your very flesh and blood
>   Be what your Eagle eats and drinks,
> You'll praise him for the best of birds,
>   Not knowing what the Eagle thinks. . . .'

If nature endows a man richly with humanity, the world will destroy him. In its greed for wealth and power (though self-deceivingly sworn to honor the Dove of peace and love also—an incredible pretension), it will break down with an impersonal cruelty whatever structures a disinterested concern has begun to erect. Thus, the concepts of success and failure become curiously reversed in the world of Robinson's poetry. Every 'successful' person is in a deeper sense a failure, as this world wags—and every failure, even Miniver Cheevy, is in some sense to be honored and cherished. There is a *mystique* of failure. We feel it in the beautiful compassion of the opening strophe of 'Captain Craig,' in the cold, sad brooding of the sestet in 'Many Are Called,' in the intense hatred of death that rises to break the Classical calm of 'For a Dead Lady' at the very end. It is man that breaks down; it is the antihuman that triumphs—and man betrays himself if he thinks the Triumph of Dollar and Eagle is his own. The sweet-souled calm of 'Isaac and Archibald' holds up an idealized past to us with delicate pity and laughter. It is a past recalled from the speaker's childhood—a remembrance of himself and of two old men. The two old men were *men:* absurd and pitiable in certain ways, no doubt, they yet lived with an earnest dignity, looked out for one another's interests, and read their own separate frailties into each other. They had no such spiritual perversity as Cassandra denounces. They respected the simple individuality of the boy, as he did theirs:

> Isaac and Archibald have gone their way
> To the silence of the loved and well-forgotten.
> I knew them, and I may have laughed at them;
> But there's a laughing that has honor in it. . . .

It is difficult to read 'Isaac and Archibald' without thinking of Robert Frost, who shares Robinson's rueful nostalgia for the past (and for the ever-dissolving present) as he does his elusive sententiousness and his way of coming against ultimate imponderables and turning from them with a shrug of bafflement that is all but a fatalistic contentment. The rural setting and detail of 'Isaac and Archibald' are a further reminder of Frost, though partly a fortuitous one; Robinson's characteristic *personae* are not farm dwellers, and he does not usually linger over the minutiae of scenes as he does here. There is an old-fashioned 'modernity,' too, that these poets share; they face certain brute realities with a shocked honesty, as in Robinson's 'John Evereldown' and Frost's 'The Subverted Flower' which have this in common despite their differences. Both speculate darkly on the life of woman, and both emerge often with the same elegiac sadness for the death of her beauty and innocence mixed with a harsher pity for the way life betrays her. Robinson in 'The Gift of God' and Frost in 'The Lovely Shall Be Choosers' are akin to Yeats in 'Among School Children' and Eliot in 'Portrait of a Lady' with their helpless notations of life's betrayals of womanly expectations and ideals, in love and in motherhood. Eliot, it is true, does not speak directly of motherhood in the 'Portrait' (his Lil in *The Waste Land* is another matter), and Yeats speaks of nuns as well as of mothers and 'lovers,' but the sense of where the pity lies is much the same in all.

Frost rises above Robinson partly in the greater specificity of his impressions of places and persons and experiences: 'Isaac and Archibald,' as I have suggested, brings us close to the world of Frost but is unusual for the older poet. The kind of specificity I mean is inseparable from the fabric of almost any Frost poem:

> These flowery waters and these watery flowers
> From snow that melted only yesterday.
>
> ('Spring Pools')

> I'm going out to clean the pasture spring;
> I'll only stop to rake the leaves away
> (And wait to watch the water clear, I may) . . .
>
> ('The Pasture')

> Out in the ploughed ground in the cold a digger,
> Among unearthed potatoes standing still,
> Was counting winter dinners, one a hill . . .
>
> ('The Investment')

This is the staple of Frost's reputation, of course, this lyrical and realistic repossession of the rural and the 'natural.' For most of his readers it has the charm of the completely exotic. Literate America is not, for the most part, to be found in 'the country,' and in general the world of modern poetry has been dominated by a metropolitan consciousness. Frost gives us a welcome release, puts us in touch with something 'purer,' something idyllic, which is also real. But beneath the surface appeal there lurks a further and terrifying implication. At his most powerful Frost is as staggered by 'the horror' as Eliot and approaches the hysterical edge of sensibility in a comparable way. The consciousness at work in his poetry is neither that of a plain New England farmer nor that of a Romantic rediscoverer of primitive delights. His is still the modern mind in search of its own meanings. The aim is comparable to that of the Georgians, among whom Frost first found kindred sensibilities and became certain of his true bearings. Only his work is richer than theirs in every way: it includes the nostalgic, it 'proves' the pastoral pleasures, it savors the contemplative calm the ancient poets praised, but it also seeks to encompass the dreadful and the neurasthenia-breeding aspects of man's existence as the modern consciousness feels them.

Nothing quite brings out this 'morbidity' of Frost so painfully as his poems centering on the characters of women. The wife's hysteria in 'Home-Burial' is a characteristic outlet for this poet's shocked sense of the helpless cruelty of things. Set against the husband's ordinariness—and *he* is not without feelings—it provides the decisive energy of the poem. The husband may be 'right,' but he is made to appear crude and obtuse, for the wife's voice carries the pain of a primal wound:

> If you had any feelings, you that dug
> With your own hand—how could you?—his little grave;
> I saw you from that very window there,
> Making the gravel leap and leap in air,
> Leap up, like that, like that, and land so lightly
> And roll back down the mound beside the hole. . . .

More than his women, Frost's men, with some exceptions, play the game according to the rules. They take pride in their workmanship, like the poor home-burier, and thereby can hold life's destructive terrors at bay. Perhaps in the confessional stanza of 'Two Tramps in Mud Time' the poet implies the same thing about himself as well as guilt for remaining aloof from public causes:

> Good blocks of wood it was I split,
> As large around as the chopping block;
> And every piece I squarely hit
> Fell splinterless as a cloven rock.
> The blows that a life of self-control
> Spares to strike for the common good
> That day, giving a loose to my soul,
> I spent on the unimportant wood. . . .

The women are more likely to be overborne by an ultimate emptiness or grossness or fear. In the speaker's own *persona*, or that of some other male figure, there is almost always some saving humor or sense of valued mystery or deliberate understatement such as we find in 'The Demiurge's Laugh,' 'Storm Fear,' 'An Old Man's Winter Night,' or 'Stopping by Woods.' Poems like 'The Hill Wife' and 'A Servant to Servants,' on the other hand, show the naked terror through women's eyes. At its most intense 'The Witch of Coös,' despite its wild folk-humor, does the same thing as 'The Subverted Flower' does despite its ambiguities. The latter poem gives the character of a young girl a surprising turn; she is shown as mean and narrow—so that we are almost diverted from the glimpse of sexual squalor she has shared with her shamefaced would-be lover. The abyss yawns in this poem as in perhaps no other by Frost. Its mixture of disgust and fear is like the death-horror of the first stanza of 'Design' in its portrayal of the perversion of life values implicit in the very structure of existence. That feeling in 'Design' derives from the awful silence, the grotesque acrobatics of the little circus act Frost says he has come upon:

> I found a dimpled spider, fat and white,
> On a white heal-all, holding up a moth
> Like a white piece of rigid satin cloth—
> Assorted characters of death and blight
> Mixed ready to begin a morning right,
> Like the ingredients of a witches' broth—
> A snow-drop spider, a flower like a froth,
> And dead wings carried like a paper kite.

In the sestet of this sonnet, Frost lapses into a tiresomely 'profound' questioning reminiscent of Hardy and Robinson—its point being to find in this unique configuration (including the whiteness of the usually 'blue and innocent heal-all') some purpose:

> What but design of darkness to appall?—
> If design govern in a thing so small.

What oft was thought, and oft as well expressed. Despite his great virtues, you cannot read a great deal of Frost without this effect of the *déjà vu*. Sententiousness and a relative absence of formal daring are his main defects. Even in his finest work, the conventionality of rhythm and rhyme contributes a certain tedium, temporarily relegated to a dim corner of the reader's consciousness. But he does give richly of detail about nature and life as he has known it:

> Ten million silver lizards out of snow!

He has absorbed one kind of regional experience, and its voices and shadings, as well as any poet has done; he has given us its comic notes, its dramatic crises, its familiar imponderables, its vivid surfaces. But also, he echoes its dreary 'wisdom' and overdependence on a less and less meaningful past. Thought and form in Frost seem therefore weaker, at once more smug and more timid, than they might be.

2. WILLIAMS AND STEVENS

> *so much depends*
> *upon*
>
> *a red wheel*
> *barrow*
>
> *glazed with rain*
> *water*
>
> *beside the white*
> *chickens*
>
> ('The Red Wheelbarrow')

Just that keener and more adventurous insight into the aesthetic of existence that we miss in Frost is found in William Carlos Williams. He is remarkably alert to the subtler life of the senses: how it feels to be a growing thing of any kind, or to come into birth; how the freshness of the morning or the feel of a particular moment in a particular season impresses itself upon us; what impact the people glimpsed in myriad transitory situations have upon us at the moment of the event. This alertness is intimately related to his faith in the power of art to reveal the meaning of experienced reality and even as he says, 'to right all wrongs.' The poem 'The Red Wheelbarrow,' just quoted, states and embodies the principle perfectly. In each little stanza the opening line, with its two stressed syllables, prepares for a flight of thought and imagination, while the second weighs the tiny unit down with a turn of idiom or the name of a familiar concrete object. The poem's design is a striving for value, for significant realization, against the resistant drag of the merely habitual. Everything 'depends' on the way we see color, shape, relationships; the scope of our understanding of life depends on it, the freedom of our consciousness, the way we transcend limitations and communicate with one another as human beings. The artist's task of 'lifting to the imagination those things which lie under the direct scrutiny of the sense,' Williams once wrote, is at once a 'virtual impossibility' and a task whose very difficulty 'sets a value upon all works of art and makes them a necessity.' *

The ability to project such universals out of the near-at-hand has made it possible for Williams to immerse himself in the local and immediate without loss of larger perspectives. To be Dr. Williams of Rutherford, New Jersey, has enabled him, in a way his friend Pound never could, to learn the landscape of American experience. Both share the driving, almost evangelical conviction that man's best possibilities, brutally subverted and driven underground, must be brought to the surface through a freeing of pagan impulses, a 'revelation' which is also a moral and cultural revolution. Both attack the main directions of American society, both radically reject modern economic practice, and both call for the violent breakthrough of human creativity. Williams's inclusion of a social-credit propaganda leaflet in the poem *Paterson* and his portrait in *In the American Grain* † of Poe striving desperately to

* Williams, *Selected Essays*, p. 11.

† William Carlos Williams, *In the American Grain*, New Directions, New York, 1925, pp. 216-23.

originate a truly American poetry amid the corruption and imitativeness of the national drift are two obvious examples of his closeness to Pound in general attitude. But while his large frame of values has resembled Pound's, his specific materials and the emphases they imply are very different. Among these materials are what he calls the 'secret gardens of the self' to which he has been admitted as a physician—'deaths and births,' the 'tormented battles between daughter and diabolic mother, shattered by a gone brain,' the 'gulfs and grottos' of the life of 'the poor, defeated body.' * Among them too are the potentialities and the 'poison' Williams finds in native American life and, set against every kind of disillusioning impact, an ultimate deification of the sensual and the earthy:

> The world is cleanly, polished and well
>   made but heavenly man
> is filthy with his flesh and corrupt. . . .

The most striking surface characteristic of Williams's writing, moreover, is its extraordinary empathic responsiveness, noted by many critics, to trees and flowers especially. In this respect he seems more akin to Lawrence than to Pound. Sometimes, in 'The Botticellian Trees,' for instance, he makes everything in nature seem the work of some delicately erotic artist, some Botticellian demiurge. And sometimes the terror of reality chills the skin of a poem, and we have a realization such as that in 'Spring and All' of the oneness of all initiation into life:

> Lifeless in appearance, sluggish
> dazed spring approaches—
>
> They enter the new world naked,
> cold, uncertain of all
> save that they enter. All about them
> the cold, familiar wind—

* *The Autobiography of William Carlos Williams*, Random House, New York, 1951, pp. 288-9.

> Now the grass, tomorrow
> the stiff curl of wild carrot leaf
> One by one objects are defined—
> It quickens: clarity, outline of leaf
>
> But now the stark dignity of
> entrance—Still, the profound change
> has come upon them: rooted, they
> grip down and begin to awaken

Poetry like this, in which the writer temporarily holds his own personality in abeyance and then returns to it with what he has taken from the world outside, is reality subjectively encompassed. Perception has not been falsified. Thus, the figure 'dazed spring' is more than a convenient personification. It has been derived inductively from the whole set of the poem, its verbal shaping-up of the experience of birth. It is the essential link between the objective description of a late-winter landscape and the passionately conceived subjective imagery of 'profound change' and 'awakening.'

This empathy carries us back to Williams's most precious attribute, his driving conviction (which he shares with Lawrence) of the *importance* of each individual life and of the individual moment within it. These lives and moments are so precious that one cannot ignore any truth about them. As early as 'The Wanderer,' a poem of his twenties, Williams wrote that his Muse compelled him to come to terms with his part of the real world—the industrial city Paterson with its fouled rivers, its scarred and patchy surrounding countryside, and its people,

> Grasping, fox-snouted, thick-lipped,
> Sagging breasts and protruding stomachs,
> Rasping voices, filthy habits with the hands.

The Muse held him to his task. At the age of seventy, in 'To a Dog Injured in the Streets,' he wrote:

It is myself,
          not the poor beast lying there
                    yelping with pain
that brings me to myself with a start—
          as at the explosion
                    of a bomb, a bomb that has laid
all the world waste. . . .

Here is indeed a sensibility like Lawrence's. One thinks of his close-ups of ordinary folk which strengthen our awareness of the individual flame behind the common mask of anonymity, or of his anguished description of the carnage winter wreaks on the birds, or of his feeling for the blazing life of flowers. Motifs of symbolic death and rebirth are important in both poets, and in parallel form; Lawrence's 'New Heaven and Earth' might serve as a credo for Williams. Williams does part company with him in his un-faltering confidence in art's redeeming and healing powers, al-though the poets' difference on this score can easily be exagger-ated. The salvation implied in Williams's localist program from 'The Wanderer' on is, despite its compassion and anger, primarily an aesthetic one, not a purely religious, mystical, or social one. The poet, seeking to awaken the people to their own rich poten-tialities, purifies himself by taking into his own being the whole degradation of modern traditional life bereft of all traditional graces. The waters of the 'filthy Passaic' enter his heart and soul and transform him. But it is a transformation like that of which Yeats writes in 'The Circus Animals' Desertion' when he speaks of the 'foul rag-and-bone shop of the heart' out of whose wares are ultimately created the 'masterful images' of 'pure mind.'

This sacramental-aesthetic theme enters most of Williams's work. Take the three pieces in *Al Que Quiere* each of which he entitles 'Pastoral.' In them he applies the pastoral tradition, with its elegant connotations, to the vileness and poverty all around, transforming what he sees through the saving humor sometimes found in that tradition and through 'appreciation' of the design and colors, the brawling earthiness, the majesty, the dream of an opposite state of pure beauty evoked by the various sights and sounds of which he treats. Even in poems that seem little more than sharp, objective snapshots—poems such as 'To a Poor Old Woman,' 'Proletarian Portrait,' and 'The Girl'—there is this motif of transformation. No speculation, but mostly clean, economical, dramatic presentation, with only the *design* suggesting anything beyond the picture itself. But the design is there: the refrain 'They taste good to her' in the first; and the completed actions, in all their necessary simplicity, and the inclusiveness and point of movement in the second and third. Each picture reaches a certain point of rest or minimal satisfaction, and each implies by its vibrancy and animation the unlimited possibilities of life.

Even in a darker mood, Williams answers along the same lines: poetic repossession of the intractable.

> The justice of poverty
>   its shame its dirt
> are one with the meanness
>   of love
>
> ('The Descent of Winter')

At its bleakest, as in 'The Raper from Passenack,' the poetry lets the human condition speak for itself. Some of Williams's most effective work is of this sort, with the center of the stage held by a single character—anguished, humble, vituperative, or whatever. As a doctor he has come to know a great variety of people intimately: Polish immigrants, Negro laborers, and many others outside the range of acquaintance of most American literati. He is much concerned with the problem of finding a way to express these people—a way for the poet to communicate, a means for them to express themselves. This concern, and the despair he has felt in trying to solve this problem, is the chief motivation behind his *In the American Grain*, which attempts to sum up the materials of an informing American myth. This book, one of the truly germinative American prose works of this century, is a perfect complement to his fiction and to those of his poems (such as 'To Elsie') which provide close-ups of the splintering violences and innumerable undeveloped sources of strength in our culture.

His greatest poetic effort to deal with this problem and predicament is the *Paterson* sequence. Here Williams chose to base his structure on the movement of the 'filthy Passaic'—that river whose native symbolism had intrigued him from the start of his career. He sought an open structure like that of Pound's *Cantos*. 'I decided there would be four books following the course of the river whose life seemed more and more to resemble my own. . . . above the Falls, the catastrophe of the Falls itself . . . below the Falls and the entrance at the end to the great sea.' At the beginning the city of Paterson (an epitome of the American scene, with the poet, sometimes called 'Dr. Paterson,' its unrecognized prophet) is seen as a sleeping stone-giant. The people, automatons to whom he *might* give more vital existence, walk 'unroused' and 'incommunicado.' They do not know the organic relatedness that gives unconscious meaning to every moment in more primitive lives. Grossness, destructiveness, daredeviltry, and divorce are the outward signs of our condition. Everywhere the sexual life is thwarted and distorted; we are the victims of a sexual confusion inseparable from our cultural confusions. Williams shares this theme with Lawrence but gives it a peculiarly American emphasis.

We see the difficulties most compellingly in Part II, whose second section begins with the word 'Blocked.' The poet speaks of 'an orchestral dullness'; the 'massive church,' the mulcters of cash, the political interests, all interfere with creative invention and self-awareness. The closest we come to beauty is the kind of free-wheeling evangelism heard from a vigorous speaker in the park, an irresponsibly sharpshooting, half deadly accurate, half charlatan-ish operator. The pessimistic prayer, growing out of a bitter love of America, and the almost unrelieved negations of one of its sections make Part II the most intense and concentrated writing of the book. A prose correlative runs through the poem, in the form of letters, news items, and so on, providing both a continual 'outside' commentary and the raw material out of which the high poetic moments rise. One voice in this prose correlative is felt particularly, that of a woman writer whose loneliness, dissatisfaction with herself, and inability to develop her talents properly are seen as aspects of the national indifference to the ideals of civilization.

Her reproaches to the poet—the cry of failure reaching through to him, irrevocable and tragic, from the sea of desolation (that sea pictured so brilliantly and painfully in 'The Yachts')—are part of the burden of the creative spirit in America. The block to communication between man and man, man and woman, man and his land, is the result of centuries of violation of the human need for *concern:* the rape of the land which *In the American Grain* pictures, betrayal of the Indian, power monomania, brutalization of the frontier woman, and civil war.

The first four books of *Paterson,* completed in 1951, were intended to be the whole work. They constitute a devastating comment on every phase of our life, though one relieved by momentary oases of perceived or imagined beauty, and they 'end' modestly and familiarly, as they began, in the midst of things, in the midst of predicament. In the *fifth* book, however, published in 1958, Dr. Williams reopens the issues; or rather, he refocuses them. The transcendent, saving power of the aesthetic imagination is played like a brilliant light over old archetypal oppositions and symbols— sexuality versus chaste love, reality versus the ideal, the Virgin and the Whore, the hunted-down unicorn pictured, in a famous tapestry now at The Cloisters in New York, amid a setting both natural and courtly. Such themes and images do the refocusing, placing the poet's perspectives in sharper relation than before to the bedeviled perspectives of the culture at large; they represent a mellowing without loss of energy—*Paterson's* 'roar of the present' removed just enough to give the poem another and much needed dimension, that of the 'measured dance':

> Yo ho! ta ho!

> We know nothing and can know nothing
> > but
> the dance, to dance to a measure
> contrapuntally,
> > Satyrically, the tragic foot.

As various critics have noted, the first two parts of the sequence hold together in a way that is not quite true of the whole work.

However, the design is that of search, a continuity, rather than of a self-contained, watertight structure. It would have been easy to end with Part II ('catastrophe'), but Williams chose to reopen the poem, to stick with his own understanding of the nature of things, pragmatically and stubbornly hopeful in the midst of tragic confusion: 'Say it, no ideas but in things.' So long as the poet does not accept the 'failure of speech' in modern civilization as final, so long can he insist on the reality of the possible.

This aesthetically reinforced pragmatic faith Williams shares with Wallace Stevens. The relation of the two poets can be seen in a delightful circumstance: Stevens's writing of the poem 'Nuances of a Theme by Williams,' based on the latter's early four-line 'El Hombre.' Williams had written:

> It's a strange courage
> you give me ancient star:
>
> Shine alone in the sunrise
> toward which you lend no part!

Despite the brighter glow of the sunrise, the morning star remains uniquely apart. It does not yield to the greater cause, and therefore encourages the poet to go his way also. But, as in 'The Red Wheelbarrow,' the inner dynamics of the little poem make for its real life. Very quickly a double relationship between poet and star and between star and sun emerges. In the climactic apostrophe to the star a single aspect of the scene fixes our attention; the poem seems to reorganize itself around this. The preceding motifs are now subordinated to the final center—the star's faint yet independent morning light. Looking back over the four lines, we can see that the strangeness of the courage which the poet says the star gives him derives from the cold, lonely impersonality of this central image. It has no intrinsic meaning for mankind; for anything the external universe may show to the contrary, men must learn to be bravely themselves without hope, to create their own meanings.

That is, of course, authentic Williams. Stevens's 'Nuances' begins by quoting 'El Hombre' in full; then it begins to embroider on it:

I

Shine alone, shine nakedly, shine like bronze,
that reflects neither my face nor any inner part
of my being, shine like fire, that mirrors nothing.

II

Lend no part to any humanity that suffuses
you in its own light.
Be not chimera of morning,
Half-man, half-star.
Be not an intelligence,
Like a widow's bird
Or an old horse.

The major differences are Stevens's cultivation of stylistic elegance and wit for their own sake and his greater emphasis on the autonomy of art. Where Williams found an instructive analogy between the 'independence' of the star and that which he must cultivate as a man, Stevens would go further. He reminds us that the star 'mirrors nothing,' after all. Thus, Stevens stresses the self-containment of the poetic symbol more than Williams does; and his simile 'shine like bronze' suggests the desirability of cultivating a brilliant surface for its own sake. Neither star nor poem should be considered only half itself and half an 'intelligence.' The poem is not a means of consolation ('a widow's bird') primarily, nor is it an emblem of human pathos or of life's burdens ('an old horse'). Stevens, like Yeats, seeks a transcendent impersonality through giving a certain prior importance to form.

One is likely to forget Stevens's passionate side in pondering his pure designs of color and sound, his dandyisms and buffooneries, the way he has of teasing his own characters, and his richly elaborated subtleties. 'Earthy Anecdote,' first poem in his first volume, is a simple example of joyous verbal geometrics. The 'bucks' go 'clattering over Oklahoma.' They clatter right, they clatter left, but always blocking their way is the 'bristling' and 'leaping' of the 'firecat.' It is a magnificent, self-limiting, animated design, with a comic pathos that suggests a world of frustration without emphasizing anything but the design itself. The bucks clatter 'in a swift, circular line' this way or that; the firecat leaps before them. It is movement and limit, will and fate, fear and power, and, less portentously, herbivore and carnivore. Something grim, though, is hidden in the brief stanza that brings the stylized fireworks to an end:

> Later, the firecat closed his bright eyes
> And slept.

'The Plot Against the Giant' presents three girls, each of whom in turn tells how she will conquer the giant. The first will 'check' him with the 'civilest odors' of 'geraniums and unsmelled flowers.' The second will 'abash' him with delicate colors 'small as fish eggs.' The third will 'undo' him with sound and speech; she will run before him with a 'curious puffing' and will whisper 'heavenly labials in world of gutturals.' The girls want to capture, not kill, the 'yokel' giant as he comes 'maundering' and 'whetting his hacker.' He is the crude, sexual life-force in itself—unlicked nature. And the weapons of civilization are aesthetic. As in 'Earthy Anecdote,' the chaotic and the cruel are to be conquered rather than eliminated—they *cannot* be eliminated, though the world of the senses (which is their world also) can be exploited in such a way as to impose a controlling order on itself.

The rationale of Stevens's method and overriding thought throughout his work is presented in the beautifully written essay 'The Realm of Resemblances,' first published in 1947. Poetry is built, says Stevens, around reality as its 'central reference,' and is related to reality by 'the resemblance between things.'

> Take, for example, a beach extending as far as the eye can reach bordered on the one hand, by trees and, on the other, by the sea. The sky is cloudless and the sun is red. In what sense do the objects in this scene resemble each other? There is enough green in the sea to relate it to the palms. There is enough of the sky reflected in the water to create a resemblance, in some sense, between them. The

sand is yellow between the green and the blue. In short, the light alone creates a unity not only in the recedings of distance, where differences become invisible, but also in the contacts of closer sight. So, too, sufficiently generalized, each man resembles all other men, each woman resembles all other women, this year resembles last year. The beginning of time will, no doubt, resemble the end of time. One world is said to resemble another.*

Resemblance, then, binds together all the various aspects of nature; indeed, all relationships really come under the heading of 'resemblances,' since, by a simple extension, we can say even opposites resemble one another in being contrasting aspects of whatever principle puts them into opposition. Poetry, too, the essay argues, binds parts of reality together, but through metaphor— a general term for images of any kind in Stevens's vocabulary. Metaphor is the 'creation of resemblances' by the imagination, a process in which all things undergo transformation. 'In metaphor . . . the resemblance may be, first, between two or more parts of reality; second, between something real and something imagined . . . as, for example, between music and whatever may be evoked by it; and third, between two imagined things as when we say that God is good. . . .' Both nature and the imagination are unceasingly creative, but the former is the controlling element. The limits of art are determined by the ultimate range of resemblances in nature.

Thus, Stevens affirms an interdependence of art and nature which, on the surface, his poetic practice would often seem to deny. The whole aestheticist movement, as we saw in our review of Yeats, is based on a similar paradox. The principle of the autonomy of art frees the artist from tendentiousness and vulgar moralizing, from making his work a 'widow's bird' or an 'old horse.' A cut below the surface, however, are the whole world's concerns, though at an 'aesthetic distance.' Something like a pleasure principle connects the 'independent' surface and the

* Wallace Stevens, *The Necessary Angel*, Knopf, New York, 1951, pp. 71-2.

'involved' depths. It is a kind of 'Narcissism,' says the poet, the ego's loving search for images of itself. But turn the thought another way and the poem becomes a search by the unrealized, still 'inhuman,' self for a 'human self.' In so attempting to define an ideal he grapples, as he says, with a variety of 'Platonism.' Within an exploratory and pragmatic frame of thought his mind plays over the paradoxical and interpenetrating relations of nature and art. His method gives him freedom to indulge in that 'satisfying of the desire for resemblances,' natural, he believes, to man.

The ambiguous but compelling poem 'Anecdote of the Jar' offers an excellent example. 'I placed a jar in Tennessee,' the poet informs us grandly; he 'placed' it high on a hill, and the 'slovenly wilderness' found some order for the first time. The jar, 'tall and of a port in air,' dominated the landscape, 'no longer wild.' That is the burden of the first two stanzas. The third, however, after telling us the jar 'took dominion everywhere,' jolts us in a terse sentence, the shortest of the poem: 'The jar was gray and bare.' And then the two closing lines follow with another abrupt, deliberately awkward shift:

> It did not give of bird or bush,
> Like nothing else in Tennessee.

These knotty negatives seem to make the jar something less than the wilderness after all. Everything else in Tennessee is of nature's world and is alive in that fact; not so the jar, which is but artifact. This outcome is implied in the first stanza in two ways not especially noticeable on first reading. For one thing, there is the whimsical, self-mocking tone of the opening line. 'I placed a jar in Tennessee' is oddly pretentious; and besides, it sounds like the beginning of a humorous folk-song rather than of a poem of intellectual import. Secondly, each of the two sentences in the first stanza ends on the word 'hill,' calling attention to the jar's immediate location rather than to the jar itself. The unconventional structure reinforces this emphasis: the repetition of 'hill' gives the poem its only identical rhyme, and the short fourth line, 'Surround that hill,' breaks the four-stress pattern sharply. If the jar, by contrast and example, imposes an order on the wilderness, it nevertheless depends on the wilderness for a context and a source of possible meanings. So the two perspectives, that of a world given formal pattern through man's imagination and that of the blankness of art not informed by the living proliferations of nature, are advanced side by side, the latter gaining precedence by the poem's end.

Stevens is an intriguing poet. Indeed, his work has so much surface charm and elegance that far too many readers have dismissed him as precious,* not perceiving the highly relevant and highly serious mind that is present. 'Peter Quince at the Clavier,' for instance, provides four kinds of melodic effect—the erotically colored octosyllabic triplets of Part I; the even more sensuously erotic, wavering effects of the varied, but usually shorter, lines and irregular stanzas of Part II; the tripping couplets, speeded up by anapests, which give Part III its flutteringly feminine quality; the philosophical cast of Part IV, with its longer lines and calmer effects. These effects alone would give the poem great appeal since they are woven together ingeniously, each section having certain echoings of the others, all building up in a truly musical sequence. The title itself suggests the author's fanciful love of sound; and also, it suggests that the speaker sees himself as an oafish fellow (like the Quince of A *Midsummer Night's Dream*) who, most unsuitably, is trying his hand at some delicate keyboard instrument. That is the first hint of an irony cutting below the level of whimsey and lovely sound.

The thought of the poem progresses within the atmosphere of these effects. The speaker appears first as a lover who, as he sits playing at the keyboard, is thinking romantically of a woman he loves. He compares his desire for her with the effect of music on the spirit. That effect, and indeed 'feeling' generally, is what music really is, and thus his desire *is* music. All this is in the grand Romantic tradition, and if there is an erotic strain in what is being said, it is of an 'approved' variety; no lady would be offended—quite the contrary—to have these observations directed at her. Without warning, though, the speaker shifts to a comparison of

* On the puritanical premise, apparently, that too much richness is bad for the spirit whether it is ultimately serious or not.

his 'music' with that of the elders in the apocryphal Biblical tale who tried to rape Susanna. Most of the poem—the remaining stanzas of Part I, all of II and III, and a good portion of IV—is an elaboration of that comparison. Watching Susanna bathe, those 'red-eyed elders' felt their 'thin blood' pulsing 'pizzicati of Hosanna.' Susanna, in her sensual self-awareness in the water where she lay and then after her bathing, made and felt a sighing music of her own before the 'cymbal crashed' and the 'roaring horns' were upon her. Her Byzantine maid-servants rush in and out of the scene, simpering and shocked and twittering, 'with a noise like tambourines.' All desires, all the permutations of sense and sex, are compounded of a complex of music; the speaker has cut himself down to the level of those nasty old lechers, but simultaneously he has raised them to the level of all who are touched by beauty. He shares their lust, they his 'feeling.'

The final section draws the conclusion that true immortality is to be found only in recurrent physical and emotional sensations:

> Beauty is momentary in the mind—
> The fitful tracing of a portal;
> But in the flesh it is immortal.

Thus Stevens reverses the usual Platonic formula. Individual bodies die, but there are always new bodies, with new beauty; 'so evenings die, in their green going,' and gardens, and maidens. But all of these are renewed endlessly in nature—that is the only immortality we shall know. The key to it, therefore, lies just in that realm shared by romantic lover and bawdy elder. The poem ends speaking of a 'constant sacrament of praise' evoked by beauty and its memory. The religious connotations of 'sacrament' recall Stevens's 'Sunday Morning,' in which Christian assumptions and attitudes are set against those of a secularism based on intensity of experience and a sort of as-if religion of the sun and nature:

> the heavenly fellowship
> Of men that perish and of summer morn.

Both poems tinge with sadness their proposals for joyous self-fulfilment within the limits of what life has to offer. They face

common mortality half in dismay, half stoically; and this divided
emotion is what gives impulse to their hedonistic 'program.' It
is because of our turbulent awareness of mortality that we dream
and create so intensely—projecting at last a vision of its opposite
in which our most poignant griefs are healed:

> Death is the mother of beauty, mystical,
> Within whose burning bosom we devise
> Our earthly mothers waiting, sleeplessly.
>
> ('Sunday Morning')

Stevens broods much more darkly over this theme in other
poems. 'Thirteen Ways of Looking at a Blackbird,' for instance,
moves progressively through its thirteen haiku-like stanzas toward
a terrified sense of death's inexorability. Each stanza can be read as
a separate poem, a clever or penetrating turn on the theme of
'blackbird.' But they are woven together along two main strands
of thought. One strand has to do with the blackbird as a symbol
of the inseparability of life and death in nature. Thus the first
stanza contrasts its tiny but lively eye with the massive lifelessness
of 'twenty snowy mountains.' In the third stanza, though, we
see the bird as 'a small part of the pantomime' of autumnal death.
Then, in the next stanza, we see it in still a third way: 'A man and
a woman/ Are one,' but add the blackbird and the scene is still
unified. What does the blackbird add to the relation of man
and woman that yet is integrally absorbed into the picture? Doubtless the sense of common mortality again, half the assertive
thrust of life against death, half the acceptance of the universal
lot. Into our awareness of the cycle of sexual intercourse, birth,
growth, and family life, the truth of death insinuates itself inevitably.

The second strand of thought is the poet's attitude toward his
symbol. In stanza II he introduces himself with a witty reference
to its triple significance:

> I was of three minds,
> Like a tree
> In which there are three blackbirds.

In stanza V he adds another dimension when he says he doesn't know whether he prefers contemplating his symbol directly or thinking of its ramifications—whether he prefers the 'beauty of inflections' or that of 'innuendoes.' Whichever it is, he says later in the poem, he knows that the blackbird is inextricably a part of his art and his knowledge. The exquisite tenth stanza states the issue with climactic poignancy:

> At the sight of blackbirds
> Flying in a green light,
> Even the bawds of euphony
> Would cry out sharply.

The juxtaposition of tragic knowledge and the keen relish for life makes even poets, professional traffickers in voluptuous sounds, 'cry out' in pain and excitement.

It is the development of the blackbird symbol itself, however, that dominates the organization of the poem. The sixth stanza plunges the poem into a mood of dread, its 'indecipherable cause' the shadow of the blackbird seen through ice ('barbaric glass') on the window. The eleventh stanza, with its picture of a man 'pierced' by fear because he mistook the 'shadow of his equipage' for blackbirds, heightens this feeling of dread.* At the end of the poem, we see a picture of complete darkness and cold and endless snow. Now the blackbird sits in 'the cedar-limbs' like Satan in *Paradise Lost* when he flew up on the Tree of Life in Eden and 'like a cormorant,' huge and evil, brooded over the whole doomed scene.

'The Emperor of Ice-Cream,' one of Stevens's bitterest poems, is an act of mordant revulsion against the brutality of death and the self-deceptions of the ritualizing, aestheticizing mind itself. A loved woman has died, and the poem calls ironically for an appropriate celebration. Let the life-force, or God, the muscular 'roller of big cigars,' continue to whip up human passions—'in

* The man, incidentally, was riding in Connecticut (Stevens's state) 'in a glass coach'—showing that even a New Englander is vulnerable! The poet indulges in this regional teasing in stanza VII also, when he appeals to the 'thin men' of Haddam, Connecticut, to stop dreaming of a golden afterlight and observe the blackbird walking 'around the feet/ of the women about you.'

kitchen cups concupiscent curds.' Let 'the wenches dawdle' in
their usual provocative clothes. Let boys bring flowers 'in last
month's newspapers.' All the values that Stevens usually celebrates
he here reduces to staleness and paltriness. 'Let be be the finale of
seem,' he cries. For once let the supposedly transforming imagination be still, and let us take things for what we so bleakly see they
are. There is no order except the one so childishly and self-in-
dulgently imposed by the imagination—an 'ice-cream' of the mind,
whipped up by that 'muscular' deity who does not exist, 'the
emperor of ice-cream.' All this in the eight lines of the first stanza.
Then the horror and shock are expressed more directly; the concluding second stanza speaks of the dead woman outright. Let her
face be covered with a sheet on which she 'embroidered fantails
once.' Still, neither art nor piety can deceive, and

> If her horny feet protrude, they come
> To show how cold she is, and dumb.
> Let the lamp affix its beam.
> The only emperor is the emperor of ice-cream.

It will be clear that Stevens, exquisitely though he savors the
possibilities of sound and language even in a poem as serious and
passionate as this, is a speculative poet. And what he speculates
about is the subject matter of 'The Realm of Resemblances,' the
reciprocities of reality and imagination and the relationship of
aesthetic to other forms of imagination. Religious beliefs and moral
systems he is likely, as in 'A High-Toned Old Christian Woman,'
to relegate to the level of an inferior imaginative expression—inferior because they are hardened and limited forms in a universe of
infinite possibilities. Their 'tink and tank and tunk-a-tunk-tunk'
are but one tune among many, while poetry, which follows all implications through, 'is the supreme fiction, madame.' Yet poetry, all
imagination, must yield—as 'The Emperor of Ice-Cream' shows—
to a disciplining reality. Follow through the thought of one of
Stevens's more complex structures, for example 'Sea Surface Full
of Clouds,' and this ultimate discipline generally comes into play.
'Sea Surface,' in fact, deals with this question exactly. It has five
movements, and contemplates the same scene in each of them.

In the first we see the simple workings of imagination, evolving 'sea-blooms from the clouds,' making a calm morning seascape a vision of 'rosy chocolate' and 'gilt umbrellas' and 'paradisal green.' In the second, it is seen as a sinister vision of false calm until, at the very end of the movement, 'blue heaven' spreads a brilliance that dispels 'the macabre of the water-glooms.' Then we see it as primal nature transformed by human imagination—made 'porcelain,' 'polished'—and by the sexual energy that informs it. The fourth returns us to the deeper sources of power in the objective world, capable at any time of negating the transformations envisioned in Part III. And the final movement pushes this insight relentlessly, showing how, when imagination seems to become mere triviality and drollery, external reality itself brings 'fresh transfigurings of freshest blue.' Throughout the poem, of course, the actual seascape has limited the terms in which the imagination could work on it, and the imagination itself has been shown to have sources in the physical reality of the observer.

This sort of aesthetic metaphysics is characteristic of Stevens's poetry from beginning to end. He has dealt with many matters that have troubled the minds of thoughtful and sensitive people not only in our century but often in the past: poverty, war, social change, desire, old age, familial memories, religious belief. As he grew older, his work took on a slower-paced contemplative cast, though it never lost its elegant curlicues and laughters, its elusive, subtle emphases. He envisioned an as-if, pragmatic god, meditating on 'the full of fortune and the full of fate,' a God of perhaps and probability. And yet the aesthetic remained uppermost, and he took pains to embody his speculations in such melody and color— the playing of the 'man with the blue guitar,' the woman singing in 'The Idea of Order at Key West'—that he will always be the great Dandy of American letters. What is constantly surprising is how much he is, at the same time, a poet of power too.

3. MacDiarmid and Muir

The great surge of 'modern' poetry in the English language in the second and third decades of this century was, except for Yeats, and Eliot since his transference of citizenship to England, and Lawrence largely American in its most forceful and influential aspects. Housman, Kipling, Æ, Monro, Sassoon, Stephens, Aldington, De la Mare, Graves, the Sitwells—these names have loomed large at one time and have their places; a few have a distinguished place indeed. But the main drift has passed these writers by. It was only in the 'thirties, with the coming of Auden and the new poetry of the Left, that British verse once again came to the fore as a body of new and exploratory work. Of the older British generation, Hugh MacDiarmid and Edwin Muir have the most staying power although individual poems by Herbert Read have extraordinary interest also.

MacDiarmid is probably the least known of poets in our language who might conceivably be called 'great.' When I say 'our language,' I must correct myself at once. His finest work is in Scots, and to this fact is due his relative obscurity. He at first seems a very special kind of acquired taste, writing as he does in a half-foreign tongue that requires a sympathetic ear and, often, a glossary to be understood.

> O wha's the bride that cairries the bunch
> O' thistles blinterin' white?
> Her cuckold bridegroom little dreids
> What he sall ken this nicht.
>
> For closer than gudeman can come
> And closer to'r than hersel,
> Wha didna need her maidenheid
> Has wrocht his purpose fell.
>
> O wha's been here afore me, lass,
> And hoo did he get in?
> —*A man that deed or I was born*
> *This evil thing has din.*
>
> And left, as it were on a corpse,
> Your maidenheid to me?
> —*Nae lass, gudeman, sin Time began*
> *'S hed ony mair to gie. . . .*

MacDiarmid in this poem ('O wha's been here afore me, lass') does a quietly extraordinary thing. He has written a modern poem which repossesses not only the diction and rhythm of the medieval folk-ballad, but also its implicit mentality—in this instance, its thrilled awe and terror of the supernatural. It is difficult to think of more than two or three other 'literary' ballads that approach this achievement. A poem like 'The Rime of the Ancient Mariner' uses many folk-elements, but makes of them an elaborate embroidery with much sophisticated overlay. MacDiarmid's poem, it is true, is a sophistication also; without really violating the native simplicity and 'rudeness' of the form, he has buried intellectual sharpness and paradox within the demonic mystery and, as part of this effect, has given us a more suggestive imagery than we ordinarily find in the folk-ballad.

> But I can gie ye kindness, lad,
> And a pair o willin hands,
> And ye sall hae my briests like stars,
> My limbs like willow wands.
>
> And on my lips ye'll heed nae mair,
> And in my hair forget,
> The seed o a' the men that in
> My virgin womb hae met. . . .

What is the 'significance' of a poem of this sort? An instantaneous linking of past and present, I think, one mercifully free of ratiocinative expansiveness or of proliferating juxtapositions. It is not a mere exercise but a rediscovery; and a rediscovery, not of a superstitious dread of the unknown but of the terrible mystery to which such dread makes abject obeisance. MacDiarmid establishes (not without wit) the 'traditional' sense of terror, then overbalances it by the equally awesome yet real consolations offered by the bride. Contemplation of the poem inevitably summons up the story of the Virgin Mary, though there are important differences (for instance, the allusion to 'a' the men' in the next-to-last line) and though the woman calls that strange ravishment of her by one 'wha didna need her maidenheid' an 'evil thing.' But with all this the simplicities, melodic beauty, and the elemental immediacies of the poem are not dissipated. They are in fact reinforced through this subtle twentieth-century recasting of the spiritual mold which gave them their original powerful character.

Among living English dialects it is a peculiarity of Scots that, while vigorous and full of homely and racy and humorous idiom, it also has the richness and dignity of a formal literary and even scholarly tradition. MacDiarmid is sometimes called the modern Burns, but the line out of which he works goes back to the Scottish Chaucerians and even further back. His 'Love' sounds like Burns but is sharper and harder, as informed by the earthiness of folk-speech yet more rapid in its turns, passionate without sentimentality:

> A luvin wumman is a licht
> That shows a man his waefu' plicht,
> Bleezin steady on ilka bane,
> Wrigglin sinnen and twinin vein,
> Or fleerin quick and gane again. . . .

His 'Harry Semen' moves far out beyond the elusive simplicities of these poems, which hint at the sexual mysteries of life as the clue to its meaning. Here MacDiarmid, like Yeats and Pound, creates a symbolic center of attention transcending both the form he employs and the frame of mind peculiar to this one poem. His intellectually concentrated yet beautifully lyrical Scots seems entirely conversational and spontaneous despite its rich density of thought:

> Hoo mony shades o white gaed curvin owre
> To yon blae centre o her belly's flower?
> Milk-white and dove-grey, wi harebell veins;
> Ae scar in fair hair like the sun in sunlicht lay;
> And pelvic experience in a thin shadow line;
> Thocht canna mairry thocht as sic soft shadows dae.
>
> Grey ghastly commentaries on my puir life,
> A' the sperm that's gane for naething rises up to dam

> In sick-white onanism the single seed
> Frae which in sheer irrelevance I cam. . . .

Look too at the hard objectivity of thought in 'At My Father's Grave' which gains tremendously in emotional charge from the Scots as well as from the implied feeling:

> We look upon each ither noo like hills
> Across a valley. I'm nae mair your son. . . .

or at the moral passion of 'First Hymn to Lenin,' a passion which enabled the poet to face directly, and accept, the post-Revolutionary terror of Russia:

> As necessary, and insignificant, as death
> Wi a' its agonies in the cosmos still
> The Cheka's horrors are in their degree;
> And'll end suner! What maitter's't wha we kill
> To lessen that foulest murder that deprives
> Maist men o real lives!

The 'First Hymn' was published in 1931, in the heat of that same wildfire movement which produced Auden's '1929' and Spender's 'Not palaces, an era's crown,' as well as Aragon's 'Red Front,' translated by Cummings for Ezra Pound's *Active Anthology*. The perspective is that of great revolutionary events, the impulse of rejection one common to most Western sensibilities in the years following World War One, the rhetoric unmistakable:

> Churchills, Locker-Lampsons, Beaverbrooks'll be
> In history's perspective less to you
> (And them!) than the Centurions to Christ
> Of whom, as you, at least this muckle's true,
> —'Tho pairtly wrang he cam to richt amang's
> Faur greater wrangs.'

MacDiarmid's Communist attitudes, though sturdier than those of Auden and his English fellows for the most part, were functions of an independent, antiphilistine spirit rather than of a doctrinaire one, as can easily be seen from his relatively late poem

'Reflections in a Slum' and his disdainful 'British Leftish Poetry, 1930-1940' in which he dismisses the achievement of the Auden group. In both his Scottish and his English poetry he deals more directly than most poets with theoretical and political subjects, using his verse not only for the familiar purposes of our century but also for extended exposition in the Classical manner. He may not always be as 'free of ratiocinative expansiveness,' therefore, as in 'O wha's been here afore me, lass,' but his more extended works have the force of sustained thought electrified by intense conviction.

In contrast to the more insular English poets of the 1940's and 1950's, MacDiarmid stands with another Scotsman, curiously, as a dynamic type of the British writer as a *European* man. Born five years earlier (1887), Edwin Muir embodied in his career much of the development, and motivation, of advanced thought of his time. He belonged to a Scottish farming family that was uprooted and brutally proletarianized. This ordeal, described in his autobiography, led him to socialism. Later, he tried to heal the wounds of early traumatic experience through psychoanalysis. He became absorbed, too, in Continental romantic, existential, and mystical thought. Increasingly, he came to feel that our century has all but beaten the humanity out of modern man:

> It was not time that brought these things upon us,
> But these two wars that trampled on us twice,
> Advancing and withdrawing, like a herd
> Of clumsy-footed beasts on a stupid errand
> Unknown to them or us. . . .
>
> ('The Good Town')

We Americans too have been through these wars, but not in this European sense. We do not believe that we and whatever we build must again and again be literally trampled down. We still think that any morning we can rearrange the rules and start everything all over again in a completely new way; we even think that any one of us, if he really puts his mind to it and does the proper exercises (and, especially, eats the proper food), can remake the world in the divine image. If we feel guilty, it is because we cannot find the time to bring about this necessary reform. But when a European like Muir feels guilty, it is because he seems part of an inexorable fatality for which he is irrationally responsible as Agamemnon and Oedipus were responsible for the deeds of their ancestors. For Muir the vision of Kafka, which influenced him deeply, was an expression of actual experience, while for Americans it merely adds a sobering dimension to a world of confusing possibilities. Muir's poems—like Kafka's stories—are not difficult, but very often their heavy oppression of tone half paralyzes the reader as if he were enmeshed in a slow-motion nightmare.

> At the dead centre of the boundless plain
> Does our way end? Our horses pace and pace. . . .
> Time has such curious stretches, we are told,
> And generation after generation
> May travel them, sad stationary journey,
> Of what device, what meaning?
>
> ('Variations on a Time Theme')

Or:

> There is a road that turning always
> Cuts off the country of Again.
> Archers stand there on every side
> And as it runs time's deer is slain,
> And lies where it has lain.
>
> ('The Road')

The baffling question in such poems as this is: What lies behind the agony of men lost within 'the stationary journey' of existence? In any one lifetime, generation, historical cycle we can see only so far: a succession of individual deaths, exhaustions of inspiration, recurrent defeats of the humane ideal. There are heroic journeys and quests in Muir's poetry, and he wants them to come out right. He experiments with an aestheticism in which, through pure imagination, man returns to a state of innocence like Adam's or like the poet's own remembered childhood. In certain poems he experiments with a suspension of skepticism and of reason generally—an as-if projection of pure faith, such as Wallace Stevens sometimes attempts. Characteristically, though, the language and tone belie the 'happy' projections. Muir has a way of providing a vision of beauty and joyous acceptance but surrounding it and, as it were, outnumbering it with notes of sorrow and horror so that its integrity is destroyed. Thus, in 'Oedipus,' he shows the Sophoclean hero accepting his lot as necessary and good, but in words ringing with tragic knowledge; the acceptance becomes a defeated acquiescence in a principle of evil the gods themselves cannot escape. 'All,' says Oedipus,

> must bear a portion of the wrong
> That is driven deep into our fathomless hearts
> Past sight or thought; that bearing it we may ease
> The immortal burden of the gods. . . .

Muir's poetry is tortured with the sense of history and personal life as governed by a compulsion to follow a maze of roads that 'run and run and never reach an end.' In one poem the victorious Greeks, returning from Troy to their longed-for homes and families, find only disappointment and triviality; if they could they would turn back to that dread wall against which they battered their prime years—the mystery of destiny is rendered unheroic by its banality, and ironic by men's utter ignorance of where they really are and what really awaits them. But neither an Oedipus nor an Odysseus has any choice; heroic or not, man is driven along. He cannot rest, cannot retrace his way to the irrevocable through the 'sweet and terrible labyrinth of longing,' cannot take any sure bearings for the future.

What makes this poetry so difficult to contemplate for very long at a time is its infinite sadness, and the repressed hysteria that underlies it. The horror of 'Then' and 'The Combat,' poems in which the essential discovery of life's cruelty is at once abstracted and condensed into the most elementary dramatic imagery, cuts at us like a sword slash at the face. The shock of 'Troy' or 'The Interrogation' or 'The Good Town' is rooted in contemporary political experience, the experience of heartless torture and of human beings become scavengers among the ruins of civilization, of the systematic displacement of peoples, of a restless evil eating away at all we consider meaningful. 'The Usurpers' stares into the blank face of a world 'liberated' from every old concern and value and finds no answer but 'black in its blackness'—

> There is no answer. We do here what we will
> And there is no answer. . . .

The most heartbreaking poems are the ones which, like 'Horses,' 'The Animals,' 'The Myth,' and others, picture or seek to evoke the primal innocence of man. If in MacDiarmid we have a driving spokesman for the revolutionary, secularist mentality of European man, in Muir we have a tragic spokesman for his foiled humanist idealism and for the era in which that idealism began to lower its flag in utter discouragement. What Muir implies is a cosmic sadness that once again the stars have 'thrown down their spears' and 'watered heaven with their tears.' The work over the past two decades or so of Herbert Read, and of the British and American writers who first emerged as Left poets of the early 'thirties, can in some ways be understood as falling within a polarity defined by MacDiarmid on the one hand and Muir on the other. The mood of the latter has held the mastery, however, at least since Auden's 'Spain, 1937.' Intended in the main as a trumpet call to action in support of the Spanish Republic, this poem ends:

> The stars are dead; the animals will not look:
> We are left alone with our day, and the time is short and
> > History to the defeated
> May say Alas but cannot help or pardon.

Read's '1945' is even closer to Muir's Sophoclean music of universal betrayal. It is only one example among many we might proffer from the storehouse of contemporary poetry:

> . . . I was invested with the darkness
> Of an ancient quarrel whose omens
> Lay scatter'd on the silted beach.
> The children came running toward me

But I saw only the waves behind them
Cold, salt and disastrous
Lift their black banners and break
Endlessly, without resurrection.

4. MOORE, CUMMINGS, SANDBURG, JEFFERS

Modern American poets have been more 'experimental' on the whole than have their British fellows. MacDiarmid and Muir, for instance, do not, like Williams and Stevens, express their originality through the externals of form (unless we consider MacDiarmid's use of Scots a more idiosyncratic formal 'technique' than we should). Williams has argued that a poem is a 'machine' made for a certain purpose,* and it may be that stubborn American individualism inclines us more readily to design machines to suit our own temperaments and aims. There are, of course, many reasons for this, and one in particular—the recurring concern to discover or create an 'American myth.' For our lack of a deep-going tradition of either revolutionary or conservative political and social thought with rich lodes for the independent thinker to explore poetically is even more important than our lack of an established church with native intellectual and aesthetic associations. On the other hand, the American does have a heritage of pragmatic, skeptical idealism that requires rigorous self-discipline if it is not to sour into cynicism. Thus, relying more on his own ingenuity than does the European, he tries sometimes to re-invent the language, sometimes to explode it, and always to reconquer it—for it is the Englishman's language after all, and when an American (or an Irishman) uses it he never quite has the relaxed, familiar feeling that so often makes the English poet too much at home with the medium of his art.

In these senses Marianne Moore's experimentalism is peculiarly American. She has invested heavily in 'expertness' both of style and of knowledgeableness. Her tone is always, as are Pound's and Eliot's, that of the insider—the skilled mechanic who knows his machine inside out, and who is also a distinguished engineer,

* Williams, *Selected Essays*, p. 257.

cyberneticist, and, for that matter, theoretical physicist. Her subject matter underscores this characteristic. To make a vivid, moving design out of precise factual information is for her almost the highest value. There is a certain whimsey in her use of any and all sources: a *Times* sports column, a laboratory report on 'plastic sponge imports in surgery,' a telephone company leaflet, or the following poetically rearranged quotations and data from *The Abbé Berlèse; Monographie du Genre Camellia:*

> Camellia Sabina
>   with amanita-white petals; there are several of her
>
>   pale pinwheels, and pale
> stripe that looks as if on a mushroom the
> sliver from a beet-root carved into a rose were laid. 'Dry
> the windows with a cloth fastened to a staff.
> In the camellia-house there must be
> no smoke from the stove, or dew on
>   the windows, lest the plants ail,'
> the amateur is told;
>   'mistakes are irreparable and nothing will avail.'
>
> ('Camellia Sabina')

But, as this passage shows, neither her aim nor her feeling is essentially whimsical. She is intrigued by the professional mastery reflected in her source book even though, throughout the poem, she gently mocks the pedantic, narrowly practical outlook of French horticulture, arguing that 'the gleaning is more than the vintage.' The concluding line of the quotation amuses her with its solemn, intransigent tone and unintended portentousness. Less solemn but just as serious, she has lavished all her own professional skill on the passage, and has turned what was literal exposition into delicately evocative decription. Notice the sensuous freshness of the first five lines, culminating in a figure as vivid as it is precise and restrained, and, further, the subtle lacework of sound, rhyme, and rhythm. Like all the other stanzas, the stanza beginning 'pale pinwheels' and ending 'nothing will avail' forms an ordered sequence of three-line units despite its relaxed manner of speech.

The first unit expands in length with each line, the second contracts the line length slightly, holding the factual content steady, and the third contracts sharply and then expands again. This design permits the handling of the colloquial and intellectual materials in a formally structured way that allows for continuity and ease from stanza to stanza, and within stanzas, without becoming too loose. The pains that go into maintaining such a pattern in stanzas of some length are obviously very great and demand a virtuoso's almost compulsive pride of craftsmanship. The rhymes too maintain a certain order, unobtrusive as they are. Miss Moore employs exact rhymes ('pale,' 'ail,' 'avail'), inexact rhymes (for instance, 'dry' and 'be'—the open vowels of which, as in Anglo-Saxon verse, are felt to match one another in the kind of sound they make), and light rhymes (the matching of stressed and unstressed syllables, as in 'be' and 'the'). A large number of *l*'s are worked into the entire passage, as often as possible combined with *a*'s and *e*'s ('pale pinwheels,' 'laid,' etc.) but not so often as to weigh too heavily on the general movement.

This massing of special information, discriminatingly but somewhat arbitrarily selected, and its orchestration, as it were, by a witty mind with a fastidious sense of form, are characteristic of Miss Moore's work by and large. Obviously, a poet working in this way cannot avoid precious and recherché impressions as well as a certain initial effect of condescension. As readers we may at first react with indifference to the difficulties presented by this sort of thing. They may seem irrelevant to our lives, as might the conversation of specialists in ostrich breeding. But there can be passion in such conversation, and the more we know about what is being said, the warmer the passion will seem. Miss Moore's role is not really that of an ostrich expert, but of a fascinated overhearer who, having assimilated some of the more striking points about ostrich breeding, makes use of them in her own conversation. Humorously but interestedly she tells others about her views on art or on the nature of integrity or on death, building up her theme by putting together all the fine things she has heard about ostriches and about other subjects. She finds sermons in

snails, steam rollers, camellias, skunks: naturally allegorical embodiments of the functioning principles of life.

> . . . The inky thing
> adaptively whited with glistening
> goat-fur, is wood-warden. In his
> ermined well-cuttlefish-inked wool, he is
> determination's totem. . . .
>
> ('The Wood-Weasel')

> the inextinguishable
> salamander styled himself but presbyter. His shield
> was his humility. . . .
>
> ('His Shield')

> The illustration
> is nothing to you without the application.
> You lack half wit. You crush all the particles down
> into close conformity, and then walk back and
> forth on them.
>
> ('To a Steam Roller')

The first two of these quotations illustrate the poet's special admiration for the quieter virtues of a principled existence—adapt-
ability that is not self-betrayal, unaggressive readiness to defend the
right to be one's perhaps eccentric self. The third illustrates her
satirical powers; Miss Moore can be sharp and direct, in the negative especially, as when she writes, in 'The Paper Nautilus,' about

> . . . authorities whose hopes
> are shaped by mercenaries

and

> Writers entrapped by
> teatime fame and by
> commuters' comforts. . . .

The theme of the negative, indeed, is the clue to much of the
feeling in Marianne Moore. The resistance to destruction of straw-

berries, hedgehogs, starfish (some of the heroes of her poem 'Never-theless') wins all her admiration—

> The weak overcomes its
>   menace, the strong over-
>   comes itself. What is there

> like fortitude! . . .

Her fastidiousness consists, poetically, of a closing-in on right atti-tudes of taste through a considered rejection of more vulgar atti-tudes. 'Distaste which takes no credit to itself is best,' she writes in one poem. The tone is that of a person of sensibility thinking aloud. 'The deepest feeling,' she writes elsewhere, 'always shows itself in silence.' Then she corrects herself: 'not in silence, but restraint.' Her portrait of the true 'hero' is of one who corrects his own natural fears and inadequacies by accepting the demands of situations not necessarily to his 'personal liking.'

Yet the poetry as a whole does not have the pallor of mere negation. Not even the curious poem 'Marriage' with its finely Jamesian distinctions lacks vigor or a ground sense of the physical side of its subject. The note of life's terrors sounds clear and pure in 'A Grave' or 'Snakes, Mongooses, Snake-Charmers and the Like.' The bold, clean impressions of 'The Steeple-Jack' give an incomparable picture of a New England sea coast town and at the same time provide a necessary groundwork for the poem's aesthetic and moral, as well as tragic, implications. 'Poetry,' in which the speaker toys with an implied hard-headed 'practical' man's objections to 'all this fiddle' (granting his assumption that only the real article, skillfully made, is worth anything) and moves with brilliant, irrefutable force to one of the great triumphs of verse-rhetoric of its kind, is a high-spirited, rapidly darting, excit-ing piece of work. Because of her unique effects, we can too easily overlook her artistic kinship with Stevens, Pound, Eliot, and Williams. Yet there is an important family resemblance to them in her exclamatory outbursts, her lyrical ironies, her subtly threaded metaphysical and imagistic argumentation, and her attempts to root her work in concrete observation. Moreover, her emphasis on the details of subhuman organic life makes her poetry alive with symbolic inwardness. Sometimes her famous 'imaginary gardens with real toads in them'—her figure for genuine poetic creations—are very close to Blake's tiger-haunted forests.

E. E. Cummings shares with Marianne Moore a reputation, in each instance earned by special gifts, for intriguing surface pyrotechnics. Each has fashioned a highly individual art, adaptable enough to influence others powerfully but particularly expressive of the poetic personality that emerges within it. Miss Moore has a poem that begins:

> THE MIND IS AN ENCHANTING THING
>
> is an enchanted thing
>   like the glaze on a
> katydid wing
>   subdivided by sun
>   till the nettings are legion. . . .

The speculative, self-correcting attempt to 'define' the mind, advanced through an imagery of light refracted from a smoothly shining yet living, active surface, is true Marianne Moore in both its quiet abstractness and its detailed excitement. The poem becomes even more characteristically Marianne Moore as it advances through a series of similes ('like Gieseking playing Scarlatti,' 'like the apteryx-owl,' like 'the kiwi's rain-shawl,' 'like the gyroscope's fall') for the mind in action and then, as it nears completion of the figurative network of definitions, through a series of metaphors that gather the intensities of its dominant conception into one last concentrated statement.

Cummings, though as dazzling a juggler of verbal effects, is of course in an entirely different world from Miss Moore's. The immediacies of

> i like my body when it is with your
> body.   It is so quite new a thing. . . .

or of

> i sing of Olaf glad and big
> whose warmest heart recoiled at war:
> a conscientious object-or. . . .

do not at all recall Miss Moore's world of self-disciplined candors
surrounded by restraints, that chastely frank world of the sensitive
lady arguing for things of earth from somewhere not quite of it.
Yet Cummings too is absorbed in the problem of definition
through the trapping of a state of awareness. Few other poets
besides Marianne Moore could catch an *aperçu* so beautifully and
sculpturally as Cummings does in Poem 40 of 95 *Poems:*

> silence
>
> .is
> a
> looking
>
> bird:the
>
> turn-
> ing;edge,of
> life
>
> (inquiry before snow

'Silence is a looking bird; the turning edge of life; inquiry before
snow.' The images, arresting in themselves, accumulate a range
of connotation belied by the poem's physical brevity. Punctuation
and line arrangement control the pace at which the connotations
come into view. First there is the isolated *silence,* emphasized by
the space below it and then by the period, which is not final but
musically transitional: Silence (pause) *is.* Then the 'is' becomes
a bridge in its turn: Silence is a *looking.* The gerund turns to
participle as we move on: a looking *bird*—and perhaps, by association, a *mocking bird* as well? By the poem's end we have crossed
many boundaries between subjective awareness and objective uni-

verse. Silence seems a confrontation of two states whose terms of reference are always changing. With the concluding (but un-closed) parenthesis, the whole mysterious, freshly felt experience of silence has become a relationship between the clear-eyed, awed, but uncowed observer and the imponderable, relentless nature of things.

Every unorthodoxy of punctuation, spacing, and noncapitaliza-tion in this poem, and in Cummings's poems generally, can be read functionally in much the way that we have read the uncon-ventional placing of the period in line two of the poem just quoted. The visual element cannot always be conveyed by the way the poem is read aloud, though it very often guides the reader to the right duration of pauses and to the right tone. The unclosed parenthesis, for instance, walls off what has gone before just enough so that the wondering, rather chilled awe of the poem's final moment is given tremendous emphasis, and the absence of a period suggests that this last effect is of a realization that must continue without a stop. Yet a good reader would not really need these 'visual aids' to expression, and their chief value is pictorial—an added dimension for the reader actually looking at the page. Some of the poems, for instance, the grasshopper poem in *no thanks* which begins 'r-p-o-p-h-e-s-s-a-g-r' and rises to the first cli-max of 'PPEGORHRASS' and the second of '.gRrEaPsPhOs' *cannot* be read aloud at these key points. The whole life, and joke, of the poem consists in a pictorially kinetic effect typographi-cally created to represent the insect bunching itself up to leap—distorting itself and scattering itself about in the sense that its normal appearance in repose is scrambled during its various move-ments—and then coming to rest rearranged, or, as Cummings shows it,

to
rea(be)rran(com)gi(e)ngly
,grasshopper;

—that is, to 'rearrangingly' become a normal grasshopper, but only momentarily, as the poet suggests by placing a semicolon rather than a full stop at the end of the poem. The gay life of this poem is ideogrammatic rather than aural. One might make a sputtering attempt to *say* it; however, there would be more dance and pantomime than sound to the effort. The poem is a kind of mechanical toy, but an ingenious one that works.

Generally the aural values of a Cummings poem are the most important, with the visual fireworks serving as they do in 'silence,' to guide the reading typographically rather than to replace it. Two simple instances are 'Buffalo Bill's/ defunct' and 'who's most afraid of death? thou.' The former of these poems begins with the flat statement of Buffalo Bill's death, *presents* his particular talents in language that evokes his quick-shooting, smooth-riding virtuosity, breaks into excited admiration, then suddenly turns and asks:

> how do you like your blueeyed boy
> Mister Death

The irony is directed against both Death and Death's 'blueeyed boy,' the folk-hero whose carnival yet murderous abilities have been so mock-naïvely praised in the early lines. The poem's structure is based on this rhetorical build-up of tone. The tough 'defunct' of the second line is sardonically echoed in the 'blueeyed boy' of the end—both terms show something less than awe toward both the hero and 'Mister Death.' In the poem's mechanical structure words are run together ('and break onetwothreefourfive pigeonsjustlikethat') and lines are staggered in length and design, in accordance with this rhetorical basis. The poem thus stands as a perfect example of what is commonly meant by free verse.

'who's most afraid,' on the other hand, is a free use of the sonnet form. Here too the lines are staggered to emphasize movement of thought and feeling, and the lengths of stanzas (three of them have only one line each) are varied to bring out shifts and pauses in this movement. Moreover, the lines are mainly run-on, and the unconventional visual design Cummings gives them, together with his use of half rhymes and light rhymes as well as exact ones, further hides the essential sonnet from us; nor is the line length always the conventional iambic pentameter. But the underlying pattern is still very much present, a Petrarchan octave and a sestet made up of rhyming couplets, and contributes heavily by its felt presence to the way the poem moves into ever more passionate statement. It is a poem which, though not sensual, is about an aspect of intense erotic love: especially, the lover's compassionate, tender feeling of his beloved's vulnerability to death. The feeling directs both lovers to a swooning awareness of life's precious fragility and of the vast, terrible meaninglessness of all that negates it—Mister Death and his 'enormous stride' through 'the mysterious high futile day.' The last moment of the poem becomes a poignantly romantic gesture in the face of this awareness:

> (and drawing thy mouth toward

> my mouth, steer our lost bodies carefully downward)

Cummings's great forte is the manipulation of traditional forms and attitudes in an original way. In his best work he has the swift sureness of ear and idiom of a Catullus, and the same way of bringing together a racy colloquialism and the richer tones of high poetic style.

> (ponder,darling,these busted statues
> of yon motheaten forum be aware
> notice what hath remained. . . .

The thought of the poem which begins thus might make it but one more of the hundreds of thousands that have been written on the themes of mutability (à la 'To the Virgins to Make Much of Time' or, more pointedly even, 'To His Coy Mistress'). What makes the difference is the humorous, slangy, hard-boiled language and speech tones expertly mixed in with the resounding motifs from the heritage of the past. This is how he 'makes it new,' and in this sense his virtuosity is very much in a great Classical tradition. As Browning did in 'Two in the Campagna,' so Cummings in '(ponder,darling' reintroduces an ancient motif through a completely contemporary voice. He is quite capable of writing a poem without using the colloquial tack—witness 'who's most afraid' or 'all in green went my love riding' or 'my love.' In the first of these the 'modernity' consists in the free handling of the sonnet, in the 'private' allusiveness of the tone, and in the momentarily ambiguous images. In the second it is a matter of a sharper, more complex imagery and a modification of the traditional ballad that tightened it into a polished, compact lyrical instrument. In the third it is again the free handling of line and stanza, and the subtle complicating of the figures. Where the 'Song of Songs' in the Bible has a sequence of chanted similes, all quite simple in themselves—'Thine eyes are as doves behind thy veil' or 'Thy two breasts are like two fawns that are twins of a roe'—Cummings gives us metaphors that extend the feeling beyond the immediate praise of a woman's physical beauty:

> thy head is a quick forest
> filled with sleeping birds
> thy breasts are swarms of white bees
> upon the bough of thy body. . . .

> in thy beauty is the dilemma of flutes. . . .

The deliberate archaism of some of the diction and syntax in all these poems contributes, paradoxically, to their modernity. The archaic elements, side by side with the imagery of modern sensibility, simply add a note from the past that after all remains part of our consciousness.

Beyond this technical consideration, the archaisms help Cummings express his often sentimentally romantic feeling, whereas his more colloquial tones help him keep it in check, or at least take some of the curse from it by giving him one or another comic mask—that of a sarcastic guide to the ruins of Rome, or a wisecracking down-and-outer, or a circus barker:

> ladies and gentlemen this little girl
> with the good teeth and small important breasts. . . .

The mask of the tough guy with a heart of mush is often fixed over the speaker's face in Cummings's less successful poems:

> goodbye Betty, don't remember me
> pencil your eyes dear and have a good time

with the tall tight boys at Tabari'
s, keep your teeth snowy, stick to beer and lime,
wear dark, and where your meeting breasts are round
have roses darling, it's all i ask of you——

The opening lines of this sonnet are wonderfully memorable in a brittle, Noel-Coward way, and the poem as a whole catches the bittersweet feelings of young love in a manner peculiar to the 1920's. Its nostalgic sentimentality expresses a genuine mood of youth, and the surface sophistication recalls scenes in Hemingway and, even more, in F. Scott Fitzgerald. (What is always missing in Cummings is the more negative or sour side of romantic experience, which both novelists take into account and which John O'Hara makes one of his central themes. Not that a poet *should* necessarily give a view of his subject in such sober perspective, but there is something callow about many of his pieces.) In the second half of the poem the wit of the beginning is forgotten, however, and a too heavily perfumed speech takes over. It is comparable to the cloying effects in 'somewhere i have never travelled, gladly beyond.' Except in a few lines, this poem's effort to show the infinitely delicate, revelatory responsiveness of one lover's spirit to another's substitutes affectation for convincing emotion; the affectation is especially glaring in the gauchely exquisite culmination: 'nobody, not even the rain, has such small hands.' As further examples of the failure of taste which is Cummings's most recurrent weakness, one might list 'anyone lived in a pretty how town,' the 'Chansons Innocentes,' and even the elegiac 'my father moved through dooms of love.' It is hard to imagine that the same poet could have been the ruthless satirist of 'POEM, OR BEAUTY HURTS MR. VINAL' and 'next to of course god america i' or the hard-riding bacchanalist of 'she being Brand.'

The truth about Cummings seems to be that he reveals an enormous talent within a quite narrow range of thought and sympathy, much of it adolescent and *poseur*-ish. He was not put upon this earth to publish enormous *Gesammelte Werke* but to issue forth little sheaves, each of them containing a few poems of astounding sensuous vitality, some intransigent jeers and shockers against a repressed, war-tormented, 'progress'-ridden civilization, various visual aids to verbal explosion, and two or three poems like 'who's most afraid.' His main triumphs have been in these modes, and have included a large proportion of pieces that are pure prestidigitation or in the spirit of the comic strip *Krazy Kat* (often extolled by Cummings) or of old-time burlesque. His lapses into sentimentality and some of his pettier political and racial satires show how easily a great natural ability and real poetic temperament can be used for self-defeatingly trivial ends. His prose works, especially *The Enormous Room* and parts of *Eimi*, are further evidence of the distance the poetic gift can carry a man with no great weight of intellect to burden him (or give him ballast either) as he goes. Yet it may have been just this combination of endowment and ordinariness that has made his achievement what it is. The chief effect of Cummings's jugglery with syntax, grammar, and diction was to blow open otherwise trite and bathetic motifs through a dynamic rediscovery of the energies sealed up in conventional usage. Though in some important way such success depends on the writer's sharing the assumptions he thus reopens, there is little question he succeeded masterfully in splitting the atom of the cute commonplace.

A fruitful comparison can be drawn between Cummings and Carl Sandburg—the former at his heights all but pure stylist, the latter only minimally one. Sandburg at his most effective is a movingly 'poetic' socialist (or populist) orator, a political dreamer whose *mystique* is centered on Lincoln, The People, the anonymous and carefree or pathetic poor. One can imagine Upton Sinclair's heading each section of his protest anthology *The Cry for Justice* with a quotation from Sandburg. Sandburg has real, if secondary power. For one thing, he has a delighted ear for the common speech, so that his poetry is a great repository of idiomatic folk-wisdom. (One can read his books, especially *The People, Yes*, with pleasure for hours just for this particular richness.) For another, it is full of 'shocking' portraits and home-truths, though by now much of the charge has gone out of its proletarian and muckraking features, which seem largely derivative from Whitman and Masters and Sherwood Anderson, and from the general atmosphere of the radical movements and the 'new' spirit of the second and third decades of this century. He is one of Whitman's many less sensitive, less inward heirs, but he can also be hard as Bertolt Brecht is hard:

> Why is there always a secret singing
> When a lawyer cashes in?
> Why does a hearse horse snicker
> Hauling a lawyer away?
>
>   ('The Lawyers Know Too Much')

And Sandburg, like Cummings, can be suddenly gentle, delicate. A poem like 'Fog,' with its curiously Oscar Wildean daintiness, suggests Cyclops having tea with the ladies. The poet of the open democratic spirit, the immigrant workman's son fresh from the prairies who was once a Socialist organizer, learned much from the Imagists:

> bright accidents from the chromosome
> spill   from the color bowl of the
> chromosomes   some go under in early
> bubbles   some learn from desert blos-
> soms   how to lay up and use thin
> hoardings of night mist
>
>   *(The People, Yes)*

What Sandburg is *not* may best be seen through contemplating an account by Yeats of how he came to write one of his greatest poems:

> I wrote 'Leda and the Swan' because the editor of a political review asked me for a poem. I thought, 'After the individualist, demagogic movement founded by Hobbes and popularized by the Encyclopaedists and the French Revolution, we have a soil so exhausted that it cannot grow that crop again for centuries.' Then I thought, 'Nothing is now possible but some movement from above preceded by some violent annunciation.' My fancy began to play with Leda and the Swan for meta-

phor, and I began this poem; but as I wrote, bird and lady took such possession of the scene that all politics went out of it, and my friend tells me that his 'conservative readers would misunderstand the poem.' *

'As I wrote, bird and lady took such possession of the scene that all politics went out of it.' Sandburg never comes near such a transcendence; his pictures always illustrate an implied or stated text, never shape it up in their own right. If Yeats and Pound (in *Canto* 13, for a simple example) and Eliot are the great masters of the age, they are so because of this indispensable achievement. MacDiarmid's 'Tarras,' Auden's 'September 1, 1939,' do not quite manage it, but they are at least of the order of work which reaches out (and within) toward it. Whether what all these writers believe they realize is always defensible in the forum is beside the question. Hart Crane may be horribly wrong when he speaks of love, in *The Bridge*, as 'a burnt match skating in a urinal.' Eliot may be wrong about history and about what he considers the evils of humanitarianism in the Stetson passage of *The Waste Land*. But Sandburg's most famous poem, his 'Chicago,' is emptily swaggering by comparison with such unsqueamish, unblinking moments of violent revelation as Eliot and Crane have shown us. 'Chicago' speaks of brutality:

And they tell me you are brutal and my reply is: On the faces of women and children I have seen the marks of wanton hunger. . . .

But there is no brutality, no shock of insight, in the line, or the poem, itself.

It may be argued that Sandburg gives us something almost as good. He holds in solution, as it were, the vast *un*realized possibilities of a native American radicalism that has never found its fullest expression in our literature. Not entirely unrealized, it goes without saying, in Sandburg himself, in a poem like 'Balloon Faces'—

* *The Variorum Edition of the Poems of W. B. Yeats*, ed. Peter Allt and Russell K. Alspach, Macmillan, New York, 1957, p. 828.

> Poets, lawyers, ad men, mason contractors, smart-alecks
> discussing 'educated jackasses,' here they put crabs
> into their balloon faces,
> Here sit the heavy balloon face women lifting crimson
> lobsters into their crimson faces. . . .

or in his sardonic comment on the rich man's fence:

> As a fence, it is a masterpiece, and will shut off the rabble and all
> vagabonds and hungry men and all wandering children looking
> for a place to play.
> Passing through the bars and over the steel points will go nothing
> except Death and the Rain and Tomorrow.

('A Fence')

or in his fine, free-thinking scorn toward moral and religious pre-
tentiousness, expressed in the language of an old-time Wobbly
orator:

> You come along . . . tearing your shirt . . . yelling about Jesus.
> Where do you get that stuff?
> What do you know about Jesus?

('To a Contemporary Bunkshooter')

These motifs are inseparable in Sandburg from his sense of racy,
colorful life and speech, which he has in even greater abundance
than Cummings. Like Cummings, he comes back repeatedly to the
theme of Shelley's 'Ozymandias'—the mutability of things. The
difference lies in the lower pitch of Sandburg's technique, as well
as in his emphasis, which is not erotic but partly 'philosophical'
in the popular sense and partly political—as in the brooding over
the fate of great nations and personalities in 'Four Preludes' and
'Cool Tombs.' It is his 'sad' side—the reverse of his constant
praise of the land and its past and future. But in the main his is
a zestful, an emphatically 'popular' poetry, as is that of Lindsay
and Masters—and as Whitman's is not—a poetry to enchant and
stir a listening audience, to make it laugh or grow sweetly grave,
'thinking' about deep, melancholy things. Not too savage, not too
committed, not too unpleasant or 'difficult' for contemplation, free
of those brooding depths we find in Muir or those harsh, pedantic

insistences of a MacDiarmid, it is a half-poetry which, nevertheless, few of us would want to do without.

The problem Robinson Jeffers presents is a little different. If Sandburg can be charged with incomplete commitment to his art, Jeffers is in his way—it is some kind of West Coast disease—overcommitted. That is, he pushes too hard against the limitations of his own formal resources. Having a genuine but hardly overwhelming gift for swift narration, for subtle and evocative description, and for impassioned argument—all in a basically conventional though loosely manipulated verse-patterning which gives the illusion of being 'free'—he tries to squeeze out of these talents every drop of symbolic and didactic inference he can. In such longer works as *Roan Stallion* and *Tamar* the effort is disastrous. As with Cummings, one is occasionally shocked by the immature level of conception. The unresolved jumble of life-force-ism, cosmic pronouncements, and erotic daydreaming cloys feeling and forces an all too willing suspension of belief, rather than of disbelief. *Roan Stallion* is the more successful of these two poems, largely because it is the shorter one and because Jeffers has had the grace to make the most important 'event' in the narrative one that is experienced in the mind, rather than literally:

> The fire threw up figures
> And symbols meanwhile, racial myths formed and dissolved in it,
>   the phantom rulers of humanity
> That without being are yet more real than what they are born of,
>   and without shape, shape that which makes them . . .
> Out of the fire . . . a crucified man writhed up in anguish;
> A woman covered by a huge beast in whose mane the stars were
>   netted, sun and moon were his eyeballs,
> Smiled under the unendurable violation, her throat swollen with
>   the storm and blood-flecks gleaming
> On the stretched lips. . . .

The cruel sexuality of this purportedly archetypal picture dominates *Tamar* also. Violence, and violation, is the means by which

male and female come together—the two poems are full of scenes
in which the heroines strip off their clothes and seek out or imagine
brutal possession; they are replete with 'bruised breasts,' flogging,
rapings, and submission without love. Behind this lurid fantasy
(itself forced by a deliberate frothing-up of imagination beyond
what the given premises of the poems and of the kinds of characters involved will carry), there lies an insistent rhetoric. Man has
outworn his achievement, trivial as it was in the first place; the
poet can but await his self-destruction with the tragic patience of a
Cassandra, pointing bitterly to the nature of that self-destruction,
which is also self-betrayal, in the hypocrisies and *hubris* of modern
politics and modern thought generally.

Humanity is the mold to break away from, the crust to break
   through, the coal to break into fire,
The atom to be split.
         Tragedy that breaks man's face and a white fire flies
               out of it; vision that fools him
Out of his limits, desire that fools him out of his limits, unnatural
         crime, inhuman science. . . .

It is his own sensuous intensity that fools Jeffers. Its vigor is
naturally convincing, and its intellectual overflow, as it were, per-
suades him that the implications he reads into what he has summoned up in fantasy or really observed will be equally convincing.
The subject need not be sexually centered. Thus, the first half of
'The Purse-Seine' brilliantly captures the experience of the sardine
fishermen of the Pacific Coast as they 'circle the gleaming shoal' of
'crowded fish,' each fish a 'comet's tail wake of clear yellow flame,'
while outside the 'floats and cordage of the net' the sea lions
watch, 'sighing in the dark,' and 'the vast walls of night' rise 'erect
to the stars.' Jeffers's particular glory, perhaps, lies in his mystically
sensitive Pacific regionalism. But he too rarely restricts himself
to the boundaries of this glory. In the second half of 'Purse-Seine'
Jeffers must needs 'interpret' for us, lest we ponder the scene for its
intrinsic beauty and implications rather than for the thought he
wants to impose on us:

> I thought, we have geared the machines and locked all together
> into interdependence; we have built the great cities; now
> There is no escape. We have gathered vast populations incapable
> of free survival. . . .

The netting of the fish becomes a parable to show we are fore-doomed to greater and greater authoritarianism in government, a development which revolution would only accelerate, or to 'anarchy, the mass-disasters.' No wonder, says Jeffers, that our poetry is either fatalistic or hysterical. Still, he concludes,

> There is no reason for amazement: surely one always knew that
> cultures decay, and life's end is death.

The elaborated, arbitrary comment, taking up over half the poem, is characteristic of the violence Jeffers does to his own work. But even in the opening stanzas he intrudes with just enough flatly expository diction and just enough facile use of adjectives to suggest he will reduce his startling sense impressions to a subordinate position. For instance:

> I cannot tell you
> How beautiful the scene is, and a little terrible. . . .

Go through Jeffers's most famous poems, and you will find this kind of blunted, hackneyed diction growing in scattered weed patches everywhere:

> . . . life is good, be it stubbornly long or suddenly
> A mortal splendor. . . .
>
> ('Shine, Perishing Republic')

> . . . the ever-returning roses of dawn.
>
> ('Apology for Bad Dreams')

> The immense vulgarities of misapplied science and decaying
> Christianity. . . .
>
> ('Prescription of Painful Ends')

And you will also find the bland profundities, such as the ending of 'The Purse-Seine' itself, or the beginning of 'Science':

Man, introverted man, having crossed
In passage and but a little with the nature of things this latter
   century
Has begot giants. . . .

Jeffers does not always miss. He *can* convince our minds as well
as our senses, and often the strength of his voice carries the day
despite everything. As Sandburg sees the great theme of possibility implicit in American and modern life, so Jeffers sees the
great tragic working-out of man's doom and tries to salvage a
perspective which will render it less painfully significant. As Sandburg delights in the surfaces of our varied American world and
plays lightly with common moods and themes, so Jeffers seeks out
the solitary passionate figure, the hawk as symbol, the impersonal
and nonsocial sources of value. Both writers have made their
mark, yet neither has taken advantage of the modern poetic revolution as he might have done. Sandburg has 'experimented,' but
save in isolated, incomplete instances such as 'Four Preludes' and
some of the passages in *The People, Yes* has never gone far beyond superficial assault on the problems of form. And Jeffers, like
Conrad Aiken, John Crowe Ransom, John Peale Bishop, and a
host of other writers all admirable in their several ways, has maintained a certain traditionalism in his art and thought—at a crucial cost, however. All these writers have forgone that ultimate
expenditure of energy which can harness the past to new formal
and psychological directions and thus give it truly renewed meaning and power.

SIX

New Heaven and Earth

1. D. H. LAWRENCE

The extraordinary influence of D. H. Lawrence is largely based on his evangelistic call for the return by modern men and women to what he called 'phallic consciousness.' 'My great religion,' he wrote, 'is a belief in the blood, the flesh, as being wiser than the intellect.' There is a magnetically, violently hostile side to this 'religion.' In order to break down the false worship of the intellect and 'make a new world,' Lawrence held, one must yield to the subconscious 'urge of life that is within.' One must forget self-consciousness and surrender to the 'stirring half-born impulse to smash up the vast lie of the world.' * So Lawrence takes the revolutionary directions of modern thought and gives them a special turn. The suppressed physical life must burst into its own; the mechanized cerebral, overpurposive character of our civilization must be exploded away. Lawrence did not invent this program; Yeats and Pound go a good part of the way with him, and Blake and others foresaw that way long ago. The difference lies mainly in a certain tone, or emphasis, behind Lawrence's subordination of everything, even his art, to the program. Also, it lies in the nearness of his work to common life. However alienated his argument and however exotic his subject matter may at times be, he is at the same time extremely interested in the details of life among the most ordinary men and women. The interest is intimate, gossipy almost—the kind of interest one has in people one knows unusually well. Finally, Lawrence always speaks in his own right, and directly to the point. He dares to expose his emotions, to risk seeming sentimental or ludicrous.

* The Letters of D. H. Lawrence, ed. Aldous Huxley, Heinemann, London, 1932, p. 94, and The Portable D. H. Lawrence, ed. Diana Trilling, Viking Press, New York, 1954, p. 667.

When I am in a great city, I know that I despair.
I know there is no hope for us, death waits, it is useless to care.

For oh the poor people, that are flesh of my flesh,
I, that am flesh of their flesh,
when I see the iron hooked into their faces
their poor, their fearful faces
I scream in my soul. . . .

('City Life')

Lawrence, even more than Williams, takes his own life and the things and people he sees seriously *in themselves*. They are important to him not because they illustrate a thought or a tradition but by virtue of their simple existence. When he was a young teacher, he set down his feelings about his work with absolute directness—not ironically, not aloofly, not in any sense pretentiously:

No longer now can I endure the brunt
Of the books that lie out on the desks; a full threescore
Of several insults of blotted pages, and scrawl
Of slovenly work that they have offered me.
I am sick, and what on earth is the good of it all?
What good to them or me, I cannot see!

('Last Lesson of the Afternoon')

Not a great poem, but it expresses a real mood of teachers. (He also wrote happier poems about his classes.) Such a poem assumes the plain necessity of expressing what we really are. Similarly, the pathetic 'Monologue of a Mother' focuses unashamedly on the exact feeling of the woman who speaks. Her son, in his need to be free of her, has sentenced her to the death of spiritual loneliness:

Like a thin white bird blown out of the northern seas,
Like a bird from the far north blown with a broken wing
Into our sooty garden, he drags and beats
Along the fence perpetually, seeking release
From me, from the hand of my love which creeps up, needing
His happiness, whilst he in displeasure retreats.

The later 'mother-poems,' occasioned by the final illness and death of Mrs. Lawrence, go beyond this 'monologue' in concentrated emotional power. A poem like 'Sorrow' or 'Brooding Grief' goes at once, quite simply, to the heart of something Joyce too dealt with in *Ulysses*, giving us the normal dimensions of that which Joyce makes a unique and complex agony.

In the same forthright way, many of Lawrence's poems of love go straight to the heart of the sexual mystery (as James's *The Ambassadors*, in its equally valid way, goes tortuously to it). The early poems show an obvious Hardy influence, and sometimes the lilt and swoon of Meredith, but they have also a quality of empathy and sheer awareness that makes them Lawrence's own. He *knows*, for example, the desire that overwhelms disgust and fear in the girl of 'Love on the Farm.' And he too has been touched by the amazed clarity about himself of the speaker in 'Hymn to Priapus.' In the 'Hymn' the speaker deliberately intermingles references to two kinds of love: his grief-stricken love for his dead mother and his physical passion for the 'ripe, slack country lass' he has just seduced. He sees Orion in the winter sky, witness of his other love-makings and of his last 'faithlessness' to his mother's memory. Orion's indifference is the clue to the speaker's acceptance of his lot. He sees his own sorrow and grief and the 'debonair' satisfying of his lust in the cold light of that ancient constellation, and a half heartbroken objectivity toward himself takes over for the moment:

> Grief, grief, I suppose and sufficient
> Grief makes us free
> To be faithless and faithful together
> As we have to be.

Lawrence has a number of candid, youthful pieces in which the speaker is tortured by a girl's refusal of his love, or at least of the consummation of it. The situation in 'Lightning' is characteristic; they are making love at night in the countryside, moving toward the sexual act itself, when

> the lightning flew across her face
> And I saw her for the flaring space

> Of a second, like snow that slips
> From a roof, inert with death, weeping 'Not this! Not this!'

The woman's fear of the act, her inertness or suffering during it, her self-defeating prudery or frigidity despite her great yearning are repeated themes, growing directly out of the poet's experience. It is a common enough sort of experience but hardly ever treated by others so frankly, keeping so intact all its frustration and mingled sympathy and anger—'Almost I hated her, sacrificed.' Lawrence does not forget, either, the added complication of the man's fear of dependence through love:

> Helen, had I known yesterday
> That you could discharge the ache
> Out of the wound. . . .
> I should have hated you, Helen.
>
>   ('Release')

Against these poems stand the marriage-poems, celebrating the new-found lands in which there is a resolving of all that has kept male and female from realizing themselves in each other. We have the almost Provençal revelation of 'Gloire de Dijon,' for instance, in which the woman bathing in the sunlight is seen as a glowing goddess:

> She stoops to the sponge, and the swung breasts
> Sway like full-blown yellow
> Gloire de Dijon roses.

And we have the strangeness of 'River Roses,' one of Lawrence's most satisfying poems despite the Poe-like tintinnabulation of some of the rhymes:

> By the Isar, in the twilight
> We were wandering and singing,
> By the Isar, in the evening
> We climbed the huntsman's ladder and sat swinging
> In the fir-tree overlooking the marshes,
> While river met with river, and the ringing
> Of their pale-green glacier water filled the evening.

By the Isar, in the twilight
We found the dark wild roses
Hanging red at the river; and simmering
Frogs were singing, and over the river closes
Was savour of ice and of roses; and glimmering
Fear was abroad. We whispered: 'No one knows us.
Let it be as the snake disposes
Here in this simmering marsh.'

'No one knows us,' say the protagonists of Lawrence's poem.
We can take on the full burden of the knowledge of good and
evil as 'the snake' taught us to do in the Garden. We can make
our own *vita nuova* without benefit of Christ or the prophets. It
is the 'intolerable music' of Yeats's 'News for the Delphic Oracle.'
The ringing waters, the chant of the frogs, our own singing are
the keys to salvation—not the Paradise of the Church, but the
profane, earthly paradise that comes into its own when darkness
falls. The theme parallels that of another of Lawrence's great songs
of discovery, his 'Song of a Man Who Has Come Through.'

If only, most lovely of all, I yield myself and am borrowed
By the fine, fine wind that takes its course through the chaos of the
    world
Like a fine, an exquisite chisel, a wedge-blade inserted;
If only I am keen and hard like the sheer tip of a wedge. . . .

What is the knocking?
What is the knocking at the door in the night?
It is somebody wants to do us harm.

No, no, it is the three strange angels.
Admit them, admit them.

As with 'River Roses,' this 'song' is the outgrowth of Lawrence's
fearless concentration on human experience. The speaker coaching
himself to 'yield' to 'the fine, fine wind that takes its course
through the chaos of the world' is both a physical lover and a
man who wants to be in right relation to the whole of being. The

life force will take him up, 'borrow' him, if he is receptive enough. Here the language is feminine, almost passive. But the next lines show that such yielding will prepare him for the purest maleness, will make him 'like a fine, an exquisite chisel,' the sheer tip of a wedge.' Literally, of course, the poem speaks neither of femaleness nor of maleness at this point, but rather of a state of responsiveness, and readiness, for the penetration of life. Nevertheless, the figurative language does bring sexual connotations into play. It suggests, however ambiguously, the necessary attitudes toward sexual experience of both woman and man. In the second and third quoted stanzas, there is a similar controlled ambiguity. If we read them literally, the voice in the second stanza speaks for the more timid side of the protagonist and the voice in the third stanza for his self-correcting courage. But here again we have the clear suggestion of a man and a woman. She is afraid, while he encourages her to admit the unknown with joy. Waiting outside, he tells her, is not someone who 'wants to do us harm' but 'three strange angels.' They will reveal to us a new realm of holiness, if only we can forget our fear and self-consciousness.

Lawrence took as his main theme the need for modern man and woman to 'come through' in this way. They must rediscover true communion with one another and with the whole of existence, the instinctive communion possessed by ancient civilization but destroyed by the death drive of latter-day civilization. Death of the old ego-self, resurrection of the bodily self, are needed. The process is described in 'New Heaven and Earth,' the eight-part sequence in which Lawrence recounts the entire mystical experience of death and resurrection he advocates and, for symbolic purposes at least, says he has undergone. He describes the modern ego-corruption in which no identity is possible:

I was so weary of the world,
I was so sick of it,
everything was tainted with myself,
skies, trees, flowers, birds, water,
people, houses, streets, vehicles, machines,
nations, armies, war, peace-talking. . . .

The agony of this condition lay in the self-enmeshing of the mind. Everything was felt as merely an emanation of the ego-self, an emblem and definition of some phase of man. The speaker felt all other beings were merely facets of himself, a feeling which, by definition, violates the integrity and energy of each uniquely alive individual creature.

I was a lover, I kissed the woman I loved,
And God of horror, I was kissing also myself.
I was a father and a begetter of children,
And oh, oh horror, I was begetting and conceiving in my own body.

The only relief from the horror comes with the absolute deadening of the sensual life. 'I buried my beloved; it was good, I buried myself and was gone.' To this kind of self-betrayal society adds the total annihilation of modern war, with its 'thousands and thousands of gaping, hideous foul dead.' So the false ego, the self inseparable from this bestially mechanized civilization, is at last 'trodden to nought in the sour black earth.' Now the hitherto *unconscious* self can rise into its own:

risen, not born again, but risen, body the same as before,
New beyond knowledge of newness, alive beyond life. . . .
here, in the other world, still terrestrial
myself, the same as before, yet unaccountably new.

When the false social self has been destroyed, at whatever cost, then each one can feel the separate existence of himself and others. The risen speaker touches his wife as a being apart from himself for the first time:

I touched her flank and knew I was carried by the current in death
over to the new world, and was climbing out on the shore. . . .

The sequence ends with a paean to the 'new world' by the speaker, now 'a madman in rapture.' The landscape of the new world is that of the human body; the energies set free in it are those which suffuse all the physical universe. The woman is an exotic country with 'land that beats with a pulse,' and 'valleys that draw close in love,' and 'strange-mounded breasts and strange sheer slopes, and white levels.' As in his story *The Man Who Died*, Lawrence here revises the image of Christ by celebrating an earthly instead of a Heavenly Bridegroom. With this secular displacement of values, not only in 'New Heaven and Earth' but also in much of his other poetry and fiction, Lawrence creates a free floating symbol of the private revolution in the modern sensibility. He had a keen sense, in his own life and personality, of the clash between bourgeois and lower-class values, and between both of them and the aristocratic tradition. Rejecting socialism and democracy fairly early, he was attracted to fascism through his belief in great, magnetic individuals but not to the concept of mass-man essential to fascism. His real contribution in this realm was to transpose the perspectives of political and social revolution into private, inward terms.

In this special sense, there is no question he speaks for the times. His stress on the re-emergence of the primal self is but the desire to go behind doctrinal religious systems and recover the ancient—even the pre-historic—embodiments of the life-force principle. The chants scattered throughout *The Plumed Serpent*, with their incidental attacks on the degeneracy of modern men and their implication that the time of Christ is over and the time of the old gods come again, are one evidence. The animal poems, especially in *Birds, Beasts, and Flowers*, are another. Each of the birds, beasts, and flowers Lawrence writes about is an indomitable, sacred embodiment, a totem symbol, of that which man must find in himself also. How Lawrence used conventional religious and mythical associations can be seen in the Cross imagery of 'Tortoise Shell' and 'Tortoise Shout.' 'Why were we crucified into sex?' the latter poem asks. The cry uttered by the tortoise in coition is the same cry as that from the tortured Jesus, 'the Osiris-cry of abandonment': 'Torn, to become whole again, after long seeking for what is lost.' In other poems we see the snake as 'a king in exile . . . due to be crowned again'—archetype of the sexual mystery deep in the bowels of the earth; we are told that archangels and cherubim attend the ecstatic mating of whales; Bavarian gentians are the 'torch-flowers' of hell lighting up the 'marriage of the living dark,' of Pluto and Persephone.

Lawrence specifically rejects the term 'rebirth' for the kind of self-realization he thus celebrates. He visualizes the realization of the 'blood' self as something new, a *first* birth out of the adult state of 'non-being' which has prevented the emergence of the primal self into full growth. The point is that the state of living death or non-being of our civilization is a necessary prelude to a modern man's self-realization. He must not 'go back' to a savage state but 'has still to let go, to know what not-being is, before he can *be*. Till he has gone through the Christian negation of himself, and has known the Christian consummation, he is a mere amorphous heap.' Whether we call this process rebirth or resurrection, then, it is a matter of coming through to a higher stage of personality. The 'irritable cerebral consciousness' ceases to inhibit the vital self, and the once oversophisticated intelligence sinks deep within the personality. Intelligence is not lost forever, as it would be if we simply reverted to a literally animal existence. It is absorbed into the life participation of men restored to normal relations with the rest of the universe.

Lawrence's diagnosis of a diseased civilization seeing itself in a mirror of false, antihuman abstractions and needing to recover health through individual rebirth or resurrection is implicit in almost all major modern poetry. The means of salvation, or of *possible* salvation—for this is the great realm of the tentative, as Eliot's poetry surprisingly demonstrates—vary from poet to poet. But Lawrence's mystical conception of a state of communion, body-centered, into which we have yet to be born, illuminates a great deal of the poetry written over the past few decades. The impetus he has given to other writers comes not so much from his style—of all modern poets of real standing, he is perhaps the shakiest as a master of his craft—as from his simplifying the issues.

2. HART CRANE

Hart Crane is one of the important poets affected by Lawrence's cast of thought. He mentions Lawrence very early in his correspondence and there is evidence he studied *The Plumed Serpent* (as one would gather from the poem itself) while working on

The Bridge. A few months before his death, he wrote that *The Man Who Died* has 'more to tell me—at least in my present state of mind—than any book in the Bible.' * Various other comments show that he was especially appreciative of Lawrence's keen sensuousness and that Lawrence's writing generally was one of his windows into truth. Apart from direct influence, there is a simple convergence of interests. Thus, Crane read and was strongly indebted to P. D. Ouspensky, whose mysticism bears various resemblances to Lawrence's. All three writers share a Nietzchean influence, and Ouspensky is naturally familiar with the idea of a new heaven and earth for the man who can 'come through.' Such a man, he says, in his *Tertium Organum,* will move 'into a higher order of intuition, into a higher consciousness which will reveal to us a marvelous and mysterious world.' †

Crane's true bent, however, was not as a thinker, propagandist, or 'healer.' He had greater poetic gifts than Lawrence, gifts like those of Rimbaud or Dylan Thomas. Like them he was adept in metaphorical association and deeply inward in his thought. His attempt at a prophetic role in his long sequence *The Bridge* convinces us less successfully of the validity of his triumphant vision than of the desperate crisis of personality that motivated the vision. In this sequence, which took him almost seven years to complete, Crane tried to find sources of vitality for the modern world in the folk traditions of America, including the history and mythology of the Indian. He took some of his bearings from writers close in their concerns to Lawrence (see, for instance, Waldo Frank's *Our America* and William Carlos Williams's *In the American Grain*), as well as from Walt Whitman and Lawrence himself. The basic source of vitality he sought to exploit was the very machine culture so many other writers with similar aims have deplored. As the Marxian poets of the 'thirties were to do, he looked to this culture for symbols of modern man's ultimate crea-

* *The Letters of Hart Crane,* ed. Brom Weber, Hermitage House, New York, 1952, p. 395.

† P. D. Ouspensky, *Tertium Organum,* Knopf, New York, 1945, p. 152. See the discussion of Ouspensky's influence on Crane in Brom Weber, *Hart Crane,* Bodley Press, New York, 1948, pp. 150-63 and *passim.*

tivity, his ability to bring his splintered life into a new, harmonious whole. Crane conceived of the Brooklyn Bridge as such a symbol. His invocation to it in 'Proem: To Brooklyn Bridge,' the opening poem of the sequence, reads divinity into cold iron:

> O harp and altar, of the fury fused,
> (How could mere toil align thy choiring strings!)
> Terrific threshold of the prophet's pledge,
> Prayer of pariah, and the lover's cry. . . .

Even in the 'Proem,' however, the deeper vision stems from the speaker's 'crisis of personality.' The speaker begins with a gloriously precarious image of an escape into a realm of pure freedom that cannot be sustained:

> How many dawns, chill from his rippling rest,
> The seagull's wings shall dip and pivot him,
> Shedding white rings of tumult, building high
> Over the chained bay waters Liberty—
>
> Then, with inviolate curve, forsake our eyes
> As apparitional as sails that cross
> Some page of figures to be filed away;
> —Till elevators drop us from our day . . .

This is a dizzily anarchic vision at first. The opening stanza may be read in alternative but related ways. Either the bird builds a higher but less stable kind of freedom than is promised by the 'chained' Statue of Liberty in the bay waters below; or, if we read the stanza as a buoyant periodic construction, it is building, 'over the chained bay waters,' Liberty. (Since Crane did not put an apostrophe after 'waters,' both interpretations are possible.) Either way, we have an evanescent dream of soaring escape from a heavy mood of confinement and oppression. The contrast between the two states of confinement and flight is supported by rapidly shifting impressions of the seagull. The speaker identifies himself with the seagull just before his flight and then during it; he is at one with the bird's sense of itself awaking on the cold, swaying, 'chained' water and, a moment later, is with it high above, master-

ing the air like Hopkins's windhover. Meanwhile, as is characteristic in Crane, there is an extraordinary play of sound reinforcing
the kinetic impressions of the gull. The first crucial phrase, 'chill
from his rippling rest,' establishes the pattern with its short *i*'s,
its *l*'s, and its *p*'s. These sounds, occurring in varying combinations
thereafter (together with the related sounds *b*, *m*, and *n*), enmesh
the stanza in a single musical pattern that brings together the
opposed states of rest and movement. (In the next stanza the
psychological shift is marked by the emergence of long *a*'s as the
key sound.) But the first two stanzas considered together make a
more complete unit than did the first one alone because they develop the opposition of these two states more fully. The vision of
Liberty so carelessly improvised—'shed'—by the gull vanishes. The
poet calls it 'apparitional' only, comparing it to the day-dreams
of office workers who 'see' themselves on sailboats or sailing ships
as they go about their jobs. The words 'filed away' curtly dismiss
both 'gulls and sails,' and the letdown is given a jolting physical
reality in the line that cuts off the whole realm of dreams: '—Till
elevators drop us from our day . . .' The succession of impressions
in this two-stanza movement is particularly rich. The connotation of
an endless repetition in time of 'How many dawns,' the 'chill' sensation that follows (linking the heights of the dawn sky with the
waters below), and the unease implicit in 'rippling rest' are but
opening notes. Then the powerful energies of the seagull's movements take over, and the poet abstracts a design from them: 'white
rings of tumult,' out of which an illusion of true liberty can be
built. But though the curve of its movement remains abstractly
'inviolate,' there is no visible, permanently dependable emblem
here of the right kind of liberty, that which is both free and
ordered at the same moment. Rather, it is one marked by 'tumult,'
and it disappears. The double drop, from excited, soaring heights
to a cliché of reverie and from there to a really depressed image
for the low state of the human spirit in 'our day,' is enormous.

The third stanza adds yet another symbol of delusory promise:
'cinemas, panoramic sleights.' Here we find 'multitudes bent toward some flashing scene' which, however, is 'never disclosed.'
Again and again they hasten to this revelation which never re-

veals itself. Not as dramatic as the two that precede it, this stanza nevertheless focuses our attention most unerringly on the dead level of shoddiness beneath the glamor of a mechanical civilization. And yet the fourth stanza arises from this dead level of shoddiness in an arc as pure and gleaming as that which it apostrophizes— the Bridge. Here is a symbolic promise, out of that same civilization, that seems much more than the figment of a daydream—

> And Thee, across the harbor, silver-paced
> As though the sun took step of thee, yet left
> Some motion ever unspent in thy stride,—
> Implicitly thy freedom staying thee!

The fourth stanza, together with stanzas six through nine, deifies the Bridge. Yet some elements cast doubt on the wholehearted conviction of these stanzas. Remember that the poet felt it necessary to offer three symbols of delusory hope—the first from nature, the second psychological, the third from the machine world—before introducing this deification. The Bridge, while it stands in obvious contrast to those preceding symbols, might conceivably be thought of as actually the *fourth* in a series, the most delusory symbol of all precisely because of the contrast it appears to offer. Crane, though he capitalizes 'Thee' at first, does not do so later in the poem. Too, he says the Bridge shines '*as though* the sun took step of thee.' The suggestion is of an as-if divinity only, such as Stevens proposes in 'Sunday Morning.' In the seventh stanza he says the 'guerdon' this deity has to offer is an 'obscure one'—'obscure as that heaven of the Jews.' Finally, at the end of the poem, the speaker describes himself as standing 'in darkness' and bleakness—'Already snow submerges an iron year'—and prays that the Bridge *become* the divine force he has willed it to be:

> Unto us lowliest sometime sweep, descend
> And of the curveship lend a myth to God.

Symbolically this means that the poet's faith in industrial man's capacity to triumph over himself is too unsure to be asserted unqualifiedly. He certainly believed in the desirability and beauty of pure form, and the poem makes it clear that an unbroken curve is to him the purest of forms. Because of its 'curveship' which can 'condense eternity,' the Bridge can be exalted *aesthetically*. It is a modern manifestation of Olympian serenity, with its 'cloud-flown derricks' and its cables that 'breathe the North Atlantic still.' The passionate prayer to the Bridge arises, then, from the speaker's ardent desire to have confidence in the triumph of his civilization over its own inadequacies, and in his own triumph over the alienation deep within himself.

This ultimate unsureness of faith in *The Bridge* is often called a 'failure' of the poem also. Crane seems to have feared, and in at least one letter * to have been half persuaded, that his sequence was a failure in some important respects. If the sequence has failed, it is because the fifteen poems that make it up are somewhat uneven in quality and not because *The Bridge* expresses the agonized duality of the human condition (what Lawrence would call its 'crucified' condition) so honestly. Though Crane could not achieve absolute faith in the vision, he never doubted its beauty or its meaning. His real triumph lay in registering the complex state of feeling in which neither total confidence nor total despair allows the other mastery.

The sequence as a whole is ordered so as to unfold this motivation. 'To Brooklyn Bridge,' as we have seen, announces the heroic theme even while it evokes the sense of dilemma. Next, 'Ave Maria' shows Columbus's thoughts on his homeward voyage, full of his own mystical vision of triumph over terror and nothingness. Clearly he is a 'mask' for the poet himself, bringing together, as Pound often does, the sensibility of the European past and that of the American present. The *Powhatan's Daughter* section projects similar continuities with our own native past. 'Powhatan's daughter,' Pocohontas, personifies the living American earth as a female deity who inspires each generation anew and, 'virgin to the last of men,' must be taken anew by it. The lovely poem that opens this section, 'The Harbor Dawn,' evokes her quietly. Awaking beside his beloved, in a room near the Harbor, the poet notes the sounds and other impressions of the world outdoors as the morn-

* Crane, op. cit. pp. 352-4.

ing comes on. In this state not yet free of the sleep world, he sees his beloved and the ancient dream of Pocohontas blended together in a single being.

The other poems in the *Powhatan's Daughter* section pursue the Pocohontas symbolism on many levels, bringing together a large number of personal and national or mythical memories. 'The River,' for instance, speeds through a satirical view of the twentieth-century cultural landscape but touches sympathetically on the childlike feeling of hoboes for the land, the 'body under the wide rain' that the Indian at the height of his vitality once knew how to love and use. The six powerfully evocative stanzas closing this poem sing the Mississippi River's virile relation to that meaning of Indian culture and also to the white American heritage, both foul and fair. 'The Dance' moves over to the Indian theme entirely, the poet sloughing off his modern self and attempting to repossess the psychology of the mythical Indian hero and the significance of his tragic sacrifice to the future. The spirit of Lawrence's *The Plumed Serpent* is strongly evident at the climactic points here.

The final poem of the *Powhatan's Daughter* section is 'Indiana,' in which is signalized the transfer of the life-bearing native tradition from Indian to white culture. After the vast imaginative projections of the other poems in the section the prairie woman's monologue brings us back to the difficulties of the vision celebrated in *The Bridge* by reminding us of the hardships and failures of American life, the often futile restlessness, the pity of individual defeat.

The next two sections consist of individual poems. 'Cutty Sark,' taking up from a sailor theme introduced in 'Indiana,' centers on the poet's conversation with an old rum-soaked sailor in a South Street dive in New York. The poet walks home, his head full of images of Atlantis and of 'clipper dreams indelible and ranging.' Remembering the sails of 'Proem,' emblems of a caged futility, we are perhaps not surprised that at the very end 'Cutty Sark' speaks of ships sunk and missing. 'Cape Hatteras' pushes hard against a letdown into essential pessimism. The poet strives to see himself as the spokesman for cosmic evolution culminating in a

new world of power: 'The nasal whine of power whips a new universe.' Crane now swears allegiance to the inclusive, mystic vision of Whitman.

The *Three Songs* of Section V form an interlude on the theme of woman. They are rather Metaphysical variations on the Pocohontas theme. We move from lust for the ineffable in 'Southern Cross,' to the mystery implicit in the flesh described so harshly, lushly, and wittily in 'National Winter Garden,' to the easy idealization of the innocence possible within the realities of life in 'Virginia.' Indulging in free intellectual play after the affirmations of 'Cape Hatteras,' Crane reveals in these poems his versatility and lyric craftsmanship.

Section VI, 'Quaker Hill,' strikes down these perspectives to plunge into a bitter contemplation of the philistinization of American life. All the artist can do is model himself on such forerunners as Emily Dickinson and Isadora Duncan, both of whom knew pain yet were able to create 'Love from despair—when love foresees the end.' The drop in mood from the gaiety of 'Virginia' is like the elevator-drop of the opening poem. It goes still lower in the crucial next section, 'The Tunnel,' a hell vision of the dim grays and naked glares, the monotonous motion, the incoherent snatches of overheard conversation, and the general ugliness of the subway-world:

> The phonographs of hades in the brain
> Are tunnels that re-wind themselves, and love
> A burnt match skating in a urinal—

Such lines are a complete negation of the sexual idealism of *Powhatan's Daughter* and *Three Songs*. Elsewhere in 'The Tunnel' there is a similar negation of the affirmative effort of 'Cape Hatteras.' Not Whitman but Poe is the forerunner to whom Crane now feels most akin. The substitution is particularly convincing because of the dynamic imagery he uses to portray this turn. Whitman was apostrophized in fairly general terms; Poe looms before us in violent, concrete images of death-horror, some of them out of his own poetry:

Whose head is swinging from the swollen strap?
Whose body smokes along the bitten rails,
Bursts from a smoldering bundle far behind
In back forks of the chasms of the brain. . . .
And why do I often meet your visage here,
Your eyes like agate lanterns—on and on
Below the toothpaste and the dandruff ads?

'Atlantis,' the paradisally ecstatic paean which closes *The Bridge*, does not, of course, overcome the dark conviction of 'The Tunnel.' It strains against it, but together the poems proliferate and sustain the duality of spirit established in 'Proem.' 'Atlantis' has certain questioning and hypothetical moments of the sort we noted in 'Proem,' but they are only minor restraints on its upward leaping effort toward pure affirmation of the Bridge's character as a 'swift peal of secular light, intrinsic Myth.' The dream of Atlantis, considered either as a city of the mythical past or as a usable hope for the future, is by definition dangerous—'apparitional.' But it is to Crane's credit that he took the risk, although perhaps he 'builded better than he knew.' Everything about the sequence is risky in this sense. Like the Bridge itself, its ancillary symbols—Columbus the voyager between two worlds, Pocohontas the earth goddess linking two civilizations, the rivers and railroads and tunnels and ships cutting across space and time, and finally Atlantis bridging reality and myth—confirm the need to accept the challenge with all its dangers. Without the negatives of the poem the challenge would be meaningless. The threatening sea-imagery of 'Ave Maria' betokening the antihuman terror of the universe; the equally antihuman flow of history represented in the closing section of 'The River'; the savagery of 'The Tunnel'—these, together with other portions of the poem, including the allusions to Crane's own unhappy childhood and youth, open the yawning depths which the seeker after pure affirmation must take into account. The poetic problem lies in the manner in which he undertakes the affirmation, not in its success or failure.

'Coming through' meant something quite different to Crane than it did to Lawrence. Where Lawrence visualized a fearful strangeness he *knew* he could count on an accompanying paradise of 'valleys that draw close in love.' Crane accepted the need to be 'born' in Lawrence's sense, without believing he would arrive in the new life at anything more than a quintessential terror or sordidness. Many of his shorter poems bring out this difference quite simply. 'The Idiot,' for instance, broods over an elementary grossness in life.

> That boy straggling under those mimosas, daft
> With squint lanterns in his head, and it's likely
> Fumbling his sex. That's why those children laughed
>
> In such infernal circles round his door
> Once when he shouted, stretched in ghastly shape. . . .

So in its way does 'Passage,' though it is a much subtler poem. 'Passage' breaks down the Lawrence dream of coaching oneself into realization through death of the 'false' self. The Laurentian program is stated ironically in the opening stanza:

> Where the cedar leaf divides the sky
> I heard the sea.
> In sapphire arenas of the hills
> I was promised an improved infancy.

The poet goes on to tell how the 'promise' kept receding, while his 'false,' civilized self proved ineradicable. He had tried to put away his memory of his 'chimney-sooted heart,' but it had manifested itself, in all its sickness, in his character and art after all. All along, his writing had been the art of a furtive, thieving, self-loathing being: his 'natural' as well as his social self. The poem ends with a sequence of images of the universe's indifference to man:

> . . . And from the Ptolemies
> Sand troughed us in a glittering abyss.
> A serpent swam a vertex to the sun
> —On unpaced beaches leaned its tongue and drummed.
> What fountains did I hear? what icy speeches?
> Memory, committed to the page, had broke.

Yet, for all his panic in the face of such a universe, Crane was in love with its very intransigence. In 'Passage,' written in 1925, the poet seemed to take a certain grim satisfaction in demeaning himself so that the 'glittering abyss' might the more easily triumph. A year later, 'Repose of Rivers' shows him entirely seduced by the dazzling emptiness which had aroused such horror in 'Passage.' Now he tells how the sea brought back to him the memory of marshlands seen in his childhood and the profounder racial memories of prehistoric, even pre-human times:

> . . . drew me into hades almost.
> And mammoth turtles climbing sulphur dreams. . . .

Had it not been for the archetypal associations the sea stirred to life in him, he would have 'bartered' away all the primal memories of the blood and become victim to the city's amnestic 'scalding unguents' and 'smoking darts.' These, we were told in 'Passage,' are insurmountable barriers to the poet's desired realization. But in 'Repose of Rivers' the sea has liberated him, not merely mocked him. It has drawn his consciousness irresistibly below the barrier of adult experience, instead of assaulting it head-on. So, in the Lawrence way, he has been 'carried' through to the *vita nuova*.

> . . . There, beyond the dykes
>
> I heard wind flaking sapphire, like this summer,
> And willows could not hold more steady sound.

The imagery and language here, especially the 'sapphire' figure, are almost identical with those of the first stanza of 'Passage.' But what was mere illusion there, albeit tragic illusion, is achieved beatitude here—not Lawrence's world of 'strange angels,' but a state in which all human tensions and agonies become irrelevant and are therefore set at rest.

This dream of 'salvation' through total annihilation of the self was natural to Crane's temperament, as his exhibitionistic homosexuality, his alcoholism, his hysterical relations with friends and lovers and family, and finally his suicide at the age of thirty-three suggest. In *The Bridge* he strove to out-argue the death drive but,

after years of intermittent effort, could only hold it at bay symbolically through agonized prayer for a life-bearing meaning to
make itself manifest.

The sequence of six poems called *Voyages*, begun about the same
time as *The Bridge* but completed within two years, is much more
successful though much less ambitious in scope and structure.
It does not struggle against the death motif, does not force the
argument at any point. Instead, basing itself on the figure of the
Sea as woman, it accepts and elaborates on the equation of the
ecstasy of sexual fulfillment with death. It begins simply, its first
poem a warning to children on the beach that the elements are
deceptive. 'The sun beats lightning on the waves,' and 'The waves
fold thunder on the sand,' and as for the Sea:

> . . . there is a line
> You must not cross nor ever trust beyond it
> Spry cordage of your bodies to caresses
> Too lichen-faithful from too wide a breast.
> The bottom of the sea is cruel.

It is with those murderous caresses that the rest of the sequence
has to do. This first poem is, thus, an overture in which the speaker
advises his more childlike self (symbolized by the 'bright striped
urchins' near the water) not to take the risks he knows he *will*
take. The intriguing thing the speaker has to tell us here is that
adult love and life's terror are for him synonymous. It is pity for
himself, of what will become of him in the ensuing 'voyages,' that
makes the three stanzas of this overture so poignant. And it is
on himself that he lavishes these images and these movingly varied
tones of affectionate admonition.

Then, with *Voyages II*, all this is in the past. Here is the Sea fully
personified as a voluptuous goddess, and the speaker is lost in the
'wrapt inflections of our love.' The previous poem had concluded
with the warning: 'The bottom of the sea is cruel.' This one
begins with the words 'And yet.' That is, 'The bottom of the sea is
cruel'—and yet there are other considerations. We see them at once,
for *Voyages II* from the first describes the Sea as an all-engulfing,
almost lewd female—a 'great wink of eternity,' whose 'undinal

vast belly moonward bends,' a creature of 'samite sheeted' undulations and secret, joyous meanings. The second stanza presents her wielding the impersonal justice of the universe, passing sentence on all things that exist. The full range of her music, her 'diapason,' knells death for all things that exist. So she is cruel, 'and yet' endlessly erotic, 'and yet' just. But perhaps our love will, if intense enough, enable us to escape the destiny she holds in store for us. That is the climactic suggestion of the long periodic sentence which makes up the first two stanzas. She respects only 'the pieties of lovers' hands,' a thought made more concrete in the third and fourth stanzas. She herself, we have already been told, is a being 'of rimless floods, unfettered leewardings,' something more than is contained in space and time. She dances 'adagios of islands,' and 'her turning shoulders wind the hours.' So perhaps she can bestow immortality on lovers, who have at least *felt* themselves beyond space and time. The poem ends in a way that has by now become familiar to us—a prayer that these things should indeed be so. Let us, says the speaker to his beloved (who is also the Sea herself), hold this moment of possibility above fate 'in one floating flower.' And he prays to the Seasons and the waves—the 'minstrel galleons of Carib fire'—for such an epiphany. The concluding lines epitomize the human predicament and all yearning:

> Bequeath us to no earthly shore until
> Is answered in the vortex of our grave
> The seal's wide spindrift gaze toward paradise.

Voyages III images forth the sexual union with the Sea for which the poem has been preparing. Its language is Shelleyan, but the rapture it sings is of death as well as love:

> And so, admitted through black swollen gates
> That must arrest all distance otherwise,—
> Past whirling pillars and lithe pediments,
> Light wrestling there incessantly with light,
> Star kissing star through wave on wave unto
> Your body rocking!
>   and where death, if shed,
> Presumes no carnage, but this single change,—

Upon the steep floor flung from dawn to dawn
The silken skilled transmemberment of song;

Permit me voyage, love, into your hands . . .

Voyages IV then describes, in a spirit of wonder like that of
Lawrence's 'New Heaven and Earth,' the mystical concentration of
all reality, all form, all potentiality in that act of union containing
'the secret oar and petals of all love.' In these two poems of sexual
exaltation the sequence reaches the climax of its literal theme.

But the most intensely felt poem is the fifth, in which the same
mood of cold terror that dominated 'Passage' cuts across the lovers'
illusion of triumph over life's limitations. Just as in that poem 'Sand
troughed us in a glittering abyss,' so here the lover becomes aware
of an ultimate nothingness:

. . . that godless cleft of sky
Where nothing turns but dead sands flashing.

'The cables of our sleep,' the rapt love-sleep of the two preceding
poems, are now 'swiftly filed' and cut through by the hard light
of the moon that turns the bay estuaries into 'one merciless white
blade.' It cuts the human lovers' understanding of one another
apart, and makes the Sea-love a ghostly illusion out of 'drifting
foam.' Without transition, with the absolute certainty of experience itself, the whole vision of triumph over death has been
slashed away.

Voyages VI concludes the sequence. It is a poem of pain, but
still celebrates the lost vision of love transcendent. The vision,
however impermanent, was in itself 'unbetrayable.' The speaker, a
'derelict and blinded guest' whose eyes are 'pressed black against
the prow' of an unnamed ship (the influence of Rimbaud's 'The
Drunken Boat' is evident here as throughout the *Voyages*), still
maintains in the magnificent opening stanzas of this last poem his
now tragic worship of the universality of the Sea:

O rivers mingling toward the sky
And harbor of the phoenix' breast. . . .

Speaking for all 'creation,' he insists that the 'blithe and petalled Word' still holds its meaning for the goddess though it means ultimate destruction for man. This is Crane's 'coming-through,' then, as it was in the dual ending of *The Bridge*—an awakening into defeat redeemed only by a refusal to deny the glory of the dream. The sadness with which this poem begins cannot be undone:

> Where icy and bright dungeons lift
> Of swimmers their lost morning eyes. . . .

Yet it remains, in this poet's view, the swimmers' task forever to follow that 'imaged Word' which alone can reconcile them to their doomed selves. Lawrence, for all his talk of courage, never could have come through to the tragic assertion this sequence reaches.

3. AUDEN AND THE 'THIRTIES

> In the nightmare of the dark
> All the dogs of Europe bark,
> And the living nations wait,
> Each sequestered in its hate;
>
> Intellectual disgrace
> Stares from every human face,
> And the seas of pity lie
> Locked and frozen in each eye.

In these stanzas from 'In Memory of W. B. Yeats,' Auden describes what 'The Second Coming' had prophesied nineteen years earlier: the end of an era in the paralysis of will toward the spiritual and the humane, the drowning of the best values in a 'blood-dimmed tide.' The difference between Yeats and Auden lies in the profoundly political coloration of Auden's sense of reality, his acute sense of the 'living nations' and of the barriers of hatred between them. This is not to suggest he is Yeats's equal as a poet. He is too much the improviser, and lacks the character to push a poem through to its aesthetic limits. There is always something unfinished about his work, a restless, almost *occasional* tone. It is interesting how often a single line stands out indelibly from one of his poems, while the poem itself recedes from the memory. This is especially true of his opening lines: 'A weed from Catholic Europe, it took root'; 'A nondescript express in from the South'; 'To ask the hard question is simple'; 'O Love, the interest itself in thoughtless heaven,' and many others equally spontaneous-sounding, colloquial, and memorable.

But the very spontaneity of these lines, so much a part of Auden's improvisatory genius, is related to his feeling for the actualities of the political life. His *Collected Poetry* has title after title like 'Hongkong 1938,' 'In Memory of Ernst Toller,' and *In Time of War*. One wonders whether it was not an unconscious desire to parody himself that led him to end the book with his 'Christmas oratorio' called *For the Time Being*. To be of the moment and speak out of it is to sacrifice a certain goal of perfection in art. As Hugh MacDiarmid pointed out: 'You cannot light a match upon a crumbling wall.' Nevertheless, this occasional motivation of his work is, with an amazing virtuosity which makes him something like a modern Dryden, Auden's greatest strength in practice.

Three representative poems, '1929,' 'Spain 1937,' and 'September 1, 1939,' are obviously political in their concerns, and taken as a group, show not only Auden's development but that of his whole literary generation. '1929' begins like *The Waste Land*, but soon takes a different direction. Where Eliot's 'April is the cruelest month' leads quickly to voices other than the poet's and to a rapid accumulation of images and emotions, Auden keeps to the same voice throughout and to a fairly explicit logical sequence. (Generally, his ambiguities and 'difficulties' are more of language and syntax than of the relation of images and ideas to one another.)

> It was Easter as I walked in the public gardens
> Hearing the frogs exhaling from the pond,
> Watching traffic of magnificent cloud
> Moving without anxiety on open sky—
> Season when lovers and writers find
> An altering speech for altering things,

An emphasis on new names, on the arm
A fresh hand with fresh power.
But thinking so I came at once
Where solitary man sat weeping on a bench,
Hanging his head down, with his mouth distorted
Helpless and distorted as an embryo chicken.

So I remember all of those whose death
Is necessary condition of the season's setting forth . . .
The death by cancer of a once hated master,
A friend's analysis of his own failure,
Listened to at intervals throughout the winter
At different hours and in different rooms.
But always with success of others for comparison. . . .

The literal argument of this opening is self-evident. The sight
of the suffering man in a season of regeneration and newly emer-
gent powers reminds the speaker of a melancholy principle: that
'the necessary condition' of one's growth and success is the defeat
and failure of others. The ironic reciprocity of joy and suffering
is conveyed especially in the image of the weeping man who looks
'helpless and distorted as an embryo chicken.' Compare the figure
with Shelley's of the West Wind as 'destroyer and preserver'; instead of Shelley's wholehearted advocacy of revolutionary change,
which once led Marx himself to praise him unreservedly, Auden's
poem is heavy with consciousness of the suffering such change
must cause. The image of what is brought to birth, 'an embryo
chicken,' is deliberately chosen to suggest weakness, awkwardness, ugliness, and confusion.

Yet '1929' *is* a revolutionary poem. First, it asserts that change
is inevitable and, though not without tragic implications, desirable. Next, the second and third sections contemplate the relation between the inexorable forces making for change and the
internal search of the 'frightened soul,' after the trauma of birth,
for the right kind of love and security. In these sections, as elsewhere in Auden's early poetry, we see him juxtaposing Freudian
assumptions with those of dialectical materialism. Part 2 of '1929'

begins with a typical Marxian formulation of the interdependence
of thought and being:

> Coming out of me living is always thinking,
> Thinking changing and changing living,
> Am feeling as it was seeing. . . .

The syntax is squeezed together telegraphically in the effort to
convey a general state of sentiency. Moving some stanzas later
into Freudian formulation, Auden uses a similar collapsed syntax:

> And I above standing, saying in thinking:
>
> 'Is first baby, warm in mother,
> Before born and is still mother,
> Time passes and now is other,
> Cries in cold air, himself no friend.' . . .

The starkness, alliterations, and falling rhythms of these passages
combine to suggest a primitive sub-awareness like that of Old
English wisdom-verses or of Browning's Caliban when he cries out:

> Setebos, Setebos, and Setebos!
> 'Thinketh, He dwelleth in the cold o' the moon. . . .

Auden, like Hadrian and like Dante, is re-creating the consciousness of the naïve, growing ego—*animula*, 'the simple soul'—
as it emerges into the world. Touched by life's inexorable cruelty,
it would model itself after the indifference of animal nature if it
could. The speaker tells of seeing a colony of ducks as they sit,
preen, doze, paddle, and fish in the water. It is political as well as
psychological truth that interrupts his dream of becoming like
them.

> Those find sun's luxury enough,
> Shadow know not of homesick foreigner
> Nor restlessness of intercepted growth.

Like Hart Crane's gulls, those ducks create a momentary illusion
of meaningful freedom for the soul-sick observer. The illusion is

rejected here too, of course, partly in the light of attitudes that again recall Crane. The speaker remembers once hearing men's voices singing in unison in a village square; he finds another sign of man's power to make his own destiny glorious in the 'strict beauty of locomotive'; in the stanza closing Part 3, he seeks a way to love fatality and even death; and he comes through to a final vision of a new world's birth. Inevitably, however, Auden departs from Crane in the political turn he takes when he speaks of refugees 'shooting and barricade in street,' and police violence, and when he sounds his trumpet note for the revolutionary destruction of capitalist society. 'It is time for the destruction of error,' he proclaims. The self can never find its bearings in a world whose living-dead rulers have already reduced love to a 'degenerate remnant' and have committed themselves to destruction of 'efflorescence of the flesh' and the 'intricate play of the mind,' and to enforcing

> Conformity with the orthodox bone,
> With organized fear, the articulated skeleton.

Personal love or ascetic self-denial—'the admiring excitement of union,' 'the abrupt self-confident farewell'—is but an incomplete form of what is needed now. The new, paradisal but man-made love will need

> . . . death, death of the grain, our death,
> Death of the old gang; would leave them
> In sullen valley where is made no friend,
> The old gang to be forgotten in the spring,
> The hard bitch and the riding-master,
> Stiff underground; deep in clear lake
> The lolling bridegroom, beautiful, there.

But if this is a revolutionary program at the point of the most drastic action, it is also deceptive and ambiguous in some important ways. Here, at the very end of the poem, the speaker identifies himself with the hated bourgeoisie by calling not for 'their' but for 'our' death. 'We'—including himself—must kill the selfishly in-

dividualistic in ourselves. The program now is reminiscent of
Lawrence's and of Christian teaching as well. Moreover, the image
of 'the lolling bridegroom, beautiful, there' again suggests Lawrence's teachings in works like 'New Heaven and Earth' and *Lady
Chatterley's Lover*; and it suggests Christ the Bridegroom rather
more than it does a resurrection of the human spirit in a classless
society. 'Deep in clear lake' is both a baptismal image and a womb
image, and very possibly goes back to the same sources in Frazer's
The Golden Bough as Eliot's 'Death by Water.' The poem is revolutionary and Marxian, yet clearly not doctrinaire. The traditions
and symbolism it draws on are more powerful than its explicit
argument, which is needed to provide a certain outline and direction but is in the long run chiefly valuable as one important element in the picturing of a complexly disturbed state of mind.
Much has been made of Auden's deliberate mystifications in his
early work, and most of the more puzzling moments have to do
with this kind of ambiguity of commitment. Political thought,
rhetoric, and action demand partisanship, while religious self-
questioning, psychological self-identification, and the aesthetic tradition look to the encompassment of opposites and the breaking
down of dogmatic formulations. Turning away from '1929' for a
moment, we need no rare perspicacity to observe that in many
other poems Auden's emphasis on disease and healing, his interest
in physical maladies as outward manifestations of personality dis-
orders (each with its social dimensions), and his romanticizing of
the voyaging sensibility hardly bespeak the disciplined Communist.
His prose poem 'Letter to a Wound,' in *The Orators*, treats the
undefined wound with a depraved affection that might be satirical, might be sincere—the context does not tell. This kind of
ambiguity runs through the whole of *The Orators*, which deals
specifically (especially in *The Journal of an Airman*) with the mysteries of commitment. The speaker, cherishing his wound (variously interpreted as the wound of homosexuality, or of vaguer
perversions; the ulcer of self-consciousness; the disease of a class-
society, etc.), loves what he should normally abominate. As the
wiseacre voice in 'The Questioner Who Sits So Sly' shows, the

temptation to yield to the beloved enemy is great. Will you have the power, the will to resist, he asks the voyager:

> Will you turn a deaf ear
> To what they said on the shore,
> Interrogate their poises
> In their rich houses;
>
> Of stork-legged heaven-reachers
> Of the compulsory touchers
> The sensitive amusers
> And masked amazers?

And, without wishing violence (a strangely pacific note in a Marxian-oriented poem), will you have the courage to risk death constantly and the patience to accept the boredom of the spiritual revolutionary's life? Can you bear not to succeed or be honored?

> Will you wheel death anywhere
> In his invalid chair,
> With no affectionate instant
> But his attendant?
>
> For to be held for friend
> By an undeveloped mind
> To be joke for children is
> Death's happiness. . . .
>
> Remembering there is
> No recognized gift for this;
> No income, no bounty,
> No promised country. . . .

The half rhymes, which often seem puns, and the indefinite use of definite pronouns, as well as the generally riddling tone, are smart-alecky devices that appeal especially to a small, 'private' group. At the same time the thought is serious and insistent, and the lyrical movement is compelling, so that these initial barriers to communication are easily overcome. The 'questioner' is obviously needling himself first of all. The same sort of thing happens, just as obviously, in ' "O where are you going?" said reader to rider.' This song from *The Orators* sets the timid representative of the old order—described variously as 'reader' and 'fearer' and 'horror'—against the searcher for the new—'rider' and 'farer' and 'hearer.' Reader–fearer–horror describes the charnel terrors of the unknown, the groping in the dark to come, the dread figures waiting to pounce, the leprous or cancerous condition attributed to those who go too far from 'normal' expectations. Rider–farer–hearer presumably silences him with a stanza full of crisp rejoinders, but the challenging questions put to him hang oppressively in the air.

The early Auden, then, was far from a tendentious writer in any hackneyed programmatic sense. '1929' was as honest an effort as *The Bridge* to build a symbolic argument toward affirmation, and Auden tried to take into account similar confusions of perspective. Now let us digress a little further and examine one small poem, 'The Decoys,' from that complex sequence of verse and prose *The Orators*.

> There are some birds in these valleys
> Who flutter round the careless
> With intimate appeal,
> By seeming kindness trained to snaring,
> They feel no falseness.
>
> Under the spell completely
> They circle can serenely,
> And in the tricky light
> The masked hill has a purer greenness.
> Their flight looks fleeter.
>
> But fowlers, O, like foxes,
> Lie ambushed in the rushes.
> Along the harmless tracks
> The madman keeper crawls through brushwood,
> Axe under oxter.

Alas, the signal given,
Fingers on trigger tighten.
The real unlucky dove
Must smarting fall away from brightness
Its love from living.

Not ideology-burdened like '1929,' 'The Decoys' gives us a clearer impression of Auden's lyrical talent, the passion underlying it, and the subtlety with which he gives idiosyncratic shape to both. This poem too employs alliterations and uses approximate rhymes to gain freedom while maintaining a patterned effect. For instance, 'valleys' is rhymed with 'careless,' 'completely' with 'serenely,' and so on. But this poem has a tighter arrangement: a scheme of *aabaa* for each stanza, and a regular though subtly varied line-length pattern. The whole poem has a grace and balanced composition impossible without true virtuosity. At the same time, it is highly concentrated narrative, in which Auden has 'loaded every rift with ore.'

At first 'The Decoys' presents a lovely, yet sinister picture. Soon the sinister aspect becomes heightened until mad terror seems to reign, and then at last we have the ultimate sad irony of the death of innocence. The decoys of the first stanzas 'feel no falseness' because they themselves have been trained to betray without knowing what they do. The symbolic connotations of these stanzas would be clear enough without further comment, but the image of the 'madman keeper' in the third stanza almost instructs us to read the symbolism explicitly—that the leaders and teachers of our society ('these valleys') are conditioned, in all innocence, to lead us to our doom. And the 'fowlers,' agents of the destruction that follows, are but doing their appointed work. As for the 'keeper,' whether he is a Hardyesque embodiment of the sense-lessness of things, or the death principle that makes everything meaningless and crazy anyway, or the principle of destructiveness driving a society mad, or the society itself gone mad, he too goes along 'harmless tracks.' Nevertheless, things are so arranged that the true innocence of life, 'the real unlucky dove,' is inevitably deceived and killed. Thus Auden brings out the tricky moral ambiguities of our condition, in language simultaneously open to social, religious, philosophical, and, especially, political interpretation. In this respect 'The Decoys' has many similarities to '1929,' though it keeps its ideological implications at sufficient distance to allow its specifically lyric qualities to hold the center of the stage.

'Spain 1937' is in general simpler than either of these poems. It argues that the great issue of whether or not man shall have a future has now thrust itself upon us. Yesterday there were great triumphs of science, religion, thought, art; tomorrow there may be even more miraculous ones; 'but today the struggle.' Man has reached the point beyond unconscious evolution, and now he must create the image by which he will guide himself henceforth. The Spanish Civil War, the poem tells us, is the moment of decision; man must look into his own mystery for his own bearings, for there are no outside clues to guide him. (Out of similar considerations the American Kenneth Fearing entitled his 1938 volume of poems *Dead Reckoning*.) Described so, the poem appears well meant but obviously propagandistic; actually, Auden's wit and imagination save it, as do his rhythms and diction. He can pull a way of putting things out of the common speech, out of the language of textbooks, out of the half pomposities of oratory— his ear catches the music peculiar to each mode of communication: the parallel constructions and 'sloganising' of the eloquent speaker, the idealist's dreams of the perfect life, half-humorously elaborated, the candors of the radical-intellectual, the tragic awareness of man's fall that is part of our Western heritage:

Yesterday the installation of dynamos and turbines;
The construction of railways in the colonial desert;
      Yesterday the classic lecture
On the origin of Mankind. But today the struggle. . . .

Tomorrow, for the young, the poets exploding like bombs,
The walks by the lake, the winter of perfect communion;
      Tomorrow the bicycle races
Through the suburbs on summer evenings: but today the struggle.

Today the inevitable increase in the chances of death;
The conscious acceptance of guilt in the fact of murder;
    Today the expending of powers
On the flat ephemeral pamphlet and the boring meeting. . . .

The stars are dead; the animals will not look:
We are left alone with our day, and the time is short and
    History to the defeated
May say Alas but cannot help or pardon.

'Spain 1937' is a beautiful instance of political poetry that remains poetry. From the moment of its ringing but curiously expository beginning—

    Yesterday all the past. The language of size
    Spreading to China along the trade-routes. . . .

it maintains the seriousness of revolutionary politics and the passion of its oratory while at the same time leaping clear of the obvious clichés that could so easily drag down such poetry. Auden's
survey of the past and daydreams about the future actually seem
nonpolitical, unless in the phrase 'Liberty's masterful shadow.'
Two stanzas of the poem do describe the volunteers, Spanish and
foreign, who 'came to present their lives' to the cause of Loyalist
Spain. But the language concerns the places ('remote peninsulas,'
'sleepy plains,' 'aberrant fishermen's islands') from which these
volunteers came and the means by which they came, not their
motives and ideals. This description is preceded by a dialogue
between human petitioners—the poet, the scientist, the poor, the
nations—and the life principle. They beg for divine intervention,
whatever form divinity may take: 'dove' or 'furious papa' or 'mild
engineer.' 'The life' replies that the time has come for them to
look to their essential selves; destiny is whatever they find themselves to be. Though this is a political poem the issue is left open,
almost as it is in Yeats's 'Easter 1916.' The poem is programmatic
and partisan, but for the poet the political situation is simply the
clearest manifestation of the modern malaise:

On that tableland scored by rivers,
Our fever's menacing shapes are precise and alive.

The closing stanza, quoted earlier ('The stars are dead . . .'),
leaves the poem more forlorn than heroic, as though the poet already foresaw the failure of the Republic and with it the loss of
the future. With this ending, Auden matches 'Easter 1916' in the
unorthodoxy of his treatment of a political theme.

An even more depressed state of mind is recorded in 'September
1, 1939.' When this poem was written Auden could look back to the
defeat of the Republican cause in Spain, his own disillusionment
with Communism, and the recent beginning of the Second World
War. History had indeed said Alas to the defeated. The 'thirties
now seemed to him, after all, 'a low dishonest decade' whose end
was leaving 'the unmentionable odour of death' everywhere. In
this poem as in others written in the same period, Auden was
still 'political,' but like many others of his literary generation had
turned away from the activistic idealism that marked his more
wholeheartedly Marxian writing. He did not seek programmatic
alternatives to the Communist and Popular Frontist set of his
earlier thinking. Apparently the whole realm of political action
had become more or less distasteful, and with it the need to identify
with 'the people' that Communist thought stresses—although one
can say 'The people, yes,' and follow out other lines of activism
without being a Communist. Auden was still very much a political
poet, but in a new way; he used the political situation as an incen-
tive for coaching himself into a tragic vision of man's fate and
for the incantation of Judaeo-Christian-humanitarian pieties. Often
in his later poetry—in 'Musée de Beaux Arts,' for instance—the
springboard of politics may be conjectured, but it is not *in* the
poem.

There had always been a genuinely religious component in
Auden's writing, not only in the Romantic prayer for the realization of vision but also, often, in an assumption (if only ironic at
times, nevertheless important as a sign of Auden's alertness to the
theme) of the existence of God. We see this, for instance, in the

early 'Petition,' which must be intoned like the Lord's Prayer if
we are to get the real feel of it. 'Petition' is a catch-all prayer in
favor of every kind of regenerative theory, all revolutionary innova-
tions, every 'change of heart.' It wills that individuals be released
from the sick rigidities of our culture, expressed psychosomatically
as 'the intolerable neural itch,' 'the exhaustion of weaning,' 'the
liar's quinsy,' the 'distortions of ingrown virginity.' Auden in this
poem runs together ideas derived from Marx, Lawrence, Homer
Lane, Groddeck, and other 'healers.' He looks upon these figures
as a Moslem looks upon the Old Testament heroes, Jesus, and
Mohammed—as prophets of the divinity whom the poem's opening
lines address:

> Sir, no man's enemy, forgiving all
> But will its negative inversion, be prodigal. . . .

'Will its negative inversion' is the fault God (and Milton) found
in Adam, the willful misdirection of his freedom to adore the good
and to act accordingly. History, or 'the life,' gave a Miltonic reply
to man's plea for help in 'Spain 1937'—it is *you* who must choose
your future; I have but made the preparations and revealed to you
the issues.

'September 1, 1939' has not lost entire touch with the Marxian
explanation of events. Auden sees 'imperialism's face' clearly
enough in these events, and he sees that American civilization is
based on 'the strength of Collective Man.' The dream of neutrality
Americans cherished at the war's start is merely 'euphoric.' Action
must follow. But all this is less a challenge than evidence of
Original Sin and its subsequent effects. The poet is no longer
an orator; now he is but a man sitting in a New York bar, 'uncertain and afraid,' viewing himself and his fellows as

> Lost in a haunted wood,
> Children afraid of the night
> Who have never been happy or good.

We may study German history since Luther's day, he says, to un-
cover through scholarship everything 'that has driven a culture
mad,' and we may ransack the records to explain Hitler's psycho-

pathology. But the answer lies in no arcane knowledge of history, ideology, or psychology. It lies in the old moral truths, known to all, that

> Those to whom evil is done
> Do evil in return

and that war derives from that same selfish and irreligious misconception of the true meaning of love which lost us Eden:

> For the error bred in the bone
> Of each woman and each man
> Craves what it cannot have,
> Not universal love
> But to be loved alone.

Finally, the poet prays for grace to 'show an affirming flame' in the darkness enveloping the world. The poem, like many of Auden's, foreshadows his later assertions of a more orthodox Christianity and of a basic social conservatism. Aesthetically, such a development was almost to be expected. There is nothing more difficult, once strong doctrinal meat of any kind has been tasted by a writer, than to hold fast to those irresolute and tentative projections with which the ideology-free must content themselves. Yet in his later work as in his earlier, the irresolute and tentative edge of sensibility cuts across the doctrine and the dogma. Early and late, Auden is obsessed with the question of what man is to do with his terrible new responsibility for himself, now that the time of unconscious evolution, biological and social, has ended. 'It's no use raising a shout,' a song of the early 'thirties, raises the question poignantly, in jazzy, finger-snapping, Tin Pan Alley rhythm and language:

> It's no use raising a shout.
> No, honey, you can cut that right out. . . .
> Here am I, here are you:
> But what does it mean? What are we going to do?

As we have seen, too, the speaker in an Auden poem often either is, or addresses, a self-exiled voyager toward an unknown destination. It is the gesture of departure ('To throw away the key and walk away') and the perils of the journey which interest him, more than the rationale of his decision:

> But ever that man goes
> Through place-keepers, through forest trees,
> A stranger to strangers over undried sea. . . .

The appeal of Anglo-Saxon poetry, in theme as well as form, is obvious in much of Auden, as these lines from 'Something Is Bound To Happen' show. The hardships of an inescapable voyage, the workings of 'Wyrd,' or fate, are standard subjects in the Old English anthology. Auden's post-war poems have continued his questionings and his motifs of departure and exploration. In the long 'baroque eclogue' *The Age of Anxiety* four characters engage in the familiar inquiry after their own meaning, undertaking the most complex symbolic search of any of his works. It is true that this poem, like many more of his even more recent ones, points to religious orthodoxy as the best of home ports, the closest man will come to puzzling out his confusions. But it is clear that his questions, not his answers, have always been the clue to Auden's great relevancy, particularly in this most political of all anxious ages. The questions have to do with readiness for change, with uncertainties more frightful than physical terror, with ambiguities of ethical commitment. We sense them behind the eagerness of the modern sensibility to find for itself a new birth in a new heaven and earth.

Auden's name has been inseparably linked in most discussions of the British 'thirties with those of Stephen Spender, Louis MacNeice, and C. Day Lewis. Each of these poets at his best is quite unlike the others. MacNeice and Lewis are rather Classical in their intellectuality, and in their different ways they have written lyric poetry of a richly robust, masculine character, as well as vigorously humorous narrative and satire. Lewis is distinguished especially for his love poems. Spender, the most delicate lyricist of the group, has an almost Shelleyan ethereality and passion for fraternal love and beauty. It is probably unjust, therefore, that the three should be frozen into the Auden constellation as stars of relatively insignificant magnitude. The quick, simple compassion of Spender's 'Ultima Ratio Regum' is different from anything we find in Auden, and so is the exquisite sensuousness of 'Not palaces, an era's crown':

> Eye, gazelle, delicate wanderer,
> Drinker of horizon's fluid line;
> Ear that suspends on a chord
> The spirit drinking timelessness;
> Touch, love—all senses. . . .

Similarly, Day Lewis's idiom permits a strain of personal feeling combined with a 'magic' or mythological frame of reference that is very far in character from Auden's characteristic pitch of voice:

> Do not expect again a phoenix hour,
> The triple-towered sky, the dove complaining,
> Sudden the rain of gold and heart's first casc
> Tranced under trees by the eldritch light of sundown.
>
> (*From Feathers to Iron*)

MacNeice's hearty delight in the physical is yet another idiosyncratic key:

> World is crazier and more of it than we think,
> Incorrigibly plural. I peel and portion
> A tangerine and spit the pips and feel
> The drunkenness of things being various.
>
> ('Snow')

And, though he has written a book on Yeats from the viewpoint of a fellow countryman, we are apt to forget that he (like Day Lewis) is Irish. The easy yet melodic colloquialism of MacNeice has an Irish flavor:

> If we could get the hang of it entirely
>   It would take too long;
> All we know is the splash of words in passing
>   And falling twigs of song,

> And when we try to eavesdrop on the great
>   Presences it is rarely
> That by a stroke of luck we can appropriate
>   Even a phrase entirely.

('Entirely')

Like Auden, however, all these writers drew oxygen from the heady political air of the decade in which they rose to prominence. Spender's 'Not palaces, an era's crown,' for instance—from which I have just quoted—is a Marxist program-poem. Its argument is that we must now (1933) transfer our sense of beauty and of tradition to new objects, away from family pride and self-cultivation and toward a world without hunger or inequality. In conclusion it makes the point that the only justification for using the Satanic instruments of war and death is to effect this transference by bringing 'death to the killers' themselves. It is possible, and I think justifiable, to argue that Spender's diction betrays his doubts of these formulations just as does the ambiguity of much of Auden's political writing. For one thing, his image of the necessary transfer of values is flat as well as strained:

> The architectural gold-leaved flower
> From people ordered like a single mind,
> I build.

Indeed, the rhetorical forcing is awkward all the way through, and especially at the end. Yet the language of the *rejected* values ('beauty's filtered dusts') and of the delight of the senses is always immediate and convincing. The poet's diction gives away reservations of attitude that suggest he really loves what he is renouncing more than what he purports to advocate. But as with Auden, none of this lessens the fact of the political enmeshment of this poem.

These poets are enmeshed, further, in the psychology of the Depression. Their pictures of industrial breakdown in England present a many-sided Marxian Wasteland. MacNeice's 'Bagpipe Music' is so balmy and bouncy one almost overlooks its revolutionary satire:

The Laird o' Phelps spent Hogmannay declaring he was sober;
Counted his feet to prove the fact and found he had one foot over.
Mrs. Carmichael had her fifth, looked at the job with repulsion,
Said to the midwife 'Take it away; I'm through with overpro-
duction.'

It's no go the gossip column, it's no go the Ceilidh,
All we want is a mother's help and a sugar-stick for the baby. . . .

It's no go my honey love, it's no go my poppet;
Work your hands from day to day, the winds will blow the profit.
The glass is falling hour by hour, the glass will fall for ever,
But if you break the bloody glass you won't hold up the weather.

His *Autumn Journal,* like much else by this group, is full of topical
allusions, to the Spanish war especially, but also to Hitler, the
employment situation, coming elections. One has the feeling,
reading these poets, that one of their main objects was to set down
a subjective record of the times, their day-by-day lives as well as
such events as the Reichstag trials, the street fighting in Vienna,
and the revolution in China, or such sights as the unemployed
lounging about the streets or a flight of bombing planes in the
sky—'the heavy angels,' says Day Lewis,

> carrying harm in
> Their wombs that ache to be rid of death.
>
> ('Bombers')

Lewis, whose writing was in general more abstract and tending
toward the Metaphysical than that of the others, summed up the
situation of the young radical poet in his 1934 manifesto A *Hope
for Poetry:*

> We have seen him on the one hand rendered more acutely
> conscious of individuality by the acceptance of current
> psychological doctrines; and on the other hand, rendered
> both by poetic intuition and ordinary observation acutely
> conscious of the present isolation of the individual and the

necessity for a social organism which may restore communion. He looks to one side and he sees D. H. Lawrence, the extreme point of individualism in this country's literature . . . but he has watched him . . . driven
ill and mad, a failure. . . . He looks to the other side
and he sees Communism . . . the most wholehearted
attempt ever made to raise the individual to his highest
power by a conditioning of his environment; yet here too
he notices the bully and the spy, and wonders if any system can expel and survive that poison.*

The ambivalence of this situation (described also in Lewis's
poem 'In me two worlds at war') suggests that these writers were,
like Auden, much less doctrinaire than is generally thought and
that they wrote out of a deep feeling of personal predicament
which the political issues of the day seemed to express. The choice
of Lawrence as representative of extreme individualism shows the
meaning they read into Communism at the opposite pole: a promise of the kind of communion (if only 'the bully and the spy' can
be done away with) Lawrence, in lonely if aggressive individualism,
failed, Lewis said, to achieve.

In the United States also the 'thirties produced its cluster of
Left poets, outstanding among whom were Horace Gregory, Kenneth Fearing, and Muriel Rukeyser. Both in their work then and
in their development since the outbreak of World War II, these
writers were, and remain, more interesting than any of the English
group except Auden. The lyric-elegiac talent of Gregory, together
with his brilliance as a translator and his fine ear for colloquial
nuances; the mordant satirical voice and tremendous emotional
concentration of Fearing, and his feeling for common speech
rhythms; and the extraordinary emotional commitment of Miss
Rukeyser, despite her rhetorical self-indulgences, make their trans-
atlantic 'counterparts' seem a bit pale by comparison. These three
poets have Whitman, Masters, Lindsay, Robinson, Williams, and
Sandburg behind them quite as much as they have Yeats, Pound,

* C. Day Lewis, *Collected Poems 1929-1933 and A Hope for Poetry*, Random House, New York, 1935, p. 217.

Eliot, and Lawrence. Poems like Gregory's 'Dempsey, Dempsey,' Fearing's hilarious 'Cultural Notes,' and Rukeyser's sequence *U. S.* 1 show their authors' naturalness in working with common American life and speech at many levels: a crowd at a prize fight, the world of genteel 'culture,' the dynamite-loaded flatness of Congressional inquiries and documents. These poets deserve more critical attention in their own right than they have yet been given.

Here it is more relevant to suggest the interesting parallels between them and the Auden group. Generally speaking, their relation to Marxian orthodoxy was similarly ambiguous, and they moved away from it in similar manner. Both Gregory and Rukeyser (who very early came under Gregory's influence) were profoundly affected by Lawrence's work and career. The author of a critical study of Lawrence, Gregory is especially haunted by the Laurentian plunge into darkness.* In his earlier writing (*Chorus for Survival* is an instance), he clearly attempts to merge that motif with the Marxian ideas of the rebirth of society through revolutionary change. When, like Auden, he shakes off the tendentiousness implicit in this mode of thought, as in *The Passion of M'Phail,* he is seen to be a poet of the elusiveness of the self. The purity of his elegiac voice conceals the resemblance between this sense of the pathos of trying to establish and maintain identity and Auden's recurring motif of the sensibility journeying toward a definition of itself. Fearing, too, in a sentimental poem like 'Memo,' or in his most desolate poem of lost social and personal directions, 'Green Light,' writes around the problem of the elusiveness of the self. The tortured, tangled writing of Miss Rukeyser is even more involved with the same problem. More than any of the others, she tried in her early books to build epic structures and sequences and to give personal direction to an art based partly on scientific and political materials. Like Lawrence, Crane, and Auden she has used her own feeling of psychological fragmentation as a central poetic symbol, asserting a victory over that fragmentation not entirely earned by what the poetry shows us.

The political poetry of the 'thirties helped shape some of the

* Horace Gregory, D. H. *Lawrence: Pilgrim of the Apocalypse,* Viking Press, New York, 1933; Grove Press, 1957.

most vigorous younger voices of the war years—for instance, the 'angry young men' (in particular, Philip Larkin) in England and the Charles Olson group in the United States. The current revulsion against didacticism and propaganda in literature has had the inevitable result of obscuring from many critics and readers the ways in which political truth has colored the emotional life of the contemporary world. We may reject uncritical adherence to any particular set of political attitudes, but we cannot reject the inescapable, tragic relevance it bears to the whole problem of what the self is.

SEVEN

Exquisite Chaos: Thomas and Others

1. DYLAN THOMAS AND RECENT BRITISH VERSE

> . . . I let, perhaps, an image be 'made' emotionally in me
> and then apply to it what intellectual and critical forces
> I possess—let it breed another, let that image contradict
> the first, make, of the third image bred of the other two
> together, a fourth contradictory image, and let them all,
> within my imposed formal limits, conflict. . . . Out of
> the inevitable conflict of images—inevitable because of the
> creative, recreative, destructive and contradictory nature
> of the motivating centre, the womb of war—I try to make
> that momentary peace which is a poem. . . .*

Few poets could be less like Auden than the author of that
statement. Dylan Thomas, the Welsh poet who died in 1953 at
the age of thirty-nine, is an adept in 'the logic of metaphor,' even
more than Hart Crane, with whom he has great affinities. He is
Romantic, incantatory, 'bardic,' though not really—any more than
Crane—nonintellectual. He is primitivistic but far from primitive.
His intellectuality has little in common, however, with the surface cleverness and knowingness, or the existentialist ironies, of
Auden and the poets who follow him. Rhapsodic and mystical, he
shows us the character of his thought and aims in the poem 'In
My Craft or Sullen Art':

> In my craft or sullen art
> Exercised in the still night
> When only the moon rages
> And the lovers lie abed
> With all their griefs in their arms,

* Quoted in Henry Treece, *Dylan Thomas*, Lindsay Drummond, London,
1949, pp. 47-8, note.

> I labour by singing light
> Not for ambition or bread
> Or the strut and trade of charms
> On the ivory stages
> But for the common wages
> Of their most secret heart. . . .

The poet sees himself the instrument of that same life force which makes both moon and lovers 'rage' with their separate yet implicitly related ecstasies. He writes by the moon's 'singing light'; and the lovers, like his poetry, carry all human meaning into what they do. They lie, he says 'with all their griefs in their arms'—griefs because implicit in their embrace is the whole cycle of begetting, bringing to birth, growth, suffering, and death. The tragic character of that cycle is also the poet's own theme, and it is what makes the moon, that symbol of cyclical change and mortality, 'rage' in the sky. An additionally painful aspect of this strange relationship is that only the poet is aware of it. He cannot communicate his knowledge—either to the inhuman moon or to the lovers who, he says, do not 'heed my craft or art.' If one allows oneself to be possessed by this poem, with its chanting intensity and its deeply solemn 'magic' interlacing of rhyme, the incommunicability of the essential kinship of all things (the universal analogy implied in the paralleling of the moon and human beings) becomes unbearable to contemplate.

Both the 'universal analogy' and its incommunicability are themes Thomas immerses himself in again and again, as he immerses himself also in the 'Freudian' theme of the all-pervasive sexuality of existence and the implacable death drive that is the maggot within it. He is preoccupied with the relationship of these themes to one another and to religious faith. 'Twenty-four Years,' crammed with paradoxical and lurid figures for the roistering tragedy that any one life must be, is an excellent example:

> Twenty-four years remind the tears of my eyes
> (Bury the dead for fear that they walk to the grave in labour.)
> In the groin of the natural doorway I crouched like a tailor ·
> Sewing a shroud for a journey

By the light of the meat-eating sun.
Dressed to die, the sensual strut begun,
With my red veins full of money,
In the final direction of the elementary town
I advance for as long as forever is.

This grotesquely powerful little poem reawakens the sense of
life behind the old cliché that the moment of conception is also
the beginning of death. The hero is the poet himself, looking back
to the womb and forward to the grave from the vantage point of
his twenty-fourth birthday. His piled-up years 'remind' him of
mortality—the embryo building out its own cells until it reaches
human form is a tailor sewing his own funeral shroud. When it
enters the outside world through the mother's 'natural doorway'
it is 'dressed to die'—an obvious, and typical, pun on the familiar
'dressed to kill.' Life is a 'sensual strut' toward death; the flesh-
clothed tailor-dandy is also a spendthrift—of his own vital force,
his 'red veins full of money.' He struts—actually, is impelled—in
the direction of the 'elementary town' of subhuman nature, to
whose endless processes and shiftings he must return. This last,
suddenly quiet figure has genuine religious implications. It very
closely resembles certain key metaphors in 'A Refusal to Mourn
the Death, by Fire, of a Child in London.' There Thomas speaks
of how, eventually,

I must enter again the round
Zion of the water bead
And the synagogue of the ear of corn. . . .

These latter images bring out, a little more clearly than does
the phrase 'elementary town,' the religious aspect of Thomas's
somewhat desperate and fatalistic 'philosophy.' The terror behind
the grotesque buffoonery of most of 'Twenty-four Years' is found
in many of his poems; the speaker's hair rises in horror at the
irresistible brutality of the life force, which catapults us into birth
and consciousness, then exhausts and discards us. Yet there is
often the strange, contrasting calm of metaphors such as the ones
we have just been contemplating, which seem to be a quiet affirma-

tion of the community, and more, the holy communion, of all
being. The Freudian link is obvious between the terror of death's
immanence and the longing for the state of existence which preceded birth and personality. These contradictory motifs are present
in every mind, but we usually hold them off at a dim distance as
morbid and maddening. Thomas tried to possess them fully, for
to him they are the real world of subjective awareness, and he
must throw the most violently intense light possible on them,
must pitch every resource of language into them, if he is to discover the revelation hidden within them and blaze the discovery
forth. The poet's task, for him, is to illuminate what Yeats called
'the uncontrollable mystery on the bestial floor.' In Christian terms,
that mystery may lie in the relationship between the Virgin Birth
and Jesus the man, and between Jesus the Son of God and the
crucified Christ who begged to be spared if that should be possible.
In artistic terms, it lies in the relationship between the poet as a
man, subject to the onrushing fate and 'redemption' through
death in the natural sense, and the poet as one who creates out
of the common experience and suffering a work that outlasts and
transcends them:

> By the sea's side, hearing the noise of birds,
> Hearing the raven cough in winter sticks,
> My busy heart who shudders as she talks
> Sheds the syllabic blood and drains her words.
> ('Especially When the October Wind')

Thomas's modernity lies particularly in his absorption in these
themes and in the way he pours his amazing psychic energy into
the manipulation of sound, syntax, and metaphor. At times his
exploitation of the resources of language seems reckless or vulgarly
sensational, but there is little question of Thomas's right understanding of his task. Indeed, he explicitly describes it in the poem
'Especially When the October Wind':

> Shut, too, in a tower of words, I mark
> On the horizon walking like the trees

The wordy shapes of women, and the rows
Of the star-gestured children in the park.
Some let me make you of the vowelled beeches,
Some of the oaken voices, from the roots
Of many a thorny shire tell you notes,
Some let me make you of the water's speeches.

Doubtless this investment of his energies in language—the high emotional and dramatic charge, the magnificent richness of his whole utterance considered as a music of poetic rhetoric—accounts for his public success more than any other single factor. What Lawrence says of the effect of D'Annunzio on the typical Italian reader is true also of the effect of Thomas on English and American readers:

> . . . It is the movement, the physical effect of the language upon the blood which gives him supreme satisfaction. His mind is scarcely engaged at all. He is like a child, hearing and feeling without understanding. It is the sensuous gratification he asks for. Which is why D'Annunzio is a god in Italy. He can control the current of the blood with his words, and although much of what he says is bosh, yet the hearer is satisfied, fulfilled.*

The difference, of course, is that what Thomas says is not generally 'bosh'—if Lawrence was right about D'Annunzio. On the other hand, it is possible to revel in Thomas simply for that same 'sensuous gratification.' Here are some passages from his first book, 18 Poems (1934), published when Thomas was twenty:

> I see the boys of summer in their ruin
> Lay the gold tithings barren,
> Setting no store by harvest, freeze the soils;
> There in their heat the winter floods
> Of frozen loves they fetch their girls,
> And drown the cargoed apples in their tides.
>
> ('I See the Boys of Summer')

---

* D. H. Lawrence, *Sea and Sardinia and Selections from Twilight in Italy*, Doubleday Anchor Books, New York, 1954, p. 260.

And that's the rub, the only rub that tickles.
The knobbly ape that swings along his sex
From damp love-darkness and the nurse's twist
Can never raise the midnight of a chuckle. . . .
                    ('If I Were Tickled by the Rub of Love')

Before I knocked and flesh let enter,
With liquid hands tapped on the womb,
I who was as shapeless as the water
That shaped the Jordan near my home
Was brother to Mnetha's daughter
And sister to the fathering worm.

                              ('Before I Knocked')

A candle in the thighs
Warms youth and seed and burns the seeds of age;
Where no seed stirs,
The fruit of man unwrinkles in the stars,
Bright as a fig;
Where no wax is, the candle shows its hairs.
                    ('Light Breaks Where No Sun Shines')

What is it that gratifies in these passages? Even less than with
most poets does the answer lie in their themes. The first passage
is from a poem which presents a three-cornered debate on self-
love and barren or perverted love. The second is from a poem contrasting the magnetic pull of each phase of the life cycle with its
eventual dismal outcome. This poem also seeks to define the symbolic meaning of man as the clue to all truth: 'Man be my metaphor.' The third is from a poem in which Jesus recalls the sense
of his state before conception; implicit in it was all his future, and
with it all the potentialities for suffering of all men. And the
fourth is from a poem which, again, explores the 'universal analogy.'
Recognition of these themes is essential to a full grasp of the
poems, but it is the intoxication of sound and phrase that engages
most of us at once, long before the connection of one phrase with
another, or even the meaning of individual phrases, is at all clear.

Moreover, there is a bold articulateness, very often sexual, that is startling in itself and stands out in relief from its mysterious context. Thomas, like D'Annunzio, 'can control the current of the blood with his words.' When one is reading Thomas, one wonders how poetry exists in any other fashion.

A great source of power in his work is its primitivistic orientation. There is relatively little overt intellectualizing, and a great deal of sheer assertion. He wills, and chants, primal desires and insights into the foreground of consciousness. He feverishly denies the pointlessness of life, and hurls defiance into the face of death. His insistence on the universal analogy, the incommunicable kinship of all modes of physical being, is really one form this feverish denial takes. The kinship he sees is essentially tragic; yet to affirm it is to affirm meaning, for somehow it is at the heart of the mystery 'on the bestial floor.'

> The force that through the green fuse drives the flower
> Drives my green age; that blasts the roots of trees
> Is my destroyer.
> And I am dumb to tell the crooked rose
> My youth is bent by the same wintry fever.
> ('The Force That Through the Green Fuse')

The life force, this first stanza tell us, drives both flowers and human beings through to their full growth, then discards both when it has exhausted them. All living things are thus exploded into birth, maturity, death, and each stage of the cycle implies all the others. The next two stanzas push the same principle down into the world of sub-organic nature:

> And I am dumb to mouth unto my veins
> How at the mountain spring the same mouth sucks.

Then the fourth stanza brings in sexual analogy on a cosmic scale:

> The lips of time leech to the fountain head;
> Love drips and gathers, but the fallen blood
> Shall calm her sores.
> And I am dumb to tell a weather's wind
> How time has ticked a heaven round the stars.

The basic thought of these lines departs from the simple propositions advanced hitherto. The proposition of the first stanza we have already seen; the second asserted the obvious identity of the kind of physical force that 'drives the water through the rocks' with that which 'drives my red blood.' The third extended this thought rather mechanically to the realization that this same impersonal force makes a constant death trap for man: whirlpools, quicksand, windstorms. It ended with a subtler if somewhat awkward turn, however, intended to restore the centrality of the *human* image:

> And I am dumb to tell the hanging man
> How of my clay is made the hangman's lime.

Now, in the fourth stanza, there is a projection out of despair that appears at first to break the pattern of all these propositions. In the image of 'the lips of time' that 'leech to the fountain head' is symbolized the powerful yearning of all mortality to clasp and be impregnated by the life force. Out of that yearning, with all its pain, man dreamed of a timeless paradise beyond death to console himself for his limitations of mortality: 'time has ticked a heaven round the stars.' The dream cannot, of course, be communicated to the rest of nature. The poem ends in despair, with a bizarre and deliberately ugly phallic image that, in degrading the symbolism of the fourth stanza, doubly underlines the anguish out of which it has arisen:

> And I am dumb to tell the lover's tomb
> How at my sheet goes the same crooked worm.

'The Force That Through the Green Fuse' is primitivistic, then, in its self-hypnotic incantation that brings chanter and listener face to face with the appalling destructive force with which the unity of all nature is bound up. At the same time, the element of the speaker's helpless 'dumbness' to 'tell' this universal secret is a sophistication upon the primal sense of awe, and the 'lips of time' stanza is a further sophistication bringing into the poem's scheme the entire skeptical bent, and regret for lost certainties, of modern thought. Another poem, 'And Death Shall Have No Dominion,' is doubtless closer to undiluted primitivism. The central argument is less complicated, and the repeated defiance of death at the beginning and end of each stanza gives it the character of a spell.

And death shall have no dominion.
Dead men naked they shall be one
With the man in the wind and the west moon;
When their bones are picked clean and the clean bones gone,
They shall have stars at elbow and foot. . . .

Granting the worst death can do, the poem proclaims life *will* reassert itself. In some manner the physical limits of the universe will be turned to advantage by the innermost will of life. Only the frenzy of the assertion, a frenzy so extreme that it symbolically destroys the created universe to obtain its demand, betrays the modern sensibility behind it:

Though they be mad and dead as nails,
Heads of the characters hammer through daisies;
Break in the sun till the sun breaks down,
And death shall have no dominion.

On the other hand, Thomas was capable of an infinite gentleness of tone, and sometimes his poems descend to whimsey and sentimentality (the great defects of his prose and of his play *Under Milk Wood*). His best works in a gentler mode, however, show him in his essential character as a modern Romantic, entranced in his visions and his recollections. The nostalgic 'Fern Hill' is such a poem, buoyant and vivid in its memories of childhood but at the same time weaving into its scheme an ever more piercing adult sadness. As we read, we are first taken with the gay and fanciful note of many lines, with the singing, fluent liquids and sibilants:

Time let me hail and climb
Golden in the heydays of his eyes,
And honoured among wagons I was prince of the apple towns
And once below a time I lordly had the trees and leaves
Trail with daisies and barley
Down the rivers of the windfall light.

There are so many such effects that we hardly notice the casual, deceptive presence of Time in the background. And besides, Time is kind and 'permissive' in this beginning stanza. In the next he shows his power a little more openly:

> Time let me play and be
> Golden in the mercy of his means. . . .

By the last two stanzas, though all is still gentle and melodic, the terror lurking in things has become as overwhelming as death itself:

> And nothing I cared, at my sky blue trades, that time allows
> In all his tuneful turning so few and such morning songs
>   Before the children green and golden
>   Follow him out of grace

and, concluding the poem:

> Time held me green and dying
> Though I sang in my chains like the sea.

'A Winter's Tale' has the same tone of gentle, almost naïve simplicity and sadness, though it becomes far more involved than 'Fern Hill.' 'It is a winter's tale,' the poet begins, describing the season in delicate, mysterious pastoral images of cold and stillness. The story unfolds like a fairy tale or myth:

> Once when the world turned old
> On a star of faith pure as the drifting bread,
> As the food and flames of the snow, a man unrolled
> The scrolls of fire that burned in his heart and head. . . .

The man of the tale prays for a transcendent, transforming love. He prays with so burning an intensity out of his deep deprivation that nature and time itself are aroused to sing his tale even yet. And eventually a miraculous vision does come to him, annunciation in the form of a bird-woman singing through the mysteriously opened door of his farmhouse. He pursues her, but she is beyond life and descends to him only after his death. The poem ends with a vision of combined sexual and spiritual beatitude reminiscent of the climactic moment in 'The Eve of St. Agnes.'

> And through the thighs of the engulfing bride,
> The woman breasted and the heaven headed
>
> Bird, he was brought low,
> Burning in the bride bed of love, in the whirl-
> Pool at the wanting centre, in the folds
> Of paradise, in the spun bud of the world.
> And she rose with him flowering in her melting snow.

There are other reminiscences of the story of Madeline and Porphyro: the winter landscape and intense imagery of cold and whiteness, the opposition and mingling of sacred and profane themes, the distinction between the continuing present and the long-ago character of the tale, and the ambiguity in which Keats veils the climactic union. Thomas's poem is more pervasively ambiguous, however, for he is not 'simply' telling a romantic tale which brings together holy and fleshly values. In his story of the man who sacrifices himself for love—'the believer lost and the hurled outcast of light'—and then is 'hymned and wedded' in the realm beyond life, there is more than a suggestion of Virgin Birth, Crucifixion, and Resurrection, though the order of events is altered and the roles of the sexes are reversed. The many sacramental figures, such as 'a star of faith as pure as the drifting bread' and the Dantean descriptions of the 'she bird' who is 'rayed like a burning bride,' support this interpretation. Finally, however, it is a symbolic creation out of the very nature of myth and religion that Thomas gives us. The poem has no ultimate literal referent beyond that fact, unless it be the pathos of the human condition.

Looking over his work as a whole, it is clear that this pathos is the emotion on which everything is based: the terror, the mystery, the crucified sexuality (to borrow Lawrence's thought once more), the bawdy Rabelaisian religiosity, the conception of his poetry as 'the record of my individual struggle from darkness toward some measure of light,' the preoccupation with what he called 'the crumbling of dead flesh before the opening of the womb.'

Together with the tremendous, impersonal fact of his natural gifts, this dominant pathos is what keeps his poetry of the physiology of conception, with its 'sperm's-eye view' of life, from being repulsively gross and renders it as magical as the mythopoeia of 'A Winter's Tale.'

> I would not fear the muscling-in of love
> If I were tickled by the urchin hungers
> Rehearsing heat upon a raw-edge nerve.
> I would not fear the devil in the loin
> Nor the outspoken grave. . . .

He would not, says the poet in this poem, 'If I Were Tickled by the Rub of Love,' refuse the challenge to be brought to birth if he were sperm or ovum, though lust and the 'outspoken grave' are all that lie ahead. It is the pitiful courage of all life which he here contemplates and advocates despite 'the rub' of things as they are. The dialogue between an unborn child and its mother in 'If My Head Hurt a Hair's Foot' is to the same effect. The poet imagines the compassionate fetus protesting:

> 'If my bunched, monkey coming is cruel
> Rage me back to the making house. My hand unravel
> When you sew the deep door. . . .'

But the mother takes the same position of desolate courage as the poet in 'If I Were Tickled.'

> 'No. Not for Christ's dazzling bed
> Or a nacreous sleep among soft particles and charms
> My dear would I change my tears or your iron head,
> Thrust, my son or daughter, to escape, there is none,
>   none, none,
> Nor when all ponderous heaven's host of waters breaks. . . .
>
> 'The grain that hurries this way from the rim of the
>   grave
> Has a voice and a house, and there and here you must
>   couch and cry. . . .'

A poetry based on elaboration of the self-evident, sad ironies of existence cannot entirely escape· the sentimentality of excessive emotionalism, unless concentrated power and formal control dam up this emotionalism and transfer its energy into self-contained image and statement. Thomas took the risk consciously. He kept himself close to the 'ordinary' emotions of day-by-day experience, and yet brought forth also the repressed implication hidden within them. Sometimes, as in 'A Refusal to Mourn the Death, by Fire, of a Child in London,' he is sentimental, yet something magnificent results. The child's death, this poem argues, is too 'majestic' and destructive an event to be mourned conventionally. But as he presents his argument against the usual ceremonial forms of mourning, the speaker employs the very language and intonations of lamentation in his falling rhythms, his arrangement of lines, and the solemnity of his long, periodic opening sentence (which takes up just over half the poem). The liturgical note, at certain moments resembling that in 'The Wreck of the Deutschland,' is clear in sequences like

> . . . the mankind making
> Bird beast and flower
> Fathering and all humbling darkness . . .

and the funereal note is inescapable in such phrases as 'sow my salt seed,' 'valley of sackcloth,' 'a grave truth.' The poet's negatives—'Never . . . shall I let pray the shadow of a sound,' 'I shall not murder . . . nor blaspheme . . . with . . . elegy,' and so on —actually support this note, and thus the two long sentences that make up three-fourths of the poem are anything but 'refusals to mourn.' Nor does the last stanza, with its two concentrated assertions that the girl is now with her 'friends' in the mother-earth's womb and that 'after the first death, there is no other,' relieve the tragic tone of the poem. It, too, is of the order of 'desolate courage,' and so is Thomas's allusion to his own death as a reentering of the 'round Zion of the water bead' and the 'synagogue of the ear of corn.' The poem is one of the great funeral sermons, and of the same order of conviction. That is, it says what we wish to hear, says it with the great Negative lying, as it were, there before us so dreadfully and nakedly we cannot bear to credit its unqualified factuality. But to muffle agony is not to undo it.

This aspect of Thomas, this self-consoling, pathetic, 'soft' alternative voice, diminishes his achievement. There are times when his final effects are not of what he called 'momentary peace,' with the opposed forces tensed in equal balance, but rather there is something spurious or contrived in the final direction the poem takes. If Thomas is superior to Crane in the luxuriant exuberance and daring of his language and in the equal daring of his allusive and tangential symbolic statement, he is below him in courage to renounce this kind of unearned assertion. The uncompromising self-exposure of Crane's 'Passage,' the yearning in his 'Repose of Rivers' for total annihilation of the self unrelieved by any self-indulgence such as Thomas often allows himself, his refusal to be taken in by his own dreams in the *Voyages* are not quite to be matched by anything in Thomas. Not to overstate the case, sometimes Thomas was a little too much the slick professional. 'I am so glad,' he wrote to Vernon Watkins, 'you liked the "Vision & Prayer" poem; and that the diamond shape of the first part seems no longer to you to be cramped & artificed. I agree that the second part is, formally, less inevitable, but I cannot alter it, except, perhaps, in detail. . . . Yes, the Hound of Heaven is baying there in the last verse. . . .' * (The allusion is to the idiom and thought of Francis Thompson's 'The Hound of Heaven,' which culminates in the speaker's inevitable capture after a symbolic flight from God.)

Not only is the second part 'less inevitable' than the first; it has no inevitability at all, at least after its first stanza. Even Part I, in fact, hardly sustains the tremendous, awe-struck paradoxical vision its two opening stanzas introduce. Those stanzas express fully the keen, sensually conditioned apperceptiveness of mystery which Thomas possessed. He could

* Dylan Thomas, *Letters to Vernon Watkins*, ed. Vernon Watkins, New Directions, New York, 1957, pp. 122-3.

> . . . hear the womb
> Opening and the dark run
> Over the ghost and the dropped son
> Behind the wall thin as a wren's bone. . . .

But he lets these stanzas carry the poem, and right after them the Hound of Heaven starts its 'baying.' Echoes from Hopkins mar the poem also, though Thomas denied their presence.

'Vision and Prayer' appeared in 1945, that is, toward the end of a literary career that began when the poet was twenty and virtually ended when he was thirty-two, for he wrote very little poetry after his *Deaths and Entrances* appeared in 1946. We can see a certain mellowing and relaxation of surface tension in his later work (after 1939 or so), but little development. His first two books do show a wilder, fresher fancy than his later ones, and a greater integrity of balance in the 'conflict' of feelings and values. But the 'elder' Thomas can often enough rekindle the early spark and tough-mindedness, and the 'younger' has the sad satyr-wisdom of the latest poems. All his writing seems the result of one single, if unevenly sustained, outpouring.

Probably the ten 'Altarwise by owl-light' sonnets printed in 1936, almost a decade before 'A Refusal to Mourn' and 'Vision and Prayer,' provide an important clue to the poet's failure to show real progress. Despite their relatively early composition, at least one of his critics has felt that they tower 'perhaps above all his work,' and 'are among the greatest poems of our century.' * Certainly they are richly impressive in their originality and multiple symbolism (which Elder Olson and others have accounted for at great length and most convincingly). Yet with all their ingenuity they do not justify the leap into unqualified faith implied in the closing sonnet. Their whole direction has been toward creating a difficult balance based on the *aperçu* of Sonnet II that 'Death is all metaphors, shape in one history.' From the first sonnet, in

---

* Elder Olson, *The Poetry of Dylan Thomas*, University of Chicago Press, Chicago, 1954, pp. 25, 88. See Mr. Olson's excellent analysis of this sonnet-sequence pp. 64-87.

which a Christ-like figure is seen lying 'graveward with his furies,' his genitals 'bitten out . . . with tomorrow's scream' by the malevolent spirit of reality, to the ninth sonnet with its ironic comment on the inadequacy of either the ancient Egyptian art of embalming or the writer's art to give us more than a token immortality, this grim thought is the inescapable theme of the sequence. Death is the principle behind the redundant cycles of the seasons (Sonnet III); in its light the paradoxes of faith are without conviction (Sonnets IV-VII); it bends the essential symbol of the Christian faith, the Crucifixion, to its merely human meaning: sacrifice without promise of resurrection (Sonnet VIII). Then, in Sonnet X, Thomas takes all the wishes for that promise which death has 'defeated' in the preceding poems and says, 'Let them come true'—

> . . . let the garden diving
> Soar, with its two bark towers, to that Day
> When the worm builds with the gold straws of venom
> My nest of mercies in the rude, red tree.

Let these things happen, indeed! Thomas's habit of identifying himself symbolically with Christ has in this instance led him into grandiosity, despite the loveliness of individual lines in this concluding sonnet. At times his very gift for standing back and letting the wonderful phrases soar is self-defeating, an improvised orchestral swelling and flourishing where the poetry demands more depth and discipline. But the wit and elegance of his presentation of a mood of sheer dread in the first sonnet, the heavy music of the third, and the bitter beauty of the climactic eighth make these particular poems stand with his best work. As for the sequence as a whole, the fact that Thomas never carried out his intention to make it longer doubtless has something to do with an unwillingness to face the issues beyond the point of their casual muting in the tenth sonnet. Nor did he ever face them in all their demanding difficulty. Like Rimbaud and Crane, he was one of those poets who exhaust the possibilities of their art fairly early after a dazzling breakthrough.

Dylan Thomas's precocity made him, like Muriel Rukeyser, a poet of the 'thirties and, in that purely chronological sense, out of his own generation. Unlike Miss Rukeyser (two years his junior), however, he did not fall into the pattern of political poetry that dominated the age. Politics touched his writing mainly through the war, and then in terms purely personal and characteristic of his usual concerns. 'A Refusal to Mourn,' 'Ceremony after a Fire Raid,' 'Among Those Killed in the Dawn Raid Was a Man Aged a Hundred' are hardly even 'war poems' despite their implicit pacifism. A poem like the earlier 'The Hand That Signed the Paper' (1935) is really a poem against political power itself, rather than one that takes sides. Thomas's poetry is a reaction away from the topical, the 'social,' and the ratiocinative to a realm of introspective personalism which is at the same time inclusively human. It was that reaction, as well as the native genius he revealed, which so surprised and overwhelmed Thomas's first audience and persuaded their affection. He did truly, despite his 'tough' swaggering and the barrier of difficulty he often presented,

> . . . by this blowclock witness of the sun
> Suffer the heaven's children through my heartbeat.
>
> (Sonnet VIII)

Except for Dylan Thomas, British poets, since the last war at least, have been dominated by the amateur spirit; their poetry does not bite hard or deep enough to suit our barbarous American tastes. Both its feeling and its wit are a little 'special' and insular, British in a limited way, idiosyncratic as a family joke. While art should, certainly, grow out of specifics, I cannot help thinking of Lawrence's picture of the British bourgeois:

> Nicely groomed, like a mushroom
> standing there so sleek and erect and eyeable
> and like a fungus, living on the remains of bygone life. . . .
>
> ('How beastly the bourgeois is')

Or Auden's picture of the invalidism of middle-class British society, with its obvious similarity to Lord Chatterley's condition:

> I don't want any more hugs;
> Make me some fresh tea, fetch me some rugs.
>
> ('It's no use raising a shout')

It is the disproportionate infusion of self-pity, I suppose, that makes the difference. The tragic and revolutionary perspectives of the great generation of modern poets begin to seem archaic to people embroiled in the petty particulars of welfare-state planning. Most of their passion now goes into self-loathing at being part of a protected, routine system of minimum standards and into indignation that Albion's sacred landscape is being 'modernized.' That the new security represents at least a minimal triumph after age-long struggle and sacrifice causes no exultation. Nevertheless, all this is part of the idiom in England today; and it is authenticity of voice that makes a poetry live, whatever we may think of what the voice is saying and however short its life may prove to be.

John Betjeman rings the changes on that voice more deftly than anyone else now writing in England. His poetry is in large part a sparklingly sentimental body of work whose vast success in England recalls the triumphs of our own Longfellow, a writer he dearly loves to parody. There is surely something of Longfellow, even something of Holmes's 'Old Ironsides,' in a poem like 'The Planster's Vision':

> Cut down that timber! Bells, too many and strong
> Pouring their music through the branches bare,
> From moon-white church-towers down the windy air
> Have pealed the centuries out with Evensong.

Betjeman's appeal is most often highly local, with a strong smell of wet tweed and a lively effeteness slightly offensive to us. But that is only one side of the matter. Betjeman's appeal is anchored in a burr-like specificity about places and circumstances and in a persuasive feeling for the countryside and its culture. This feeling, infused as it is with bitterness at the changes being wrought in English life, tempers his sentimentality and his occasionally squeamish horror at the increasing visibility and power of the hitherto uneducated classes. Together with his skill as a light-versifier and his familiar, humorous touches, it saves him from

being (what he sometimes is anyway) just another weepily conservative Englishman. These elements usually prevent any large accumulation of soppiness from bogging down his descriptions:

> We used to picnic where the thrift
> Grew deep and tufted to the edge;
> We saw the yellow foam-flakes drift
> In trembling sponges on the ledge
> Below us, till the wind would lift
> Them up the cliff and o'er the hedge.
> Sand in the sandwiches, wasps in the tea,
> Sun on our bathing-dresses heavy with the wet,
> Squelch of the bladder-wrack waiting for the sea,
> Fleas around the tamarisk, an early cigarette.

('Trebetherick')

Probably it is effective poems like these, together with such
rather more blatant, downright blubbering pieces as 'The Old
Liberals' and 'Church of England Thoughts' and 'Christmas' and
'Verses . . . in Aid of . . . the Restoration of the Church of St.
Katherine Chiselhampton, Oxon.,' that have made Betjeman's
work so popular. Except for a few poems on death, social caste, and
sex, Betjeman is not at his best when he is completely serious. But
in these few, 'Late-Flowering Lust,' 'Sir John Piers,' 'On a Portrait
of a Deaf Man' and 'False Security,' for example, he hits the note
of pure dismay implicit in his diatribes and satires against the new
world of dreariness he believes England's 'plansters' are building.
One of Betjeman's reactions to social service England is an old-
auntie excitement about church restoration and other such nobly
preservative causes. He exercises his talents more fully when he is
being wittily half-snobbish, half-tender, toward the dull *polloi*;
when he is mocking the traditional forms and vocabulary of the
bucolic and other popular poetry he exploits so cleverly (he is
most at home in a tradition that includes such minor, half-for-
gotten masters of swinging rhythms as Kipling, Masefield, Noyes,
and Chesterton); when he is dazzling us with the mingled humor
and pathos of 'The Arrest of Oscar Wilde at the Cadogan Hotel';
or when he is indulging himself in his curiously effeminate but
very funny love-poems about powerfully athletic females:

> Red hair she had and golden skin,
> Her sulky lips were shaped for sin,
> Her sturdy legs were flannel-slack'd,
> The strongest legs in Pontefract.
>
> ('The Licorice Fields at Pontefract')

Philip Larkin is typical of a younger group of self-snubbers and self-loathers (who, nevertheless, have never thought to put down their wretched mirrors). He is forever promising to be a wit and then appealing to the reader to pity him instead. It is another turn on that *petty* bitterness about life that Betjeman too sometimes exhibits—not a world's sorrow and loss of meaning, but the sullenness of a man who finds squalor in his own spirit and fears to liberate himself from it:

> Why should I let the toad *work*
>   Squat on my life? . . .
>
> Ah, were I courageous enough
>   To shout *Stuff your pension!*
> But I know, all too well, that's the stuff
>   That dreams are made on:
>
> For something sufficiently toad-like
>   Squats in me, too;
> Its hunkers are heavy as hard luck,
>   And cold as snow. . . .
>
> ('Toads')

As in *Look Back in Anger* or *Lucky Jim*, the speaker's assumption that he is in an inescapable predicament seems to Americans more stubborn than unavoidable. Larkin's poems of refusal to participate, such as 'Reasons for Attendance' and 'Places, Loved Ones,' have an air of spurious self-alienation, as opposed to a poem like Edwin Muir's 'The Interrogation' whose tragic authority derives from awareness of the myriads whom war and authoritarian militarism have deprived of birthright and identity. In the new British atmosphere a writer can speak of his childhood, as Larkin does in

'Coming,' as 'a forgotten boredom,' and have it accepted as a self-evident truth. He can write, seriously:

> . . . . Sex, yes, but what
> Is sex? Surely, to think the lion's share
> Of happiness is found by couples—sheer
>
> Inaccuracy, as far as I'm concerned. . . .
> ('Reasons for Attendance')

There is a good deal of this kind of defiant beating-down of straw men, in the vein of the posturings of a precocious pubescent in revolt against the prospect of happiness. But another side to Larkin appears in poems like 'Dry-Point,' 'Myxomatosis,' and 'Going.' The querulous whine and the limp squeak of defiance have disappeared; the poems are much more impersonal; and we can see from them that there is something of a deep, end-of-a-civilization sadness behind the talkative self-analyses and the almost silly little manifestoes. 'Dry-Point' is perhaps the best of Larkin's poems. It is immensely suggestive in the way its images carry through a feeling of men's helplessness within history. At endlessly recurrent crucial moments we are compelled to action amid an exalted vision which deserts us immediately the action is completed, and the dream of a concentrated, glowing perfection immune to historical destiny remains remote as ever.

> The wet spark comes, the bright blown walls collapse,
>
> But what sad scapes we cannot turn from then:
> What ashen hills! what salted, shrunken lakes! . . .
>
> And how remote that bare and sun-scrubbed room,
> Intensely far, that padlocked cube of light. . . .

The spiritual dolor of 'Dry-Point' comes not from the explicit meaning of its succession of evocative images, but from the character and arrangement of the images themselves. The abstract patterning here gathers the feeling for which Larkin strives in his lesser poems into its richest expression. Apart from rare achievements like this one, he is able to speak sharply and cleanly in poems like 'Deceptions' and 'Church Going,' in which he finds a rather satisfying middle ground of contemplative expression. The first, like Betjeman's 'An Incident in the Early Life of Ebenezer Jones, Poet, 1828,' is a gesture of keen sympathy toward the suffering of violated innocence. The second, which may be contrasted with Betjeman's propagandistic church pieces, is a moving consideration by the poet, merciless toward his own ignorance and incomplete commitments, of what churches mean to him. The English are generally better at this kind of verse exposition than we are, just as they are at thoughtful prose in the same vein. It *is* their language, and they are well trained at using it to be subtly lucid about things.

Yet it is possible to belabor national differences, and the insularity of current British poetic sensibility as well. Larkin's 'Dry-Point' is one sign among several that younger British poets are not satisfied with their special brand of dead-end and are turning to American post-Imagist models as a means of reorienting their work. The poems of Charles Tomlinson go much further in this direction. He is a sophisticated student of the French Symbolists and of Pound and Eliot, as his sequence 'Antecedents: A Homage and Valediction' makes perfectly clear. He is also indebted to Stevens and, even more, to Marianne Moore. His remarkable precision and his gift for the implication of intense passion held in reserve are not to be denied. The affinity with Miss Moore is therefore quite natural, though poem after poem is marred by certain purse-lipped, almost prissy effects that really parody her work. Tomlinson has her grave shrewdness, her trick of weaving quoted phrases into the body of his text, her manner of marshaling images and observations toward a pithy conclusion, and her wise dismissal of a subject when the time is right:

> A quick gold, dyeing the uncovering beach
>   With sunglaze. That which we were,
> Confronted by all that we are not,
>   Grasps in subservience its replenishment.
>
> ('The Atlantic')

The sea laps by the railroad tracks.
To have admitted this also defines the sea.

('The Mediterranean')

I find this derivativeness of Tomlinson's extremely distracting, though he does his exercises so well that they are more than exercises. They are, in certain respects, a belated (by forty years) perfecting of the Imagist ideal. A poem like 'Paring the Apple' is uncanny in the delicate sureness of its swerving movement, deceptively delicate since its grasp on the physical action around which its meanings are implied is so firm:

. . . . Paring it slowly,
From under cool-yellow
Cold-white emerging. And . . . ?

The spring of concentric peel . . .
The blade hidden, dividing. . . .

Sometimes the smotheringly depressed mood of young England comes through clearly, as in the dominant symbol of 'Poem' (an upended tree that 'gapes enmity from its hollowed core'), or in various pieces suggesting an attitude like Betjeman's toward the English landscape, the churches, the lost past. Tomlinson's virtuosity puts him in a special class, though there must be some doubt as to how much life there is in his art. His kind of perfectionism may feed too much on itself; one can't help wondering whether he will receive enough stimulus from the prevailing British *ethos* to break out of his present self-bondage and produce something vitally new.

2. ROBERT LOWELL AND THE POETRY OF CONFESSION

A reluctance to destroy himself any more rapidly than he was already doing may have been one of the causes of Dylan Thomas's refusal to look steadily into the abyss in his poetry. But in the most powerful work of the modern period the great push is often precisely in that direction. Eliot's interest in the 'inexpressibly horrible,' Pound's violence, Crane's suicidal symbolism, and the psychological self-probings of younger poets all point the same way. 'I get the feeling,' one of them has written me, 'that the madhouse is not far away from many poets writing now. I think there is something wrong in both my feeling that this should become accepted as part of the state of affairs and my feeling that this should be countered consciously and fiercely. . . . I think too that this kind of writing . . . will hurl poetry up a tree it can't descend from. . . . Where will it go? *Can* it make a 'return,' can it reaccept the culture that after all fed it and flung it on its way?'

No one can really answer these questions, although my correspondent supplied *his* answer to the last of them: 'No.' Emily Dickinson once called publication 'the auction of the mind,' but today many of our writers seem to regard it as soul's therapy. We are now far from the great Romantics who, it is true, spoke directly of their emotions but did not give the game away even to themselves. They found, instead, cosmic equations and symbols, transcendental reconciliations with 'this lime-tree bower my prison,' or titanic melancholia in the course of which, merging a sense of tragic fatality with the evocations of the nightingale's song, the poet lost his personal complaint in the music of universal forlornness. Later, Whitman took American poetry to the very edge of the confessional in his *Calamus* poems and in the quivering avowal of his helplessness before the seductions of 'blind loving wrestling touch, sheath'd hooded sharp-tooth'd touch.' More recently, under the influence of the Symbolists, Eliot and Pound brought us into the forbidden realm itself, although a certain indirection in their work masks the poet's actual face and psyche from greedy eyes.

Robert Lowell's poetry has been a long struggle to remove the mask, to make his speaker unequivocally himself. As with Thomas, whose style Lowell's sometimes (especially in a few earlier poems) resembles, his chief mask has been that of the 'crucified' man, overwhelmed by compassion and at the same time a boisterous participant in the human ordeal. He departs from Thomas in the specific meaning of the mask: for him it is a mask of moral guilt, like Eliot's, for the present decadence of values and the crash of a great tradition. He is after all a *Lowell*, and he charges himself with all the meanness of contemporary New England as he sees it—sunken in commercialist degradation, the net result of the nastiness behind its long history going back to the repressive Puritanism and to the heartless extermination of the Indians. A Catholic convert for a number of years, Lowell worked this perspective into his poetry as Eliot has done with his Anglicanism, but with a 'jackhammer' passion (to use a figure from his savagely depressed poem 'Colloquy in Black Rock'). He is also a social critic as uncompromising in his strictures as any Marxist. So his mask is a composite one, as his 'Children of Light' shows:

> Our fathers wrung their bread from stocks and stones
> And fenced their gardens with the Redman's bones;
> Embarking from the Nether Land of Holland,
> Pilgrims unhouseled by Geneva's night,
> They planted here the serpent's seeds of light;
> And here the pivoting searchlights probe to shock
> The riotous glass houses built on rock,
> And candles gutter by an empty altar,
> And light is where the landless blood of Cain
> Is burning, burning the unburied gain.

The driving rhymes and indignant irony in this poem and such others as 'The Drunken Fisherman' and 'As a Plane Tree by the Water' demonstrate Lowell's power even while they induce certain reservations. The feeling is genuine; it smashes home. And there is no question of its moral bearing. But in these poems from *Lord Weary's Castle* (1946), as in many of the pieces comprising Lowell's first volume, *Land of Unlikeness* (1944), the emotion is stronger and more immediate than the literal content. The level of *thought*, as opposed to that of *feeling* and *statement*, is a bit stale—even juvenile. He is shocked to realize what 'our fathers' did to the Indians and embittered by the unconscious hypocrisy of Puritanism and its historical results. While Lowell handles these set themes beautifully, we have here an instance of the problem Eliot long ago raised of finding an objective correlative for an emotion not directly expressible, an emotion 'in *excess* of the facts as they appear.' Lines 4 and 5 of 'Children of Light' will illustrate:

> Pilgrims unhouseled by Geneva's night,
> They planted here the serpent's seeds of light . . .

As an intellectual proposition these lines are merely a hedging comment on a knotty point of doctrine of little interest to anyone now except theological apologists or historians. On the other hand, if we inquire into the emotional connotations of that paradoxical image 'the serpent's seeds of light' we find that again and again in his writings Lowell uses snake and serpent images to suggest sly and furtive guilt, evil that *will* assert itself, and very often guilt or evil of a sexual character. The related meaning of 'seeds' is obvious, and 'light' suggests, if only ironically, that something not only desirable but valuable is associated with the guilt of the serpent's seeds. These implications are fully worked out in other poems. In 'Between the Porch and the Altar,' two guilty lovers, an unfaithful husband and his mistress, *become* snakes (in the husband's eyes) whenever they gratify themselves in the way that means 'light' for them:

> . . . When we try to kiss,
> Our eyes are slits and cringing, and we hiss;
> Scales glitter on our bodies as we fall. . . .

If Lowell's lovers were not so oppressed by guilt, this would be exactly like the hissing end of Lawrence's 'River Roses':

> . . . We whispered: 'No one knows us.
> Let it be as the snake disposes
> Here in this simmering marsh.'

'Between the Porch and the Altar' helped prepare the way for the maskless confessions of his most recent poems. Its adulterous, mother-dominated hero is first described in the third person, and its serpent imagery helps us see his pathological state:

> Meeting his mother makes him lose ten years,
> Or is it twenty? Time, no doubt, has ears
> That listen to the swallowed serpent, wound
> Into its bowels, but he thinks no sound

Is possible before her, he thinks the past
Is settled. . . .
Nothing shames
Him more than this uncoiling, counterfeit
Body presented as an idol. . . .

Throughout 'Between the Porch and the Altar' the sense of sin, rather than sin itself, is clearly the protagonist's main problem. He is sick with the burden of his mother and of the crushing family traditions and 'New England Conscience' associated with her, and he must throw the burden off even if it means, as his equally guilt-ridden sweetheart puts it, to 'ruin' his two children and his wife. The Roman Catholic framework hardly solves the moral problems behind all this, but poetically it separates the protagonist's viewpoint sufficiently from that of the poem as a whole to enable us to see the difference. The speaker in Lowell's poems needs most of all the strength to 'cast off remorse,' as Yeats demanded. 'Between the Porch and the Altar' begins to get at this need, and away from the half-relevant abstractions of other poems. Even 'The Dead in Europe,' with its picture of the bombed civilians who fell 'hugger-mugger in the jellied fire,' is marred by arbitrary and generalized religious rhetoric (whereas the later 'A Mad Negro Soldier Confined at Munich' is not), and the magnificent elegy 'The Quaker Graveyard in Nantucket' is almost betrayed by it. What saves the latter poem is the least pretentious thing about it, the crowded, sensuous concreteness of its description:

A brackish reach of shoal off Madaket,—
The sea was still breaking violently and night
Had steamed into our North Atlantic Fleet,
When the drowned sailor clutched the drag-net. Light
Flashed from his matted head and marble feet,
He grappled at the net
With the coiled, hurdling muscles of his thighs. . . .

and

. . . Sea-gulls blink their heavy lids
Seaward. The winds' wings beat upon the stones,

> Cousin, and scream for you and the claws rush
> At the sea's throat and wring it in the slush
> Of this old Quaker Graveyard. . . .

or

> . . . a gaff
> Bobs on the untimely stroke
> Of the greased wash exploding on a shoal-bell
> In the old mouth of the Atlantic. It's well;
> Atlantic, you are fouled with the blue sailors. . . .

Lowell introduces into this elegy for his drowned cousin, Warren Winslow, motifs from *Moby Dick* and from Christian worship. (Section VI, entitled 'Our Lady of Walsingham,' is intended to suggest the ultimate calm confidence of true faith; the statue of Our Lady, 'Expressionless, expresses God.') These motifs swell the organ music of the poem, enabling the poet to identify the death of young Winslow with that of Ahab and the *Pequod*'s crew and providing a specific religious and literary context for his contemplation of the ironies and the intransigence of existence, of 'is, the whited monster.' Though Lowell relates them skillfully to his theme of one specific death and to his sea music, they are nevertheless extraneous to the essential elegy. For this reason the poem lacks the piercing emotional authority of 'Between the Porch and the Altar' and of some less elaborate poems (for instance, 'The Slough of Despond,' 'The Death of the Sheriff,' and 'Rebellion'). Nor does it convey the terror of 'is' as effectively as the less expansive 'After the Surprising Conversions,' 'Mr. Edwards and the Spider,' 'Colloquy in Black Rock,' and 'The Ghost' (adapted from Propertius).

Lowell's 1951 volume, *The Mills of the Kavanaughs*, moves into the foreground themes more or less suppressed previously. In these poems, Lowell gives freer play to his driving motives of distorted and blocked love, mental exacerbation verging into insanity, and symbolic and actual homicide and suicide. The title sequence takes us into the mind of an elderly woman remembering her impoverished and loveless childhood and compensatory self-love, her unsatisfactory marriage and the later breakdown of her husband, a wartime naval officer, his homicidal jealousy after his return, and her own burning but unsatisfied sexual need. She thinks of herself in terms of the myth of Persephone, as one who has given 'whatever brought me gladness' to death and the grave. 'Her Dead Brother,' with its theme of incest, and 'Thanksgiving's Over,' with its sexual cruelty, would-be suicide, and madness, and other poems in this volume show how Lowell is approaching the revolutionary breakthrough of *Life Studies*.

In this book he rips off the mask entirely. *The Mills of the Kavanaughs* had one ludicrous aspect, the circumstances of the protagonists cumbersomely devised to account for their pressing psychological despair. In most of *Life Studies* there is one protagonist only—Robert Lowell. Through what he has to say about himself we discover the real, essential bearing of most of the earlier work. As a result, it is hard not to think of *Life Studies* as a series of personal confidences, rather shameful, that one is honor-bound not to reveal. About half the book, the prose section called '91 Revere Street,' is essentially a public discrediting of his father's manliness and character, as well as of the family and social milieu of his childhood. Another section, the concluding sequence of poems grouped under the heading 'Life Studies,' reinforces and even repeats these motifs, bringing them to bear on the poet's psychological problems as an adult. The father, naval officer *manqué* and then businessman and speculator *manqué*, becomes a humiliating symbol of the failure of a class and of a kind of personality. Lowell's contempt for him is at last mitigated by adult compassion, though I wonder if a man can allow himself this kind of operation on his father without doing his own spirit incalculable damage. But the damage has clearly been in the making a long time, and Lowell knows very well that he is doing violence to himself most of all:

> . . . I hear
> my ill-spirit sob in each blood cell,
> as if my hand were at its throat. . . .
>
> ('Skunk Hour')

He does not spare himself in these poems, at least two of which have to do with sojourns in mental hospitals and his return home from them. We have grotesque glimpses into his marital life. 'Man and Wife,' for instance, begins: 'Tamed by *Miltown*, we lie on Mother's bed.' It later tells how

> All night I've held your hand,
> as if you had
> a fourth time faced the kingdom of the mad—
> its hackneyed speech, its homicidal eye—

'My mind's not right,' says the speaker in 'Skunk Hour,' the poem which ends the book. It is partly Lowell's apology for what he has been saying in these pieces, like Gerontion's mumbling that he is only 'an old man, a dull head among windy spaces.' And it is partly his assertion that he cannot breathe without these confessions, however rank they may be, and that the things he has been talking about are too stubbornly alive to be ignored:

> I stand on top
> of our back steps and breathe the rich air—
> a mother skunk with her column of kittens swills the
>   garbage pail.
> She jabs her wedge-head in a cup
> of sour cream, drops her ostrich tail,
> and will not scare.

It will be clear that the first impression given by *Life Studies* is that it is impure art, magnificently stated but unpleasantly ego-centric, somehow resembling the triumph of the skunks over the garbage cans. Since its self-therapeutic motive is so obvious and persistent, something of this impression sticks all the way. But as the whole work floods into view the balance shifts decisively. Lowell is still the wonderful poet of 'The Quaker Graveyard in Nantucket,' the poet of power and passion whose driving aesthetic of anguish belies the 'frizzled, stale and small' condition he attributes to himself. He may be wrong in believing that what has happened to New England's elite is necessarily an embodiment of the state of American culture, the whole maggoty character of which he feels he carries about in his own person. But he is not wrong in looking at the culture through the window of psychological breakdown. Too many other American poets, no matter what their social class and family history, have reached the same point in recent years. Lowell is foremost among them in the energy of his uncompromising honesty.

Furthermore, *Life Studies* is not merely a collection of small moment-by-moment victories over hysteria and self-concealment. It is also a beautifully articulated sequence. I say 'articulated,' but the impact of the sequence is of four intensifying waves of movement that smash at the reader's feelings and break repeatedly over his mind. The poems that make up the opening movement are not personal in the sense of the rest of the book. They are poems of violent contradiction, a historical overture to define the disintegration of a world. In the first a train journeys from Rome to Paris at mid-century. The 'querulous hush-hush' of its wheels passes over the Alps and beyond them, but nowhere in the altitudes to which it rises does it touch the sanely brilliant heights of ancient myth and thought. For its riders there are, at one terminal, the hysteria of *bella Roma*, where 'the crowds at San Pietro screamed *Papà*' at the pronouncement of the dogma of Mary's assumption and where 'the Duce's lynched, bare, booted skull still spoke'; and at the other terminal, the self-destructive freedom of 'Paris, our black classic.' The next poem reaches far enough back in time to reveal the welter of grossly sensual, mindlessly grasping egotism that attended the birth of the modern age. Marie de Medici, 'the banker's daughter,' soliloquizes about 'blood and pastime,' the struggle between monarchy and the 'pilfering, pillaging democracies,' the assassination of her husband. The third poem returns from modern Europe and its bloody beginnings to our own American moment. All that turbulence of recent centuries now seems frozen into intellectual and moral death:

Ice, ice. Our wheels no longer move.
Look, the fixed stars, all just alike
as lack-land atoms, split apart,
and the Republic summons Ike,
the mausoleum in her heart.

But then the fourth poem hurls at us the monologue of a mad
Negro soldier confined at Munich. Here the wit, the audacious
intimacy, the acutely bizarre tragic sense of Lowell's language take
on jet speed. In this monologue the collapse of traditional meaning and cultural distinctions is dramatized in the frenzy of one
contemporary figure. Thus Lowell begins to zero in on his main
target, himself as the damned speaking-sensibility of his world.
The humiliated, homicidal fury of the Negro soldier throws its
premonitory shadow over the disturbed 'comedy' of '91 Revere
Street' which follows. It helps us to see, beneath the 'Jamesian'
nuances of relationship in a society of ritual pretensions but no
center of gravity, how anguished is this prose section's murderous
dissection of the poet's parents and its complaint against a childhood gone awry. In this way it prepares us for the personal horrors
with which the book closes.

But before that long, devastating final wave of poems, there is
a smaller one, corresponding in gathering force with the first
group. This third wave is again made up of four poems, each of
them about a modern writer with whom Lowell feels kinship as an
embattled and alienated spirit. Following hard upon the prose,
these poems clearly say: 'This is what the predatory centuries, and
the soul-devouring world in which I walked the maze of my childhood, have done to man's creativity.' Lowell first portrays Ford
Madox Ford, the 'mammoth mumbler' cheated out of his earned
rewards, scratching along in America, sick and 'gagged for air.'
Then, dear to Lowell's heart, the self-exiled Santayana looms
before us, 'free-thinking Catholic infidel.' The third poem re-
creates with sentimental bitterness a winter Lowell and Delmore
Schwartz spent at Harvard in 1946. Nothing could be more patheti-
cally open about Lowell's state of mind concerning himself and his

art than the parts of their conversation he chooses to record and
even to italicize:

> . . . 'Let Joyce and Freud,
> the Masters of Joy,
> be our guests here,' you said. The room was filled
> with cigarette smoke circling the paranoid,
> inert gaze of Coleridge, back
> from Malta—his eyes lost in flesh, lips baked and black. . . .
> You said:
> *'We poets in our youth begin in sadness;*
> *thereof in the end come despondency and madness;*
> Stalin has had two cerebral hemorrhages!'

The ironic facetiousness that so often marks Schwartz's writing
and conversation is here absorbed by Lowell into a vision of unrelieved breakdown centered on the image of Coleridge's 'paranoid gaze' in the picture. That image, together with the mocking
allusion to Stalin as one of 'we poets' who come at last to madness, brings past and present, and all political and psychological
realities, into a single focus of defeat. Then in the fourth poem,
'Words for Hart Crane,' the group comes to a climax paralleling
that of 'A Mad Negro Soldier' in the first group. Crane's brief,
self-destructive career is seen as the demand of the creative spirit,
deliberately wearing the most loathsome mask it can find, for unquestioning love from the culture that has rejected it. Here, just
before he plunges back into his major theme, the 'life studies' of
himself and his family, Lowell again, at the most savagely committed pitch he can command, presents the monologue of a drama-
tically suffering figure whose predicament has crucial bearing on his
own situation.

In large part, the fourteen poems of the final section echo the
prose of '91 Revere Street.' But they echo it as a storm echoes the
foreboding sultriness of a threatening spell of weather before it.
Apart from the obvious differences that verse makes, they break
out of the cocoon of childhood mentality that somehow envelops
'91 Revere Street' despite its more sophisticated aspects. Lowell,
like Yeats and Thomas, casts over his autobiographical prose a

certain whimsey (though often morbid) and childlike half-aware-
ness. But the poems are overborne by sadness first and then by the
crash of disaster. Side by side Lowell places memories of his confinement in mental hospitals and a denigration of his great act of
defiance as a conscientious objector in World War II which led
to his imprisonment for a year:

> I was a fire-breathing Catholic C.O.,
> and made my manic statement,
> telling off the state and president. . . .

The only poem of this group in which he does not talk in his own
person, ' "To Speak of Woe That Is in Marriage," ' is a monologue
by the wife of a lecherous, 'hopped-up' drunkard. It is placed
strategically just before the last poem 'Skunk Hour,' and after
'Man and Wife,' in which Lowell makes certain we know he is
discussing his own marriage, and it is a deliberate plunge into the
depths of the theme of degradation at all but the last moment.
Finally, 'Skunk Hour,' full of indirections and nuances that bring
the sickness of our world as a whole back into the scene to restore
a more universal vision, reaches a climax of self-contempt and of
pure symbol-making. This is Lowell's fantastic, terrifying skunk
image for the secret self's inescapable drive to assure itself of continued life:

> I myself am hell;
> nobody's here—
>
> only skunks, that search
> in the moonlight for a bite to eat.
> They march on their soles up Main Street:
> white stripes, moonstruck eyes' red fire
> under the chalk-dry and spar spire
> of the Trinitarian Church

Life Studies brings to culmination one line of development in
our poetry of the utmost importance. Technically, it is an experiment in the form of the poetic sequence looser than but comparable to Mauberley and The Bridge. To build a great poem out

of the predicament and horror of the lost Self has been the recurrent effort of the most ambitious poetry of the last century. Lowell's effort is a natural outgrowth of the modern emphasis on the 'I' as the crucial poetic symbol, and of the self-analytical monologues of the sensibility which have helped define that emphasis from 'The Love Song of J. Alfred Prufrock' to Miss Rukeyser's *Elegies*. It is also an outgrowth of the social criticism that has marked almost the whole sweep of poetry in this century. Thus, Lowell's poems carry the burden of the age within them. From this fact they derive (given Lowell's abilities) an authority not quite present in the post-Byronics of *The True Confession of George Barker*,* or in other works in which the speaker thrusts himself to the fore mainly as an *interesting* person.

It is important, I think, to remember one implication of what writers like Robert Lowell are doing: that their individual lives have profound meaning and worth, and that therapeutic confession will lead to the realization of these values. In this respect their explorations are very different from the sense of bleakness in some of Hart Crane, or in a poem like Kenneth Fearing's 'Green Light' whose predicate sentences (in which the subject is omitted) and half-images suggest a universal irrelevance of experience:

> Bought at the drug store, very cheap; and later pawned.
> After a while, heard on the street; seen in the park.
> Familiar, but not quite recognized.
> Followed and taken home and slept with.
> Traded or sold. Or lost.

To what subject do these predicates belong? Certainly the images are of the commercial world, yet they refer also to love and memory. Later, other images, absurd or fantastic or commonplace, are added: the predicates of human existence. The poet makes the point that all the impressions of daily life and of fantasy, inseparable from the self-centered and brooding mind, are 'strange, and yet not extraordinary.' A tragic pointlessness of truth is suggested, simultaneously defining the universe as zero and raising the pettiest

---

* George Barker, *The True Confession of George Barker*, Alan Swallow, Denver, 1950.

details, such as the green light of the busy corner, to a level of universal significance. If truth is pointless, then so are the facts of wisdom, morality, desire, and death. They are facts

> Bought at the drug store down the street
> Where the wind blows and the motors go by and it is always
> > night, or day;
> Bought to use as a last resort,
> Bought to impress the statuary in the park.

Fearing's poem represents a letting go, while the work of poets with a perspective like Lowell's is an attempt to hold fast to a moral perspective. Such poets, in their way, are carrying on where Yeats left off when he proposed that the time had come to make the literal Self poetry's central redeeming symbol:

> I must lie down where all the ladders start,
> In the foul rag-and-bone shop of the heart.

It is not easy so to carry on. The will, the energy, the aesthetic perspective must be sustained, as Delmore Schwartz tries to convince himself in a number of the poems of *In Dreams Begin Responsibilities*:

> Now I must betray myself.
> The feast of bondage and unity is near,
> And none engaged in that great piety
> When each bows to the other, kneels, and takes
> Hand and hand, glance and glance, care and care,
> None may wear masks or enigmatic clothes,
> For weakness blinds the wounded face enough.
> In this sense, see my shocking nakedness.
>
> > ('Prothalamion')

Schwartz's main theme has been what he calls 'the wound of consciousness.' Although he has not been able to push through to anything like the ruthless self-revelation of Lowell or Theodore Roethke, he has again and again stated the unrelenting moral crises which make it so necessary. His poetry relates them to the inescapable demands of the 'dog named ego,' the relentless insistences of the body ('the heavy bear that walks with me'), the weight of history and the physical world around us, pressures forever scrutinized by the eye of the protagonist's pervasive guilt. His earliest memories are suffused with this guilt: he talks of 'when I skated, afraid of policemen, five years old.' It enters into his poems of love, as in 'After the Passion Which Made Me a Fool.' Guilt, he thinks, is so deep in our consciousness it would spoil the meaning of revelation itself for us:

> The starlight's intuitions pierced the twelve,
> The brittle night sky sparkled like a tune
> Tinkled and tapped out on the xylophone.
> Empty and vain, a glittering dune, the moon
> Arose too big, and, in the mood which ruled,
> Seemed like a useless beauty in a pit;
> And then one said, after he carefully spat:
> 'No matter what we do, he looks at it! . . .'
> ('Starlight Like Intuition Pierced the Twelve')

This poem is from *Vaudeville for a Princess* (1950), in which Schwartz attempts to get at the heart's truth by a half-comic treatment of the romantic ego's predicament in modern life. But without the terrible bitterness and tempo of serious crisis beneath it, the comic element cannot thrust past the sentimental wryness that delimits much of Schwartz's most appealing verse. His energy fails beyond a certain point.

There is a similar limit to Stanley Kunitz's effectiveness as a 'confessional' poet. He admits to loosing 'a gang of personal devils' to 'clank their jigging bones as public evils,' but he brings them to heel a little too readily to be completely convincing. They are real enough: the oppressions of love and marriage gone bad, the pain of one generation's inability to communicate with the other (a pain compounded in immigrant families), the private impact of war and race-terrorism, and the ever-present modern lust for '*Mobility*—and damn the cost!' A heavy Baudelairean sense of secular damnation and of ennui has marked his work indelibly. An instance among many is the infinitely sad 'Father and Son,' with its account of the dreaming speaker's terrible plea for a reconciliation that will heal the break of years, while the image of the old Jewish father, unresponsive, strides relentlessly toward a swamp at whose edge he at last turns to the son 'the white ignorant hollow of his face.'

Kunitz belongs to a group of distinguished American poets whose technique is conventional but not rigidly so. He can, if he chooses, write in 'free' forms:

> The dialogue of lovers,
> And the conversation of two worms
> In the beam of a house,
> Their mouths filled with sawdust.
>
> ('Revolving Meditation')

For Kunitz, though, the traditional forms liberate more than they confine. For example, by slight modulations within and away from blank verse in 'Father and Son' and 'Reflection by a Mailbox' he gets the emotional freedom he needs while retaining the great advantages of a recognizable line that need not be wearyingly 'regular.'

> . . . the hunters of man-skins in the warrens of Europe,
> The impossible creatures of an hysteriac's dream
> Advancing with hatchets sunk into their skulls
> To rip the god out of the machine.

One does not, though, see this poet as stung by the fury of his vision and pushing against the limits of form despite the dizzying risks that lie outside. With all its passion, his writing is more rationally contained and oriented than Lowell's or Theodore Roethke's. There is in his poetry a world of restraint which is enormously expressive. A poem like 'The Waltzer in the House' is almost entirely of that world in its lightness and dry toughness and elegance. One like 'The Class Will Come to Order' sums up the case for restraint and silence:

> Decorum is a face the brave can wear
> In their desire to be invisible and so
> To hear a music not prescribed, a tendril-tune
> That climbs the porches of the ear. . . .

Despite their distinction, both Schwartz and Kunitz stop short of total concentration on the Self. They do not reach the pitch, do not take the risks that make the difference. Take up, for example, one of Theodore Roethke's longer poems and you are stunned by an agonized gibber, which the poet himself in an essay written some years ago called 'the muck and welter, the dark, the *dreck*' of his verse. The same essay ('Open Letter,' published in John Ciardi's *Mid-Century American Poets*) asserts that he nevertheless counts himself 'among the happy poets.' And indeed, Roethke at his best throws all kinds of dissimilar effects into the great, ceaseless mixer of his sensibility, stirring together notes of driving misery and hysterical ecstasy, of Rabelaisian sensuality and warm, wet regressiveness:

> Believe me, knot of gristle, I bleed like a tree;
> I dream of nothing but boards;
> I could love a duck.
>
> Such music in a skin!
> A bird sings in the bush of your bones.
> Tufty, the water's loose.
> Bring me a finger. . . .
>
> ('Give Way, Ye Gates')

Some of the allusion is a little too private. ('Tufty, the water's loose,' for example, has all sorts of obvious physiological connotations but probably has something to do with Roethke's boyhood experiences helping out in his father's greenhouse. And it is more than likely that 'Tufty' was a family nickname for Theodore.) But the passage as a whole, which begins the poem, is a wildly bawdy outcry of desire, thinly and wittily veiled in euphemism.

Later in the poem all this exhilaration withers and is replaced, first by frustration and suffering and then by a sort of minimal self-consolation. The overexcitement of the first part, in which the pain of the need was muted or hidden in humor, is balanced off by a gross, almost infantile desolateness. The images become ones of impotence and shame:

> Touch and arouse. Suck and sob. Curse and mourn.
> It's a cold scrape in a low place.
> The dead crow dries on a pole.
> Shapes in the shade
> Watch.

His projection without comment of a series of differing psychological states is characteristic of Roethke's most interesting work. A desperate exuberance that seems at one moment unrepressed joy of life, at the next the pathetic hilarity of the unbearably burdened, makes the manic-depressive mood-spectrum the law of life. Each opposite is implicit in the other, and that is the chief logic at work here. The universe of Roethke's poems is a completely subjective one; not some source of meaning outside himself, but how he feels within is the key to everything. The private sensibility is a mad microcosm; the speaker responds violently to everything that touches it, and he struggles frenetically to win through to a moment of calm realization in the sunlight of 'wholeness.' The ebullient anguish created in poems like 'My Papa's Waltz,' 'Child on Top of a Greenhouse,' and 'The Shape of the Fire' is a triumphant expression of hypersensitivity. Consider the opening stanzas of 'The Shape of the Fire.'

> What's this? A dish for fat lips.
> Who says? A nameless stranger.
> Is he a bird or a tree? Not everyone can tell.
>
> Water recedes to the crying of spiders.
> An old scow bumps over black rocks.
> A cracked pod calls.
>
> Mother me out of here. What more will the bones allow?
> Will the sea give the wind suck? A toad folds into a stone.
> These flowers are all fangs. Comfort me, fury. . . .

The reader will come somewhere near the poet's intention, I think, if he imagines the speaker to be giving a voice to the fire and responding to it. It crackles and whispers; what is the secret of its voice? There is a horror in that devouring sound that considers the wood or coals (or anything else) 'a dish for fat lips'; the second stanza gives further images for that dry, merciless sound and its terror: the receding of waters before the 'crying of spiders' perhaps the most nightmarish of them. The third stanza shows the speaker overwhelmed with the sheer dread of mutability and annihilation that has been accumulating through all these impressions. The whole process is not so much conceptual as it is self-hypnotic. This is the shaping sensibility in operation, and in this sort of thing Roethke is brilliantly successful.

But he does attempt more: he tries to conceptualize and to give his poems a further implication of victory over the frenzy through a Freudian rebirth of the Self. These efforts are not, by and large, very convincing. Thus, the last two movements of 'The Shape of the Fire' are attempts to soar and transcend in the old sense—like the ending of 'Lycidas': 'To-morrow to fresh woods, and pastures new.' But Milton had a vision of 'the blest kingdoms meek of joy and love,' while Roethke simply tells us all will be well on his own wishful authority. Something similar happens in 'The Lost Son,' whose title suggests the psychoanalytical, inward turning of the poet's eye. Roethke's essay 'Open Letter' says of this poem that it is at first 'a terrified running away—with alternate periods of hallucinatory waiting . . . the protagonist so geared up, so over-alive that he is hunting, like a primitive, for some animistic suggestion, some clue to existence from the subhuman.' So be it. This panicky hunt for pre-intellectual 'clues to existence' is without doubt one of the real, though uneasy, enterprises of thought in this century. But the poet is not ruthless enough to carry the hunt through, any more than he was able to remain true to the realizations at the beginning of 'The Shape of the Fire.' He finds another clue to salvation, an easier one than the frenzied beginning would imply was possible. It is the 'lost son's' psychological re-entry into the world of his most vivid childhood memories, the world of the 'long greenhouse' which he has called 'my symbol for the whole of life, a womb, a heaven-on-earth.'

Re-entry into this paradisic womb, one gathers, is the necessary preliminary for a rebirth of the Self. The true 'coming-through'

into mature, calm reconciliation has not yet occurred, but faith
is expressed that it will happen:

> A lively understandable spirit
> Once entertained you.
> It will come again.

The promise of a Freudian romance with a happy ending is too
pat and wishful. As in most of Roethke's longer works, the denoue-
ment does not live up to the poem's initial demands. Shorter
poems like 'The Return,' 'The Minimal,' and 'The Exorcism' are
really stronger in the way they sustain a sometimes Dantean
close-up of minutely detailed, realistic horror on the terms with
which they began. Also better are the beautiful 'The Visitant,'
the guilt-filled 'The Song,' the deeply sad and very original 'Dolor,'
the dreamlike 'Night Crow,' and the sweatily, feverishly, embar-
rassedly alive greenhouse poems of Roethke's 1948 volume *The
Lost Son and Other Poems*. Together with certain passages in
the longer poems, such pieces constitute Roethke's more lasting
achievements. Although I do not believe the special variety of
Romanticism he represents permits of consistent control, his gift
for release among the gaudy *Walpurgisnacht* images of the tormented subconscious life is unrivaled.

3. POETS OF THE NEW ACADEMY

In the 'forties and 'fifties a new world of poets and poems has
issued forth in exquisite chaos. The war against the Axis created
no significant new body of verse; in a sense the best poetry of the
traumatic shock of war had already been written, and the basic
attitudes taken. Moreover, mass bombing, concentration camps,
and purposeful genocide, as well as the engulfing of individuals
by a military efficiency and mechanization hitherto unheard of,
were so overwhelming in themselves that poetry could hardly
strike with any greater force than common knowledge of these
things had already done. (For the same reasons we have virtually
no first-rate poetry dealing with the atom bomb.) Hence, although

the war poems of such writers as Randall Jarrell, John Ciardi, Winfield Townley Scott, Richard Eberhart, and Karl Shapiro include some very sensitive work, they do not generally come directly to grips with their subject. Jarrell's 'The Death of the Ball Turret Gunner' is an exception, one of the few poems that can be considered in a direct continuum with the writing of Wilfred Owen and others like him in World War I.

> From my mother's sleep I fell into the State,
> And I hunched in its belly till my wet fur froze.
> Six miles from earth, loosed from its dream of life,
> I woke to black flak and the nightmare fighters.
> When I died they washed me out of the turret with a hose.

This is a poem overwhelmed, as Owen's poems were, by the enormity and brutal mystery of war. The three turns on the womb-symbolism that informs it take it beyond the indignation and compassion which Owen expressed to a realm of helpless awareness. 'The poetry,' Owen once wrote, 'is in the Pity.' * To the concept of Pity Jarrell adds the thought of an ultimate and absolute vulnerability in men, a virtually fetal helplessness or blamelessness. The State takes over the 'child' from his mother's womb into its metallic one. He is later reborn in the nightmare of air combat, and then is delivered yet again in the grotesque fashion the last line describes. The poem is clearly hostile to the State, yet it is not a political poem so much as one that leads us into the plain predicament of being born and alive at all in our civilization. In some of his war pieces the pity of making 'murderers' out of the docile, goodhearted young is brought out with the sadness of Auden's 'The Decoys.' 'Second Air Force,' in particular, brings us a depressed view, through a mother's eyes, of the huge, mechanized slaughter-system which has taken her son away from her, and 'A Camp in the Prussian Forest' moves into hysteria as it recalls the discovery and burial of corpses found in a German

* Wilfred Owen, *Poems*, New Directions, New York, 1949, p. 40. The sentence is part of a draft for a preface to a book of poems Owen was planning before his death in the war.

concentration camp for Jews. But in most of his war poems the feeling of innocence betrayed is less piercingly expressed.

In his 'civilian' poetry, Jarrell is often moved by the pathetic attempt of the child-mind to encompass death and life's harshness. No one can convey more sympathetically than he that hazy, dreaming state in which fantasy, dream, fairy tale, and reality are indistinguishable from one another and from the suffering in the speaker's mind:

> When the swans turned my sister into a swan
> I would go to the lake, at night, from milking:
> The sun would look out through the reeds like a swan,
> A swan's red beak: and the beak would open
> And inside there was darkness, the stars and the moon.
>
> ('The Black Swan')

In this poem, and in others such as 'Märchen' and 'The Sleeping Beauty,' Jarrell uses folklore as a rich source of insight into the 'unknown unwanted life' and its relation to innocent suffering. He sometimes seems to be echoing German Romantics like Ludwig Tieck and E. T. W. Hoffmann, whose interest in similar materials had morbid and sensational aspects and who at times seem to be foreshadowing modern psychoanalytic thought. Jarrell, however, whatever his subject, whether the death of a Negro girl in 'Lady Bates,' or the hallucinatory wretchedness of the woman who speaks in 'Seele im Raum,' or his own feeling of lost cultural possibilities in 'A Girl in a Library,' is always seeking to evoke an acute feeling of violated sensibility.

Everywhere in Jarrell the world seems to be locked in a grisly dream of the endless victimization of man. The mood is one shared by a great many other poets of his generation, including Thomas despite his heroic fatalism and theatrics. Lowell's confessional impulse is closest to it, perhaps; his need to confess supplements the feeling in Jarrell, and the combination parallels the emotion controlling such contemporary novelists as Saul Bellow, Bernard Malamud, and Ralph Ellison. This complex emotion, so pervasive in these writers, is a form of resistance to external authority and to the demands of life itself. In Richard Eberhart's 'The Groundhog,' for example, we see the theme of injured vulnerability presented as a struggle within the protagonist's own character. Here, too, the poet calls attention to our callousness, as a society, to individual death. 'The Groundhog' (like Jarrell's 'Loss') is built around the death of a small wild animal instead of a human being. Eberhart sets our primitivist sympathies in motion against everything that in its calculated insensitivity to individual suffering suggests the impersonal State—an insensitivity that accounts, ultimately, for a statistical rather than a personal interest in the victims of every sort of catastrophe from industrial and automobile accidents to war.

Eberhart, a poet of passionate if sometimes quite abstract intensities, tells how sight of the dead groundhog aroused him to a mystical frenzy of 'strange love' and a deep if not a tranquil piety in the face of death. Against these feelings he set 'knowledge,' the naturalistic understanding of death and its philosophical discounting in the rational mind. The poet tells how, trying to gain a calm perspective, he

> . . . kept my reverence for knowledge
> Trying for control, to be still,
> To quell the passion of the blood;
> Until I had bent down on my knees
> Praying for joy in the sight of decay.

After his first revulsion and excitement at seeing the maggot-swarming corpse, the poet returned at later times to the same spot. He first had seen it in June; in autumn he found it in a later stage of decay; the next summer it was a skeleton and a little hair; 'now,' three years later, there was no sign of it. And the terror of extinction grips him—the old terror of *timor mortis conturbat me*:

> I stood there in the whirling summer,
> My hand capped a withered heart,
> And thought of China and of Greece,
> Of Alexander in his tent;
> Of Montaigne in his tower,
> Of Saint Theresa in her wild lament.

Eberhart does not always write in this way. He often plays metaphysically with his own attitudes and sometimes, for instance in 'An Airman Considers His Power' and 'In a hard intellectual light,' comes up with conclusions that seem directly opposed to those 'The Groundhog' implies. At other times, as in 'The Soul Longs To Return Whence It Came,' he gives us elegiac narration that soars unexpectedly into ecstasy despite its initial theme. Drawn to the intellectual and abstract, he makes a constant effort to overcome this tendency through inducing in himself a visionary blaze that will consume everything but its own momentary revelation. Nevertheless, his most moving work is of the order of 'The Groundhog,' a poetry of the death of animals and people which is unmatched for simple, poignant directness. In this poetry he holds intact a feeling for the uniqueness of individual life that includes the kind of pathos we have seen in Jarrell also. Poems like Eberhart's 'The Fury of Aerial Bombardment,' Jarrell's 'Second Air Force,' Shapiro's 'Auto Wreck,' Scott's 'The U. S. Sailor with the Japanese Skull,' Ciardi's 'Ode for the Burial of a Citizen,' and Wilbur's 'The Death of a Toad' are the work of a generation weighed down with its consciousness of the waste and spoiling of life by the unavoidable ponderosities and indifferences of mass-society. The consciousness of this problem has made even darker (if that is possible) the prevailing attitude toward nature as fundamentally antihuman in its workings, and has sometimes led to a 'graveyard poetry.'

Karl Shapiro, whose style and thought have an improvisational character reminiscent of the 'thirties, shares Jarrell's and Eberhart's feeling for the vulnerability of life, though his method is often half-satirical. He skims over the surface of American civilization, pausing for comment here or there, often in language that is just a shade more serious than that of light verse. He gives us a really erotic love song to a Buick that neatly epitomizes the psychopathology of a machine-culture; views of tourists in Washington that seem illustrations of the nightmare-shabby culture described in *Mauberley*; an ode to a fly that turns the stomach in its epic descriptions of the insect itself and of the war against it (we are left free to decide ourselves whether these descriptions are misguided Rabe-

laisian exuberance or the overflowing of a sensibility so distraught
and disgusted it is heedless of what utters); an account of the
arrival of an ambulance and the traumatized reactions of on-
lookers after an auto wreck; a close-up of the American drugstore
and its obscene, vacuous import for the young; a savagely un-
sympathetic view of middle-class couples doing their Sunday
visiting in Shapiro's native city of Baltimore. The poet's empathy
is such that these observations are also observations about himself. He becomes a critic of hardness and vulgarity who is himself
violently colored by them, a censorious noter of nuances of the
racial problem who is most self-consciously Jewish, and a ponderer
of cultural falseness whose poetic attitudes as a soldier in the
Pacific are often sentimentally commonplace.

The 'Jewish' aspect of Shapiro is worth consideration. Like
Schwartz and Kunitz, he brings his Jewish background into his
poetry. More than either of them, however, he has called special
attention to it, even publishing a collection of his pieces called
Poems of a Jew. In this volume, he seems to define Jewishness as
a psychological state very much like the one that dominates his
poetry: 'The Jew represents the primitive ego of the human
race. . . . The free modern Jew, celebrated so perfectly in the
character of Leopold Bloom, is neither hero nor victim.' As self-
evident truths, these and like formulations by Shapiro are want-
ing. However, the choice of Leopold Bloom, who certainly suffers
from 'the wound of consciousness,' and who is so much an out-
sider and insider at once in the little world Joyce put him in, is
apt for Shapiro. In his view, the awareness of pain life thrusts
upon the helpless, the human predicament which is Jarrell's great
theme, is the essence of Jewishness. Perhaps the real clue to
what the poet feels can be glimpsed in 'The First Time.' Here
a boy is about to be initiated into sex by a prostitute. Absorbed
in his self-consciousness, he does not notice that she has been
scrutinizing his body in her mirror. Suddenly

> . . . she turns round, as one turns at a desk,
> And looks at him, too naked and too soon,
> And almost gently asks: *Are you a Jew?*

In a note to another poem, Shapiro writes that 'in Freud's view, as in that of every Jew, mutilation, circumcision, and "the fear of being eaten" are all one.' The generalization may be dubious, but it does indicate the sexual and traumatic aspects of the poet's conception of Jewishness. Sometimes the horror of this conception is conveyed without specific sexual allusion. One of Shapiro's best poems, 'Messias,' recalls his shocked recoil as a child from an old religious Jew who came to the door seeking a 'donation for the Holy Land' in the 'hieratic language of the heart.' The boy fled 'in terror from the nameless hurt.' More characteristic is the *Adam and Eve* sequence, which represents the Fall as essentially the discovery of sex. Fascinated by his phallic and vaginal imagery, which emphatically suggests at times 'the fear of being eaten,' and which is developed with a prurient, guilty, almost voyeuristic curiosity, the poet follows, as he says, his own interpretation, though influenced by cabalic symbolism and by Reich's ideas. A footnote justifies the inclusion of this sequence because its viewpoint 'that man is for the world, not for the afterworld, is Jewish.' It seems clear, however, that its connotations of sexually oriented violence and fear provide the truer reason. (See also the first of the *Five Self-Portraits*, in which the poet tells, fairly humorously but with great sympathy for his own infant wounds, the story of his birth and circumcision amid all the echoes and symbols of American and Christian tradition.)

Shapiro is one of a group of poets who, with lively vigor, combine modern technique and sensibility with a more public appeal than is usual among their peers. John Ciardi is another. His 'Elegy Just in Case,' for instance, with its half-joking treatment of his own possible death in war, presents one typical American mask. His war poems generally, and his love poems and political and satirical pieces, make him a graphic spokesman for the liberal and literate mind today, a mind in touch with earthy reality and even a certain redeeming crudeness, and also alive to the world of thought. Robert Penn Warren may also be included in this group. He is deeply yet emancipatedly Southern, and that fact, though nonliterary, does give him a special interest. He has also the initial advantage of being a great yarn-spinner in verse as in prose, grafting sophisticated (and sometimes spuriously profound) insights and states of mind onto the folk-narrative forms he so often employs. His poems almost always strive to catch a complex mood and attitude, brooding and embittered, yet punctuated here and there by a painfully awkward bleat of optimism. That bleat is all that remains of the innocence and idealism they would celebrate; it is a bleat for human possibility, amid a world of grunts, growls, and bloody chompings.

But human possibility, as presented by Warren, seems all but inaudible and invisible. Observed reality drowns it out, and his work is dominated by pieces like the long 'The Ballad of Billie Potts,' 'School Lesson Based on Word of Death of Entire Gillum Family,' 'Court-Martial,' and the seven-part 'Ballad of a Sweet Dream of Peace.' These poems are grisly and highly colloquial, with occasional 'comic' notes midway between Erskine Caldwell and William Faulkner, and with a touch of Ambrose Bierce to drive the horror home. They are suffused with that nostalgic conviction of irrevocable loss of identity which we dare not call obsession but which has for a long time been expressed with such determined repetitiveness by so many Southerners. But their locale is sometimes foreign; Mr. Warren has been in touch with the wide world of varied human experience and of the intellectual life, and one can see the liberating and liberalizing effect of his wider-ranging mind in many of these poems. This is not to deny that he lacks a final power which would enable him to tear loose from regionalism and its fixations in the most effective way. He does not break through by confronting the deepest and bitterest truths of the South, but rather begins, as it were, to change the subject. It is interesting to see how the motif of integrity within defeat and disillusionment in Warren's poems chimes in with what we find in the work of Robinson and other, more recent Northern writers. What he is doing coincides in its fashion with some of the political and tradition-hunting poetry of the 'twenties and 'thirties. If he is no revolutionary, if he slams no doors, he at least opens them to the outside world. Taking up from such elegiac regionalists as Donald Davidson and Allen Tate, he shakes up hard-set attitudes in the process of altering their perspectives.

It is no disparagement of the latter writers as poets to note that poems of Warren's like 'Eidolon,' 'What Was the Promise That Smiled from the Maples at Evening,' and 'Walk by Moonlight on a Small Farm' do alter and widen those perspectives, and that such a piece as 'Founding Fathers' is actually a small, very quiet departure from Rebel patriotism. The Southern locale is somehow transcended in those poems; their South is closer to the rest of the world than had hitherto been apparent; the tragic memory of a region becomes that of mankind at large, rather than an excuse for special pleading. If Warren's poetry is a bit relaxed in muscle and a bit overanxious to compensate by indulgence in the bizarre, the raucous, and the near-mawkish, there is still a gain in an important kind of resilience: a refusal, against the tangible evidence, to accept the tragic irrevocability of the disappointed hope.

The poets we have been considering in this section constitute a new American 'academy,' a name I have given them partly because so many are connected with colleges and universities, partly because they have established themselves almost officially as the recognized poets of their generation. But they have not lost contact with the great modern thrust as the British seem to have done. The best among them, like Lowell, have carried our poetry a little farther into the dangerous unknown territory of the 'crisis of personality' which seems to be our main poetic challenge at this time, while some poets have met this particular challenge so quietly that their accomplishment has all but gone unnoticed. For example, Winfield Scott, who follows a lyric tradition going back to Robinson, Torrence, and Whittier's 'Snowbound' for its nostalgic strain, is in his diction and imagery and outlook close to the most tough-minded moderns, as his 'The U. S. Sailor with the Japanese Skull' will show. Many of the others have created a kind of serious verse-journalism that probably takes its main impetus from Auden—a combination of witty and knowledgeable commentary with panicky looks at the world's terrors. Still others have looked to dream and myth, or the narrative repossession of moods of the past, as ways to get beyond the moment's crisis and at the same time to give it the focus of distance. Only a few have followed the perfectionistic and aesthetic-centered lead of older poets like Marianne Moore and Wallace Stevens. Most notable among these few are Elizabeth Bishop and Richard Wilbur. It is interesting that although these two writers have done exquisite and richly suggestive work they have touched the imagination of their generation very little. The reason seems to be that they remind us only of what we have already been taught to value: elegance, grace, precision, quiet intensity of phrasing. As Wilbur writes:

> Descending into sleep (as when the night-lift
> Falls past a brilliant floor), we glimpse a sublime
> Décor and hear, perhaps, a complete music,
> But this evades us, as in the night meadows
> The crickets' million roundsong dies away
> From all advances, rising in every distance.
>
> ('Marginalia')

Nothing could more beautifully recall the whole feel of modern Romanticism with its somnambulistic centering on the dream-life and the elusiveness of ultimate values. Nothing could be more engaging through sound alone and the interplay of sparkling and shadowy moments. The lines now slow down almost to motionlessness, now open to a rapid glimpse of a 'brilliant floor,' then close that instant decisively and begin to soar until that too-doubtful 'perhaps' brings them under control again, and finally, in the description of the crickets' multiple monotone, bring to mind again the ambiguities of reality.

So too, if we take Elizabeth Bishop's 'The Fish,' we have an Imagist instant of experience held and prolonged until the object perceived, the 'tremendous fish,' becomes more than the poem can encompass. The fish, though passive with age, is a dazzling super-'mobile' with his hanging strips of skin, his barnacles, his sea-lice, the hooks from former encounters in his mouth, and, in addition, the unseen but envisioned rich design *inside* him. All the surrounding color and detail, hitherto without pattern, come into formal relationship around him, as the 'wilderness around' Stevens's famous jar in Tennessee did,

> . . . until everything
> was rainbow, rainbow, rainbow!
> And I let the fish go.

If only we could settle for 'appreciation' alone, the great poets of any time would be the Bishops and the Wilburs. It would all be the smoothness of the Marvell of 'Bermudas,' the durable music of Bridges, the poignant sweetness of John Crowe Ransom, the lyricism of Marya Zaturenska, the carefully undramatic perfections of Yvor Winters. After the stormy inventors of new rhythmic idioms and new imaginative horizons had done their work, the gifted exquisites would take over—remolding, improving, getting the nuances not of a new artistic problem but of an established tradition.

Of course to put the matter this way is unfair. For, independently of the fact that they work so well within the tradition, their styles are more than the mere sums of their masters and they have some-thing to say. Miss Bishop, as I observed, extends the Imagist instant; she extends and crowds it so, in 'The Fish,' that she bursts through it, and the vision of throbbing sensuous experience, mainly visual, becomes a triumph of art over its maker. Her 'A Miracle for Break-fast' is a triumph similar to that of 'The Fish,' this time of the imagination over the irony, possibly the cynicism, with which the poem was conceived. Both this poem and 'The Man-Moth' sweep softly above the themes of physical deprivation and the dark fur-tiveness of the naked sensibility toward a reversal of their own motivations that is grounded on the most deft and antenna-quick feeling for diction. 'View of the Capitol from the Library of Con-gress' is a remarkable example of the satirical use of Imagist tech-nique. The much-praised 'Roosters' is masterly exploration, though the guiding voice of Miss Moore is uncomfortably in the near-background here. For this reason, less ambitious poems like the airily realistic 'Jerónimo's House' and the almost casual yet ab-solutely realized 'Late Air' have more genuine life. In her poems about Negroes and the poor Miss Bishop can be sentimental; these and her love poetry have just the consistency of a typical Millay poem. Her perfectionism is not such as to keep her from ex-pressing emotions spontaneously.

Nor does Wilbur wear a mask all the time. He gives the game away in 'Juggler' and 'Mind,' both of which treat of his artistic aim. The aim is to do his work so skillfully, the first of these says, that it will 'shake our gravity up' and we shall, for the moment, have 'won for once over the world's weight.' He recognizes the self-deceptiveness of this ideal in the image of the juggler who gets tired and puts his marvelous paraphernalia back 'in the dust again' so that they resume their normal heaviness in 'the daily dark.' In 'Mind,' too, though he asserts the possibility that the 'happiest intellection' may through some 'graceful error' be able to bring about a miraculous change, he at the same time grants that

> Mind in its purest play is like some bat
> That beats about in caverns all alone,
> Contriving by a kind of senseless wit
> Not to conclude against a wall of stone.

Not a new thought obviously, nor is his Nietzschean extolling of daring and commitment as against present-day timidities and con-formity, in poems like 'Superiorities,' 'A Simplification,' and 'Still, Citizen Sparrow.' He is not completely absorbed in what he is saying in these pieces. But in the poems that move with a weary splendor to the full assumption of their Existential burden ('Marginalia,' for instance, and 'Beasts,' 'After the Last Bulletins,' and 'Merlin') we feel, if still no irresistibly new perceptions, the breath of a true diver into his own meanings. And curiously enough, we feel it as strongly in those poems which, with a joyous con-noisseurship, give praise to beauty and to the variety of worldly possibility.

Something in the tone of Howard Nemerov, a poet who has less natural feeling for his art than either Miss Bishop or Mr. Wilbur, quickens our attention as neither of these writers can do. Even in his first book, *The Image and the Law* (1947), despite its stiffly brocaded derivativeness and portentousness, he brings us an urban-centered mind, nervously alive, morally concerned, but self-mocking. He has, moreover, a metropolitan humor like Fearing's,

a clear notion of the critical questions of the modern poet's relation to the heritage of the Enlightenment though, except in the
bitter 'The Triumph of Education,' he presents them obliquely
in most of these earlier poems. His next book, *Guide to the Ruins*
(1951), showed an over-all advance toward a simplification of form
and a heightening of dramatic confrontation. 'The Lives of Gulls
and Children' is an excellent example. *The Salt Garden* (1955)
registers an amazing leap. In this volume the almost macabre,
metaphysically leavened sequence 'The Scales of the Eyes,' with
its evocation of the presence of all the dead and the immanence
of the speaker's own death, is especially striking. Nemerov's new
simplicity and direction are now being used to imply brooding
complexities:

> And the rabbis have said the last word
> And the iron gates they have slammed shut
> Closing my body from the world.
> Around me all Long Island lies
> Smouldering and still. . . .

In the same book is 'The Goose Fish,' which stares down over
the edge of the abyss unflinchingly. As it begins we find two
lovers embracing on a beach in the moonlight:

> The ordinary night was graced
> For them by the swift tide of blood
> That silently they took at flood,
> And for a little time they prized
>   Themselves emparadised. . . .

Suddenly they see,

> . . . there underfoot,
> As though the world had found them out,
> The goose fish turning up, though dead,
>   His hugely grinning head. . . .
>
> It was a wide and moony grin
> Together peaceful and obscene;
> They knew not what he would express. . . .

That cold lunar grin cracks open their illusion with a pagan or sub-pagan ferocity. Nothingness yawns there below them, the ultimate obscenity, recalling what lies behind the sweaty self-revulsion of Hopkins's 'terrible sonnets.'

Humor and fancy in Nemerov's writing support his more serious intentions. 'Thou granulated thing,' says a female mollusk to a male one in one of the poems of *Mirrors & Windows* (1958), 'I deprecate on thee.' This crushing rejection occurs in a dialogue between a certain Wentletrap and his Elysia in 'Drama':

> —Ah, green Elysia
> Scuttled at last into the western sea,
> Thou crownéd, fragile sea-nymph, slender bodied,
> Thy lobes and processes have trancéd me,
> My lust begins to rule.

> —False Wentletrap!

Avaunt. . . .

The poem ends with the lover's destruction by the female, in a thorough burlesque of the heroic tradition and its modern inversions.

> —Elysia,
> Upon thy cruel tentacles I die.

Nemerov is mainly just having fun. Nevertheless, the poem tells us a good deal about what has happened to the Romantic and melioristic view. In its own way it is a memorandum on the subject of despair: beautiful Elysia will devour us at last. Yet the poem is written in joy and with the implication that the wooing, and the dreams and language that go with it, is worth that foreknown disaster. The name Elysia itself, though comically used, supports this suggestion. The dream of Elysian perfection destroys the dreamer, but without it neither art nor social existence merits the effort. Modern poets, Yeats especially, have modified this old Romantic theme by questioning the desirability of ideals that so torment and frustrate us. Yeats attacked the problem by putting a new emphasis on common experience as both the source and the referent of every vision of the ideal. But for all that, he left a place for Mlle. Elysia. Though Nemerov is well within the Yeatsian frame of thought, his idiom is more relaxed and contemporaneous, as is his general habit of thought, and his political directions are more in harmony with the main liberal-radical drift. There they stand, the thoughtful people of good will, dreaming of peace and kindness and education and progress, while their hair stands on end at the horror, moral and metaphysical as well as political, that is everywhere. Nemerov wishes to report the horror frankly. He also wishes, at least by implication, to put the case for melioristic faith. In 'The Murder of William Remington,' for example, he diminishes the shock by using the subjunctive rather than the indicative mood to describe the 'terror in each man's thought' today:

> Frightened lest senate house and prison wall
> Be quarried of one stone, lest righteous and high
> Look faintly smiling down and seem to call
> A crime the welcome chance of liberty,
> And any man an outlaw who aggrieves
> The patriotism of a pair of thieves.

The minimal idealism that causes the poet to say 'lest senate house and prison wall/ Be' instead of 'because senate house and prison wall/ Are' is like Hardy's wistful brooding over the happy song of his 'darkling thrush' at century's end, or over the oxen that just might be kneeling—though one dare not go look because of course they aren't—on Christmas Eve. In the Remington poem the wistful subjunctive is a liberal's prayer that the harshness of political reality, and the realities of human nature behind it, will prove to be significantly less than the whole picture. In another poem the sight of storm windows lying on the grass in the rain suggests a lost meaning:

> something of
> A swaying clarity which blindly echoes
> This lonely afternoon of memories
> And missed desires. . . .
>
> ('Storm Windows')

EXQUISITE CHAOS: THOMAS AND OTHERS 259

'Unspeakable,' the poet exclaims, 'this distance in the mind!' The rain falling on the windows and the grass crushed beneath them are seen in a momentary frame that gives the whole thing the illusion of having a point—though what is really being seen in the frame is essential chaos. Nemerov reduces the necessary liberal dependence on near-sentimental wish to an almost invisible point. Another poem, 'Lore,' illuminates a further aspect of his sophisticated wishfulness by playing humorously yet passionately on a theme from Robert Graves's *The White Goddess:*

> Man walks, I learn, in fear of woman,
> Possession of the constant moon;
> Because the moon has strength to summon
> Her blood to the full and ebb again,
> And gives her strength beyond her own.

In this poem and in the 'Moses' sequence, the wish for meaning compels a return to sources of myth and ritual, and the powerful heritage of past faith and abandoned certainties shines over the skeptical present with stunning effect. Of course, we are not expected to *live* by the magical lore and example of the long ago. But there is no question that the modern liberal mind derives deep comfort from the demonstration that such a course was once possible, and that the old habits still carry certain meanings for us today. Similarly, we are enthusiastically interested in primitive rituals that remain extant—Indian rain-dances and the like. We do not relish the idea of performing the dances ourselves. But we do like to think sadly that there were once Great Ages of Faith, and that the Hopis are enviably mana-driven as we cannot be and, to tell the truth, do not wish to be. The liberal mind does not like the fact that Eliot has tried to assert the literal truth of religious faith. It is ironically aware of the awkwardness of its position, but feels there are values more important as suggestions of possibility than as revealed dogma. The crucial matter of the place of religion and mysticism in modern thought is involved in these considerations.

Nemerov is notable for his large poetic grasp of these matters, the way he feels along into and through them. 'A Day on the Big

Branch,' for instance, develops his minimal idealism ingeniously, with the sharp-witted ease which makes him an effective satirist. After a night of cards and drinking, a group of friends—one ventures to guess they are college teachers, some of them writers, also—drive up to a 'stream in the high hills' with some wry hope of 'purging' themselves through communion with nature à la Thoreau and Rousseau, with touches of Dante. They are full of a facetious self-disgust, and they distrust this primitivist enterprise. But they *do* go to the Big Branch, and after a fashion they *are* purged. It is true that on the way back they see bridges that have been smashed by the flooded river in its 'indifferent rage' and that the sight quiets them down. But they have had their moment, not entirely factitious, of the rebirth of 'truth and poetry in us,' and it has to some extent inoculated them against the more extreme effects of insight into the world's emptiness.

By certain images and observations in this poem, Nemerov makes it clear that he is not sure how well this kind of stubborn balancing of values would hold up against genuine catastrophe. This is a Western sort of tentativeness, and particularly, nowadays, an American one. Perhaps a poem like 'The Town Dump' best implies its sense of its own limitations. This poem finds in a town dump a savage image of the city and its life. It is a nightmarish world of rotting and discarded things, a hell of scavengers, animal and human, 'guarded by the flies,' those 'ancient black retainers.' Such poetry betrays a terrible vulnerability to the reminder of death, the great disaster against which the secular sensibility has no weapon but courage. Yet there is a saving irony in the image of those wild birds which, like poets, are 'drawn to the carrion and the flies' and

> Assemble in some numbers here, their wings
> Shining with light, their flight enviably free,
> Their music marvelous, though sad, and strange.

The 'answer' implied by all this is that the crucial issues will never be entirely resolved. For renewing our energy and forcing patterned significance out of existence we have the devices of art. So long as we maintain a degree of resiliency they will work. 'Order,' as

Nemerov says in his subtle poem, 'Orphic Scenario,' is inevitably 'fused of . . . refuse.' And 'Eternity,' he says (echoing Blake and Yeats), 'lusts after the productions of time.' Nevertheless, we seek a perfectable identity; we envision desired shapes in the chaos all about and within, and though the illusions cry 'False Wentletrap! Avaunt' and seduce us to our own immolation, there is no other program that we could or would choose.

That, I think, is Mr. Nemerov's 'message.' Its chief contribution is in its hypothetical, liberal-tinged commitment to whatever positive can be wrung out of the 'things of this world.' The commitment is like that of Wilbur and Miss Bishop, but Nemerov more closely approximates the nervously uncertain moment-by-moment immediacies of the sensibility they all share. What would it mean to surrender the commitment altogether? The youngest of our recognized poets, W. S. Merwin, has in his best work tried to envision what the resulting sense of empty fatality, of a continuous, all-eroding wash of impersonal reality, would mean. Quietly, very quietly, without argument, he has taken it up as *the* condition of existence. In his poems we close in on panic so gently and unexpectedly, out of an almost dazed calm, that we hardly realize we are there and *have* been there all the time. Thus, his 'Evening with Lee Shore and Cliffs,' in *Green with Beasts* (1956):

> Sea-shimmer, faint haze, and far out a bird
> Dipping for flies or fish. Then, when over
> That wide silk suddenly the shadow
> Spread skating, who turned with a shiver
> High in the rocks? And knew, then only, the waves'
> Layering patience: how they would follow after,
> After, dogged as sleep, to his inland
> Dreams, oh beyond the one lamb that cried
> In the olives, past the pines' derision. And heard
> Behind him not the sea's gaiety but its laughter.

It is audacious to take this grand old archetypal symbol of the sea and use it in this way: plainly, simply, without the rhetoric and dramatics which even Williams's 'The Yachts' and Eliot's 'Marina' and 'The Dry Salvages' (and Mann's most poetic moment,

at the end of *Death in Venice*) have attached to it. Like Hart
Crane, Merwin is obsessed, in the poems of *Green with Beasts*
especially, by the sea's ambiguous seductiveness and by the shapes
and dangers it conceals and reveals. But he is writing on another
plane; he does not hug the terror so tightly, his images do not have
the same frozen brilliance, and his relation to the sea is more
literal and familiar. Where Crane's emphasis is on the tragic gap
between the dream of absolute triumph over the nature of things
and the foreboding of absolute defeat, Merwin is altogether
humbler and more yielding, in style and rhythm as in frame of
thought. The recurrent hero of twentieth-century literature becomes the entranced man in a boat, lost at sea yet as 'found'
as fatality will permit anyone to be. He 'knows sailing,' but that
knowledge can protect him for only just so long. His predicament
is best projected in 'The Shipwreck.' Merwin's picture of the
doomed sailors' physical situation and their feelings is concrete
and moving; his ending, however, is characteristically flattened out,
even bland:

> And to some it seemed that the waves
> Grew gentle, spared them, while they died of that knowledge.

He is talking about their innate 'knowledge' of sailing, which includes the knowledge of fatality itself. Always before they had
'coiled it down,' suppressed it from consciousness. Now, though
their literal death floods in from the outside, they feel what had
always been 'bursting slowly inside them.' So it seems to them that
this innate knowledge is what pushes them into death.

Perhaps this almost quietist handling of terror will ultimately
prove to be related to some inhibition of psychic energy in Merwin's imaginative make-up. I have compared him with Crane; his
work seems to lack not only Crane's dazzling violence but, what is
quite another matter, his *capacity* for it. Nevertheless, Merwin is
not merely abstract or passive, nor does he lack intensity. No one
reading such early pieces as 'Ballad of John Cable and Three
Gentlemen' and 'The Bones of Palinurus Pray to the North Star'
in his first book, *A Mask for Janus* (1952), or 'Colloquy at Peniel'
in his second, *The Dancing Bears* (1954), could miss their vibrant

feeling. Again, sailing with him in the sea poems of *Green with Beasts*, we find ourselves uneasily alive to all the uncertainties of position and direction that fog or unexpected nearness to a buoy or the sudden 'actual' glimpse of a sea-serpent can really cause. The symbolism is implicit in the situation itself, and I think it has grown upon Merwin as gradually and imperceptibly as it did upon Melville.

The quality of symbolic awareness, if not the literal imagery, carries over into his poems that stay ashore, even in the two 'Anabasis' poems that open *A Mask for Janus*. There is the same closing-in process, for instance, in one of the most haunting pieces of *Green with Beasts:* 'Thorn Leaves in March.' In this poem a free adaptation of terza rima deepens the feeling cumulatively, echoing Dante's tragic tone as from a great distance—a faint reminder of suffering and mortality in the midst of spring:

At the hill's edge, by the blue flooding
Of the arc-lamps, and the moon's suffused presence
The first leaves budding pale on the thorn trees,

Uncurling with that crass light coming through them. . . .

From this 'ghostly' sight Merwin carries us into an ever more acute consciousness of all the mysterious and 'hazardous' questions of birth, death, and time attendant on this moment of acute awareness, a moment like so many of his focal moments, caught with the most delicately sentient accuracy. 'In the Heart of Europe' carries a similar note of loss in an entirely different context; it is a momentary gesture of tribute to those peasant peoples whose tradition of feeling themselves at home is denied the protagonist and his spiritual contemporaries. So also, the love poem 'Her Wisdom' presents a woman of unusually sensitive perceptions whose psychological voyaging must, because of her identification with the sufferings of others, take place only in pain. Such poems as these three point up the humane bearings of Merwin's voyage symbolism generally. American 'academic' poetry at its best is guided by such bearings but does not forget they must be taken in Hart Crane's terrible world of 'rimless floods' and 'beating leagues of monotone.'

4. OUTSIDE THE ACADEMY

> Never
> Give up this savage religion
> For the blood-drenched civilized
> Abstractions of the rascals
> Who live by killing you and me.
> KENNETH REXROTH ('A Sword in a Cloud of Light')

Hard behind the 'academy' groundswell in the United States comes a more violent one. The poets of this second wave are very different from one another, yet are all trying in some way to find themselves outside traditional and institutional frameworks, or rather, to find more satisfying traditions and institutional possibilities. They are experimenting with Christian anarchy, heretical mysticism, the painting of Bosch, schools of Zen Buddhism, with whatever suggests nonintellectualized individualism; this is often combined with a stubborn posture of negation like that of Turgenev's Bazarov.*

Within this new tendency, the first group to receive public attention was that of the California Renascents, at first inspired by Kenneth Rexroth but soon abandoned by him as a false start. The group, whose most publicized poet has been Allen Ginsberg, had a moment of promise but lost its impetus through over-publicizing and too much bad poetry. Yet there was, and there remains, a serious meaning in its representative intransigence. It appealed to the young everywhere to lash out against almost everything, good or bad, that 'authority' has constructed. Empty as much of the poetry has been—a cacophony of revulsion from official repression that expressed itself in attacks of logorrhea, obscenities, incoherent manifestoes, and great shrieks of 'Libertad!'—it

---

* The poets of this 'non-academic' wave are most readily available in *The New American Poetry: 1945-1960*, ed., Donald M. Allen, Grove Press, New York, 1960.

has cleared a place for itself. It has created its own audiences, with a taste for its randy rhetoric, its postures of disreputability, and its compulsively repetitive vocabulary.

Rexroth's *In Defense of the Earth* (1956) showed him the strongest of these West Coast anarchist poets because he is a good deal more than a West Coast anarchist poet. He is a man of wide cultivation and, when not too busy shocking the bourgeois reader (who would like nothing better), a genuine poet. There is nothing very revolutionary about some of his most remarkable pieces, for example, 'The Mirror in the Woods.' The mirror of the title has hung in an abandoned summer house, then fallen to the floor. The speaker finds it and puts it in his daughter's room. The succession of silent mirror images—'undersea shadows' of vegetation when it was on the wall, an occasional wood rat it reflected when it lay on the floor, and now the 'ronds, escartes, relevés and arabesques' the girl performs—makes a concentrated and graduated series of impressions of the brighter and darker surfaces of life. What might be only whimsey in many writers becomes a beautifully ordered poetic conception.

Comparable are 'Blood on a Dead World' and 'Our Home Is in the Rocks.' The former begins as personal reminiscence; the poet and his wife await the moon's eclipse with their four-year-old daughter, to whom they have tried to explain it. She, for her part, cannot understand the scientific interpretation but feels the mystery and the terror more immediately than they. 'The earth's shadow is like blood,' she says, and

> 'Is it all the blood on the earth
> Makes the shadow that color?'

This 'savage' relation to truth is what Rexroth advocates. 'Our Home Is in the Rocks' is something of a reply to Richard Eberhart, to whom it is dedicated. Eberhart's poems of death are sometimes overwrought in their anguish. Rexroth's treatment has an Anglo-Saxon hardness and melancholy realism that jibe with his secular rationalism. The poem argues wryly that we *can* be immortal, that is, 'moderately' so. Its evidences are the undecayed remains in Egyptian graveyards, the brave epitaph of a Spanish Civil War veteran, the dense luxuriance of physical life, despite the stench of fresh death and the 'faint effluvium of dry death' that are never far away. The two facts, of life and death, are continuous, as his description of a dying mountain beaver shows.

Like many of Rexroth's Japanese, Chinese, and other translations, these three poems are indeed poems of *fact* in all its irreversibility, that fact which the poet's preface calls 'the only answer, the only meaning of present or presence.' But Rexroth believes also that the poet must be a 'prophet, in the Biblical sense,' and not confine himself to the role of impersonal aesthete purportedly assigned him by the 'corn belt metaphysicals and country gentlemen': that is, 'professors,' 'neo-conservatives,' and almost all intellectuals. The dangers of such poetic prophecy and rhetoric are well illustrated in the same book. Too often the poems are swathed in overblown discursiveness. Thus, 'Thou Shalt Not Kill: A Memorial for Dylan Thomas' has a magnificently passionate and bitter beginning whose power carries over to, and is taken up by, the later *ubi sunt* stanzas which call the roll of the modern poets who have died, sickened, given up, been imprisoned, or gone mad; it carries over still further to the passages on the suicide of Hart Crane and the murder of the Bodenheims. Yet the poem as a whole is sacrificed to the self-indulgent pleasure of the poet in love with his own oratory. Our Dylan (he shouts) is dead! Who killed him? The bosses killed him! The crucifiers of Jesus killed him! The lawyers killed him! The U. N. killed him! The psychoanalysts, the publishers, *The Nation* and the *New Republic*, the scientists, everybody—Einstein, Eliot, Oppenheimer, Hemingway killed him! And then the critics and the professors 'crawled off with his bowels to their classrooms and quarterlies.' Like some of the others in this book—for instance, 'The Bad Old Days' and 'For Eli Jacobson'—'Thou Shalt Not Kill' has the pure, self-intoxicated revolutionary spirit of the selections in Upton Sinclair's *The Cry for Justice*. In that anthology of social prophecy and recurrent moral anger at the 'marks of weakness, marks of woe' which have been the lot of the oppressed through the centuries, we breathe the same headily self-righteous atmosphere of the 'liberated' mind which Rexroth has about him. Of course, Sinclair's whole bent was toward organization and activism, while Rexroth, for whom the poems of *In Defense of the Earth* represent but one stage in a distinguished poetic career, has moved toward a mixture of personalism, quietism, and individualistic prophetics.

Allen Ginsberg's *Howl and Other Poems* (1956) is more representative of the Renascents. The themes are struck off clearly in the opening lines of its two most striking pieces:

> I saw the best minds of my generation destroyed
> by madness, starving hysterical naked . . .

> ('Howl')

and

> America I've given you all and now I'm nothing.

> ('America')

Isolated quotation does not convey the real tone of these poems, although their drift is not hard to define. We had had smoking attacks on civilization before, ironic, murderous, or suicidal. We had *not* had this variety of anguished anathema-hurling, in which the poet's revulsion is expressed with monomanic frenzy.

Ginsberg hurls not only curses but *everything*—his own purported memories of a confused, squalid, humiliating existence in the 'underground' of American life and culture, mock political and sexual 'confessions' (together with a childishly aggressive vocabulary of obscenity), literary allusions and echoes, and the folk-idiom of impatience and disgust. The 'best minds' of his generation as Ginsberg, aged thirty, remembered them had 'howled on their knees in the subway and were dragged off the roof waving genitals and manuscripts.' They had 'scribbled all night rocking and rolling over lofty incantations which in the yellow morning were stanzas of gibberish.'

Would we inquire? discuss? rebuke? 'I don't feel good don't bother me.'

This poetry is not 'rational discourse,' like that we find in almost all other American literature of dissent. Neither is it that flaccid sort of negation, too easy and too glib, that so often weakens the charge in the writing of Kenneth Patchen and others, although

it does occasionally lapse into mere rant and scabrous exhibition-
ism. Its dynamics lie in the undigested way it spews up its disgust
with an increasingly homogenized and blandly impersonal culture.

In his adaptations of cadence to rhetorical and colloquial
rhythms, Ginsberg shows the impact of such poets as Whitman,
Williams, and Fearing. Once in a while he falls entirely into the
cadence and voice of one or another of them. But he does display
enough originality to blast American verse a hair's breadth forward
in the process. He has sent up a rocket-flare to locate for his readers
the particular inferno of his 'lost battalion of platonic conversa-
tionalists jumping down the stoops off fire escapes off windowsills
off Empire State out of the moon,' all of them 'yacketayacking
screaming vomiting whispering facts and memories and anecdotes
and eyeball kicks and shocks of hospital jails and wars.'

There are other Renascents, among them Lawrence Ferlinghetti,
whose association with this group has not inhibited his wit, his
stylistic sophistication, and his willingness to learn from European
and American experimenters. Also emerging is an ultimately more
serious body of nontraditional verse represented by the work of
Charles Olson, Denise Levertov, Paul Blackburn, Robert Duncan,
and Robert Creeley. Their poetry shows the same intransigence as
that of Ginsberg and Ferlinghetti, the same fundamental assumption that the crack-up of values prophesied by an older generation
has completed itself. Indeed, these qualities are at the heart of
almost all the more impressive new work, traditional or not. Relatively conventional younger poets like David Galler, Donald Finkel,
and W. D. Snodgrass are alert to cultural breakdown, and they
have the advantage of being able to display it in a stanza and
metric which recall older, sharply contrasting modes of sensibility.
By the same token, though, they rarely summon the sense of absolute immediacy and spontaneity that is the great strength of Olson
and the others like him. In the Olson group, a renewed emphasis
on the feel of specific moments of awareness, as if they were totally
detachable from the rest of life, is indispensable to the reordering
of sensibility.

Denise Levertov and Paul Blackburn are the most 'open' and

sensuous writers in this group. Miss Levertov may begin a poem ('The Flight') with a quite sophisticated proposition:

'The will is given us that
we may know the
delights of surrender.' Blake with
tense mouth, crouched small (great forehead,
somber eye) amid a crowd's tallness in a narrow room.

But that is just the bending of the bow. When the conception here stated in so cramped and paradoxical a way is embodied in an anecdote about a trapped bird, the poem flies as an arrow of insight into an important subjective reality. 'The Hands' does the same sort of thing in reverse, beginning almost sensually:

Don't forget the crablike
hands, slithering
among the keys.
Eyes shut, the downstream
play of sound lifts away from
the present, drifts you
off your feet: too easily let off.

The dreaming movement into ecstasy is then translated into abstract aesthetic dimensions, a pattern of tensions like that set up by actors rehearsing 'on a bare stage.' In such pieces Miss Levertov gives us a world of awakened, contemplative self-awareness, in which sympathy with other selves may appear, but completely independent of social expectations. Even the poems which come closest to explicit statement of the toughened intransigence I have mentioned—poems like 'The Dogwood' and 'Something'—seem to regard the civilization against which they react as a sort of cobweb brushing the face, something alien and strangely cold, almost unreal.

Blackburn, too, gives this impression, but more humorously and evasively than Miss Levertov. His poem 'The Assistance' riddles out a ridiculous but real big-city predicament almost casually. The subject is trivial and embarrassing, but Blackburn conjures up a personal universe through his treatment of it. You would think, for the moment (as in actual life you might), that this was the whole of things:

> On the farm it never mattered:
> behind the barn, in any grass, against
> any convenient tree,
> > the woodshed in winter, in a corner
> if it came to that.

> But in a city of eight million, one
> stands on the defensive. . . .

Sunken into existential reality, without pride, definitive, Blackburn's poems, like Creeley's, seem at times to reduce themselves to an uncritical savoring of consciousness. Whatever is, is; and what you care about is not what it means but what it feels like. The poet's spirit floats and absorbs whatever is there; in 'The Term' he speaks of sitting in the Spanish sunlight and

> > watching
> > weeds grow out of the drainpipes
> > or burros and the shadows of burros
> > come up the street bringing sand
> > the first one of the line with a
> bell
> always. . . .

There is another, darker brooding beneath this surface acceptance; but it too is fatalistic rather than critical in its presentation:

> Another bell sounds the hours of your
> > > > sun
> > limits
> > sounding below human voices,
> counts the hours of weeks, rain, dark-
> > > ness, all with a bell.

Not all the new voices do their re-creating so unobtrusively. Charles Olson states the major cultural issues as loudly and explicitly as ever Pound or Williams did. Almost any page of *In*

Cold Hell, In Thicket or of *The Maximus Poems* will recall the older poets' driving involvement. For instance, except that they state as known principles what Pound has exclaimed over with shocked horror, these lines of Olson's in 'The Kingfishers' might well have been written for *Mauberley* or the *Cantos*:

> with what violence benevolence is bought
> what cost in gesture justice brings
> what wrongs domestic rights involve
> what stalks
> this silence
>
> what pudor pejoracracy affronts
> how awe, night-rest and neighborhood can rot

No debate is here possible; it is all over with. Similarly, when Olson employs the typical Williams metric, sliding, improvisatory, played by ear, he weighs it down. Williams's freshness and exuberance are emotional assertions Olson cannot make. Something has come to a standstill; another machinery than the one we are familiar with will be needed to get personality going again.

> people
>
> don't change. They only stand more
> revealed. I,
> likewise.
>
> (*The Maximus Poems*)

Olson has theorized in prose more than the others. In *Mayan Letters*,* he derives a slogan from his studies of ancient Yucatán: 'I keep thinking, it comes to this: culture displacing the state.' Pound, whom he much admires, overvalues the history of the state, and the history of the West as well; and so does Williams, though he developed 'an emotional system' in his poetry 'which is capable of extensions and comprehensions [that Pound's] ego-system . . . is not.' The problem is to get back to sources of

---

* Charles Olson, *Mayan Letters*, Divers Press, New York, pp. 25-9.

meaning anterior to those of our own state-ridden civilization and so to recover the sense of personality and of place that has been all but throttled. He and the mystical Robert Duncan share this aim.

Olson's verse has less natural ease than most that I have mentioned, but it does have the power of hammering conviction—something like Lawrence's but with more brutal insistence behind it. It is a dogmatic, irritable, passionate voice, of the sort that the modern world, to its sorrow very often, is forever seeking out; it is not a clear voice, but one troubled by its own confusions which it carries into the attack:

> To begin again. Lightning
> is an axe, transfer
> of force subject to object is
> order: destroy!

> To destroy
> is to start again. is a factor of
> sun. . . .

('La Torre')

Aiken, Conrad, *Collected Poems* (Oxford University Press, New York, 1954).

Auden, W. H., *Poems* (Faber and Faber, London, 1934 and October, 1935; Random House, New York, 1934).

———, *The Collected Poetry* (Random House, New York, 1945; Faber and Faber, London, 1948).

———, *The Age of Anxiety, A Baroque Eclogue* (Random House, New York; Faber and Faber, London, 1948).

———, *Nones* (Random House, New York, 1951; Faber and Faber, London, 1952).

Barker, George, *Collected Poems 1930-1955* (Criterion Books, New York, 1957).

Berryman, John, *The Dispossessed* (William Sloane Associates, New York, 1948).

Betjeman, John, *Collected Poems* (John Murray, London, 1958; Houghton Mifflin, Boston, 1959).

Bishop, Elizabeth, *Poems* (Houghton Mifflin, Boston, 1955).

Blackburn, Paul, *The Dissolving Fabric* (The Divers Press, Highlands, North Carolina, 1955).

Bridges, Robert, *The Poetical Works* (Oxford University Press, New York, 1912).

Ciardi, John, *Other Skies* (Little, Brown, New York, 1942).

———, *39 Poems* (Rutgers University Press, New Brunswick, New Jersey, 1959).

Crane, Hart, *The Collected Poems* (Liveright, New York, 1933).

Creeley, Robert, *The Whip* (Migrant Books, Highlands, North Carolina, 1957).

———, *A Form of Women* (Corinth Books, New York, 1959).

Cummings, E. E., *Poems 1923-1954* (Harcourt, Brace, New York, 1954).

———, *95 poems* (Harcourt, Brace, New York, 1958).

Day Lewis, C., *Collected Poems 1929-1933 and A Hope for Poetry* (Random House, New York, 1935).

De la Mare, Walter, *Collected Poems 1901-1918* (Henry Holt, New York, 1920).

———, *Collected Poems* (Henry Holt, New York, 1941).

Doolittle, Hilda [H. D.], *Collected Poems* (Liveright, New York, 1925).

Doolittle, Hilda [H. D.], *Selected Poems* (Grove Press, New York, 1957).

Duncan, Robert, *Selected Poems* (City Lights Books, San Francisco, 1959).

Eberhart, Richard, *Collected Poems* (Oxford University Press, New York, 1960).

————, *Great Praises* (Oxford University Press, New York, 1957).

Eliot, T. S., *The Complete Poems and Plays* (Harcourt, Brace, New York, 1950).

Fearing, Kenneth, *New and Selected Poems* (University of Indiana Press, Bloomington, 1956).

Ferlinghetti, Lawrence, *A Coney Island of the Mind* (New Directions, New York, 1958).

Finkel, Donald, *The Clothing's New Emperor and Other Poems* in *Poets of Today VI*, ed. John Hall Wheelock (Scribner's, New York, 1959).

Frost, Robert, *Complete Poems* (Henry Holt, New York, 1949).

Galler, David, *Walls and Distances* (Macmillan, New York, 1959).

Ginsberg, Allen, *Howl and Other Poems* (City Lights Books, San Francisco, 1956).

Graves, Robert, *The Poems* (Doubleday Anchor Books, New York, 1958).

Gregory, Horace, *Selected Poems* (Viking Press, New York, 1951).

Guthrie, Ramon, *Graffiti* (Macmillan, New York, 1959).

Hardy, Thomas, *Collected Poems* (Macmillan, New York, 1925).

Hopkins, Gerard Manley, *Poems* (Oxford University Press, New York and London, 1948).

Housman, A. E., *Collected Poems* (Henry Holt, New York, 1940).

Jarrell, Randall, *Blood for a Stranger* (Harcourt, Brace, New York, 1942).

————, *Little Friend, Little Friend* (Dial Press, New York, 1945).

————, *Losses* (Harcourt, Brace, New York, 1948).

————, *The Seven-League Crutches* (Harcourt, Brace, New York, 1951).

Jeffers, Robinson, *Selected Poetry* (Random House, New York, 1938).

Kunitz, Stanley, *Selected Poems 1928-1958* (Little, Brown, Boston, 1958).

Larkin, Philip, *The Less Deceived* (Marvell Press, London, 1955).

Lawrence, D. H., *The Collected Poems* (Secker and Warburg, London, 1928).

————, *Selected Poems* (New Directions, New York, 1947).

Levertov, Denise, *Overland to the Islands* (Jonathan Williams, Highlands, North Carolina, 1958).

———, *With Eyes at the Back of Our Heads* (New Directions, New York, 1959).

Lindsay, Vachel, *Collected Poems* (Macmillan, New York, 1923).

Lowell, Amy, *Selected Poems* (Houghton Mifflin, Boston, 1927).

Lowell, Robert, *Lord Weary's Castle* (Harcourt, Brace, New York, 1946).

———, *The Mills of the Kavanaughs* (Harcourt, Brace, New York, 1951).

———, *Life Studies* (Farrar, Straus & Cudahy, New York, 1959).

MacDiarmid, Hugh, *Selected Poems* (William MacLellan, Glasgow, 1944).

———, *Collected Poems* (in preparation: Macmillan, New York).

MacLeish, Archibald, *Collected Poems 1917-1952* (Houghton Mifflin, Boston, 1952).

MacNeice, Louis, *Poems 1925-1940* (Random House, New York, 1940).

Masters, Edgar Lee, *Spoon River Anthology* (Macmillan, New York, 1915).

Merwin, W. S., *A Mask for Janus* (Yale University Press, New Haven, 1952).

———, *The Dancing Bears* (Yale University Press, New Haven, 1954).

———, *Green with Beasts* (Knopf, New York, 1956).

Millay, Edna St. Vincent, *Collected Poems* (Harper, New York, 1956).

Moore, Marianne, *Collected Poems* (Macmillan, New York, 1951).

Muir, Edwin, *Collected Poems* (Grove Press, New York, 1957).

Nemerov, Howard, *The Image and the Law* (Henry Holt, New York, 1947).

———, *Guide to the Ruins* (Random House, New York, 1950).

———, *The Salt Garden* (Little, Brown, Boston, 1955).

———, *Mirrors & Windows: Poems* (University of Chicago Press, Chicago, 1958).

Olson, Charles, *In Cold Hell, In Thicket* (Published as *Origin 8*, 1953).

———, *The Maximus Poems/1-10* (Jonathan Williams, New York, 1953).

———, *The Maximus Poems/11-22* (Jonathan Williams, New York, 1956).

Pound, Ezra, *Personae: The Collected Poems* (Liveright, New York, 1926; reprinted with additional poems, New Directions, New York, 1949).

————, *The Cantos* (New Directions, New York, 1948), Cantos 1-71 and 74-84.

————, *Section: Rock-Drill: 85-95 de los cantares* (New Directions, New York, 1956), Cantos 85-95.

————, *Thrones: 96-109 de los cantares* (New Directions, New York, 1959), Cantos 96-109.

Raine, Kathleen, *Collected Poems* (Random House, New York, 1956).

Ransom, John Crowe, *Selected Poems* (Knopf, New York, 1945).

Read, Herbert, *Collected Poems* (New Directions, Norfolk, Connecticut; Faber and Faber, London, n.d.).

Rexroth, Kenneth, *In Defense of the Earth* (New Directions, Norfolk, Connecticut, 1956).

Robinson, Edwin Arlington, *Collected Poems* (Macmillan, New York, 1937).

Roethke, Theodore, *Words for the Wind: The Collected Verse* (Doubleday, Garden City, New York, 1958).

Rukeyser, Muriel, *Selected Poems* (New Directions, New York, 1951).

Sandburg, Carl, *Complete Poems* (Harcourt, Brace, New York, 1950).

Schwartz, Delmore, *Summer Knowledge: New and Selected Poems 1938-1958* (Doubleday, Garden City, New York, 1959).

Scott, Winfield Townley, *Mr. Whittier and Other Poems* (Macmillan, New York, 1947).

————, *Scrimshaw* (Macmillan, New York, 1959).

Shapiro, Karl, *Poems 1940-1953* (Random House, New York, 1953).

————, *Poems of a Jew* (Random House, New York, 1958).

Sitwell, Edith, *The Canticle of the Rose: Poems 1917-1949* (Vanguard, New York, 1949).

Snodgrass, W. D., *Heart's Needle* (Knopf, New York, 1959).

Spender, Stephen, *Selected Poems* (Faber and Faber, London, 1940).

Stevens, Wallace, *The Collected Poems* (Knopf, New York, 1954).

Tate, Allen, *Poems* (Scribner's, New York, 1960).

Thomas, Dylan, *Collected Poems* (New Directions, New York, 1953).

Tomlinson, Charles, *Seeing Is Believing* (McDowell, Obolensky, New York, 1958).

Warren, Robert Penn, *Selected Poems 1923-1943* (Harcourt, Brace, New York, 1943).

Warren, Robert Penn, *Promises: Poems 1954-1956* (Random House, New York, 1957).

Whittemore, Reed, *The Self-Made Man and Other Poems* (Macmillan, New York, 1959).

Wilbur, Richard, *The Beautiful Changes and Other Poems* (Reynal & Hitchcock, New York, 1947).

——, *Ceremony and Other Poems* (Harcourt, Brace, New York, 1950).

——, *Things of This World: Poems* (Harcourt, Brace, New York, 1956).

Williams, William Carlos, *The Collected Earlier Poems* (New Directions, Norfolk, Connecticut, 1951).

——, *The Collected Later Poems* (New Directions, Norfolk, Connecticut, 1950).

——, *Paterson* (New Directions, New York, 1946-1951).

Yeats, William Butler, *The Collected Poems* (Macmillan, New York, 1956), 'Definitive Edition.'

——, *The Collected Plays* (Macmillan, New York, 1953).

Zaturenska, Marya, *The Listening Landscape* (Macmillan, New York, 1941).

——, *Terraces of Light* (Grove Press, New York, 1960).

Zukofsky, Louis, 'A' 1-12 (Origin Press, Ashland, Massachusetts, 1959).

Divus, Andreas, 67-8
Donne, John, 14-15, 88
Doolittle, Hilda, *see* H. D.
Dowson, Ernest, 24
Duncan, Robert, 268, 272

Eberhart, Richard, 8, 14, 245, 246-8, 265
'An Airman Considers His Power,' 248
'For a Lamb,' 8
'In a hard intellectual light,' 248
'The Fury of Aerial Bombardment,' 14, 248
'The Groundhog,' 246-7, 248
'The Soul Longs To Return Whence It Came,' 248
Eliot, T. S., 5, 6-7, 11-12, 15-17, 60, 75-103, 104, 105, 107, 109-10, 132, 140, 144, 154, 168, 183, 187, 201, 224, 225, 226, 227, 259, 261
'A Game of Chess,' 92
Ash Wednesday, 80
'Burnt Norton,' 77-8, 94, 95, 96-8, 103
'Death by Water,' 92, 93, 187
'East Coker,' 94, 95, 98-100, 102
Four Quartets, 88, 94-103
'Fragment of an Agon,' 75-6
'Gerontion,' 84-8, 232
'Hamlet,' 81-3
La Figlia Che Piange,' 83
'Little Gidding,' 95, 98, 101-3
'Marina,' 80, 261
'Morning at the Window,' 77
'Mr. Apollinax,' 77
Murder in the Cathedral, 103
'Portrait of a Lady,' 83, 109-10
'Preludes,' 77-8, 83
'Rhapsody on a Windy Night,' 6-7, 8, 75, 78, 93
Selected Essays, 12, 60n, 88-9
'Sweeney among the Nightingales,' 77-8
The Cocktail Party, 77, 92
'The Dry Salvages,' 94-5, 98, 99-101, 102, 261
The Family Reunion, 79

Eliot, T. S. (Cont.)
'The Fire Sermon,' 92, 93
'The Love Song of J. Alfred Prufrock,' 77, 79, 81, 83, 84, 86, 237
'The Metaphysical Poets,' 88
The Waste Land, 5, 9, 15-17, 76, 77, 80, 84-5, 88-96, 98, 103, 110, 154, 183
'Whispers of Immortality,' 78

Fearing, Kenneth, 191, 200-201, 237-8, 255, 268
'Cultural Notes,' 201
Dead Reckoning, 191
'Green Light,' 201, 237-8
'Memo,' 201
Ferlinghetti, Lawrence, 268
Finkel, Donald, 268
Frost, Robert, 106, 109-13
'A Hillside Thaw,' 113
'A Servant to Servants,' 112
'An Old Man's Winter Night,' 112
'Design,' 112
'Home-Burial,' 111
'Spring Pools,' 110
'Stopping by Woods on a Snowy Evening,' 112
'Storm Fear,' 112
'The Demiurge's Laugh,' 112
'The Hill Wife,' 112
'The Investment,' 110
'The Lovely Shall Be Choosers,' 109
'The Pasture,' 110
'The Subverted Flower,' 109, 112
'The Witch of Coös,' 112
'Two Tramps in Mud Time,' 111

Galler, David, 268
Georgians, the, 111
Ginsberg, Allen, 264, 267-8
'America,' 267
'Howl,' 267
Howl and Other Poems, 267
Graves, Robert, 132, 259
Gregory, Horace, 19, 200-201
Chorus for Survival, 201